Environmentalism in Popular Culture

Environmentalism in Popular Culture

GENDER, RACE, SEXUALITY, AND THE POLITICS OF THE NATURAL

Noël Sturgeon

the university of arizona press | tucson

To Marion
with love

The University of Arizona Press
© 2009 Noël Sturgeon
All rights reserved

www.uapress.arizona.edu

Library of Congress Cataloging-in-Publication Data are on
the last printed page of this book.

Publication of this book is made possible in part by
the proceeds of a permanent endowment created with
the assistance of a Challenge Grant from the National
Endowment for the Humanities, a federal agency.

Manufactured in the United States of America on
acid-free, archival-quality paper.

14   13   12   11   6   5   4   3

Nature is a topos, a place. . . . Nature is also a tropós, a trope. It is figure, artifact, movement, displacement. . . . Faithful to the Greek, as tropós nature is about turning. Troping, we turn to nature as if to the earth, to the tree of life—geotropic, physiotropic. . . . Topically, we travel toward the earth, a commonplace. Nature is a topic of public discourse on which much turns, even the earth.

Donna Haraway

Contents

Illustrations

Acknowledgments

When a friend read the acknowledgments for my previous book, she joked that she was surprised that I left out my second-grade teacher. A book project is such a long time in the writing that an author can easily end up with a lengthy list of those who helped, though still someone inevitably gets left out. Yet thanking all those who made it possible is important; no one writes a book alone, and given that I was chairing a department throughout the entire time I was working on this book, this is particularly true for me.

Thus, my first essential debt is to my administrative program manager, Linda Chesser, who with grace, humor, and unaccountable loyalty took over many of my tasks, protected my time ferociously, and encouraged me when I thought I would never be able to find the time to write. The faculty in the Department of Women's Studies—Luz Maria Gordillo, Linda Heidenreich, Judy Meuth, Nishant Shahani, Marian Sciachitano, and Pam Thoma—were steadfast colleagues, always willing to stand in for me when I needed them and patient when I could not respond right away. For a wonderful year, Heather Ebba Maib was right there whenever I needed her, organizing conferences and taking over communication with colleagues with cheerful initiative and complete efficiency. Alice Coil of the Women's Resource Center gracefully did more than her share of our work together when I got bogged down, and she has taught me a lot about political coalitions. Loren Redwood, Margo Tamez, Erika Abad, Leola Dublin, Mary Jo Klinker, Serena Peters, Maggie Reed, Patti Gora, and Gail Stearns were all helpful in various appreciated ways. I also thank two deans of the College of Liberal Arts, Barbara Couture and Erich Lear, who were kind enough to appreciate the difficulty I faced in doing my own research on top of my administrative duties; they saw to it that I got the support I needed. Dean Lear in particular encouraged me to go ahead and get this book done, and

I deeply appreciate his confidence. Ellen Arnold in the dean's office also deserves thanks for her patience and cheerfulness. Susan Armitage and Joan Burbick were incredible supporters of my work in every way; I can repay them only by trying to follow their example as excellent mentors. Jo Hockenhull kept me laughing and inspired me with her dedication to women's studies, the environment, and social justice—always intertwined with creativity, good food, and excellent cat stories.

I recognize more-focused help with specific chapters in the notes, but I want to thank several institutions that gave me time and space to work, as well as the encouragement that comes with the surprise that others are interested in the questions that animate one's research. My research cluster on masculinities, militarism, and violence was an immense help, both intellectually and personally. Thanks to Jessica Alfaro, Joan Burbick, Faith Lutze, Jeannette Mageo, and Heather Streets. Thanks also to Amy Mazur and the Gendering Research across the Campuses (GRACe) research organization for giving our cluster the support to do our work. Thanks to the Institute for Sustainability and Technology Policy at Murdoch University in Western Australia, particularly Patsy Hallen and Peter Newman (Patsy for her humor, dedication to change, and wonderful singing and Peter for his graciousness in showing me the wonders of the other WA); the JFK Institute for North American Studies at the Freie Universität in Berlin, particularly Margit Mayer (whose combination of quick wit, impressive erudition, political acumen, and playfulness is an inspiration); and the Center for Cultural Studies at the University of California–Santa Cruz, particularly Gail Hershatter and Christopher Connery. While I was at the center, a group of us started a research cluster called Cultures of Environmentalisms, Biodiversity, and Nature, and I thank Donna Haraway, Ravi Rajan, and Anna Tsing in particular for the stimulating conversations I enjoyed in that group. I am also very grateful to the UCSC Feminist Studies Board for giving me the opportunity to teach a class on the topics covered in this book to such fantastic students. My involvement with three international collaborations taught me a lot about different approaches to culture and environment, and for that I thank Professors Baodi Zhou (Yunnan University, Kunming, China), Chin Shiba (International Christian University, Tokyo, Japan), Yang Ming-Tu, and Ted Yong (Tamkang University, Taiwan).

The American Studies Program at Washington State University has been an important part of the formation of my ideas, particularly through my work with graduate students. John Hausdoerffer forced me to clarify my thoughts through his persistent and perceptive questions; Jody Pepion taught me a lot about power, community, and living relationally in the world;

and Ayano Ginoza continues to teach me about the politics of indigeneity, the complexity of imperialism, and the importance of Okinawan snacks. Jean Weigand was supportive and helpful above and beyond the call of duty. Tina Krauss deserves special mention, not only for what I learned about the complexities of sexual and gender identities from her research but also for her reliable practical help in matters ranging from dog-sitting to lending me a desperately needed router when I had to be away for an extended period. Chris Lotts and Vince Gerardis likewise deserve thanks for keeping things going when I could not finish every task, as do Paul Williams, Lindy Hough, and Richard Grossinger.

My thanks to the three anonymous reviewers of this manuscript, who challenged me usefully and provided encouragement. I did not take every suggestion, though they were excellent; the perceptive comments helped me to make significant improvements. Thanks to everyone at the University of Arizona Press, particularly Patti Hartmann for her willingness to take a chance on me and to Nancy Arora for shepherding the book through production. Thanks also to freelance copyeditor Sally Bennett and to Tobiah Waldron for the preparation of the index.

Certain scholars interested in the questions I engage in this book became stimulating long-distance colleagues as we circulated through the same conferences and email lists. Cate Sandilands, Greta Gaard, Giovanna Di Chiro, Chaone Mallory, Andil Gosine, Joni Seager, Cindi Katz, Joni Adamson, Rachel Stein, Stacy Alaimo, and Julie Sze are all contributing important work to environmental cultural studies in different ways and have been great influences and (though not often enough) excellent dining companions. The passing of Val Plumwood as this book went to press is a personal as well as an important scholarly loss.

If there is an intellectual debt connected with this book that I owe to one individual more than any other, it is to Donna Haraway. Her work, her example, and her gracious support animate this book through and through (though she certainly will not agree with everything in it). While she is widely recognized as a scholar, too little is said about Donna's excellence as a teacher. Even though I am many years away from being her actual student, if I have said anything interesting in this book, it is surely because of what I have learned from her.

Faith Lutze has been a delightful and reliable friend, and I hope she is happy that I can finally accept her invitation to ride her horses. Candice Goucher is an inspiring example of how one can be an administrator, a researcher, a supportive friend, and a fantastic cook all at the same time. Zoë Sofoulis and Katie King remain both dear friends and important interlocutors for me, and they provided needed encouragement in times of despair. Ednie Garrison served as a reminder about why continuing to teach and do research is important; she made sure that I lived up to my own advice. Barry Schwartz and Terri Zucker distracted me when I really needed it with timely phone calls. To Elka Malkis, once again and always, thanks for your love, visits, and willingness to continue to partner with me in wild schemes involving various ten-year plans. Alice Reed helped me by listening, being patient, and providing a tremendous example of strength and perseverance. Linda Ware and Michelle Spencer put up with my skipping visits and my erratic correspondence. Marion, Robin, Tandy, and Timothy Sturgeon kept me in the proper amount of phone calls (that would be a lot!), jokes, political analysis, and faith in my finally getting THE BOOK done. Special thanks to Marion for all of those Science sections of the *New York Times*, sent every week for at least two years!

T. V. Reed fully demonstrated the necessary integration of nature and culture, mind and body, by putting aside his work for considerable periods of time to keep the domestic apparatus going, doing a great part of the bibliographic tasks for this book (though all errors are mine), and in general being willing to listen to ideas, provide feedback at any odd moment, watch all kinds of tedious nature-related media, and put up with the proliferation of penguins in various forms that appeared in the house. Thanks, T.V., for your constant love and support. My son, Hart Sturgeon-Reed, is recognized at many times in these chapters, because he was a substantial contributor to the ideas and material effort that constitutes this book. In addition, he kept me going in many other ways: from doing housework to making perceptive comments about my political frameworks and keeping my hope up that I would finally fulfill my desire to encounter the moose of my dreams. Hart and his generation will have to make the important choices about what kind of world we will have in the future. While it pains me considerably that he, and other young people around the world, will have to make those hard decisions, it comforts me immensely to know his fine qualities given that challenge.

Environmentalism in Popular Culture

Introduction

Developing a Global Feminist Environmental Justice Analysis to Understand the Politics of the Natural

Imagine two scenarios in response to global climate change, one optimistic and utopian, the other pessimistic and dystopian.

The utopian hope is that we will reduce or eliminate our use of non-renewable energy, including helping the industrializing economies of the Global South to put environmentally sound practices in place before they come close to matching the Global North's profligate use of oil. This will reduce our greenhouse gas emissions and stop the warming trend. We will reforest, build green roofs on all our buildings, and sequester carbon at a rate that will allow the Earth's atmospheric and oceanic systems to recover from the warming trend. Along the way, given the greater acceptance of environmental practices and the greater understanding of the need to live lightly on the earth, we will turn to organic farming and reduce the use of pesticides and herbicides (and thus protect our bird and bee populations and keep our water sources clean). We will reduce landfills and toxic waste by rejecting the throwaway society through recycling clothes and other consumer goods, composting household wastes, and reducing packaging. We will build only green housing, using environmentally friendly materials, designed to combine living, working, and shopping areas so that we walk and bicycle rather than use cars (and if we do use motorized vehicles, they will be electric, hydrogen-fueled, or hybrids). We will increase public transportation options that use renewable fuels and will cut down on long-distance transport of consumer goods, since we will encourage locally grown production of food. We will protect fisheries until they recover from overfishing, then regulate their harvesting so that they are sustainable. And . . . well, the list could go on forever.

The dystopian vision of the future generated amidst this increase in environmentalist concern is equally plausible, in my view. One can easily imagine that the Global North, especially the United States, will not be willing to rapidly make major changes in the overuse of nonrenewable energy, especially the oil we use to run our businesses and homes and to drive our cars. The quickly industrializing countries of the Global South, especially China and India, will not then be willing to sacrifice their attempt to match our environmentally exploitative ways of living. Global climate change will accelerate as a result. The increasing costs and decreasing availability of oil will legitimate U.S. military operations in countries that have oil resources (in the Middle East, South America, the former Soviet Union), increasing our military budget and shrinking our social services budget. War will also break out in new areas, for example, between the United States, Canada, Denmark, Russia, and Norway over the ownership of oil resources in the Arctic (this may seem far-fetched, but Canada, Russia, and the United States have recently moved military ships and submarines to the area to make claims on what has been considered international territory in the Arctic; see Chivers 2007; Gunn 2007). Global North countries will build more nuclear power plants and will deposit the life-threatening waste in poorer areas, such as on indigenous people's lands and in Africa. The world will be divided increasingly between those who can afford to access food, water, and good weather under the conditions of increasing weather volatility, and those who cannot. Major floods, drought, hurricanes, and food shortages will kill millions of poor people, and disease caused by these disruptions as well as increasing pests and viruses will devastate those who cannot protect themselves or gain access to medical care. A migration of elites to cooler climes will produce new fortress communities, with their own food, water, and energy sources, protecting these elites against those outside through the use of weapons, private armies, and vigilante actions. Thousands of species will go extinct in the chaos. Cities will empty out or become places of violence and extreme poverty: satraps run by warlords with access to weapons and energy sources. I could go on, but you get the idea; if you cannot imagine this scenario, you might turn to popular culture and watch the *Mad Max* movies (1979, 1981, 1985), or *Waterworld* (1995), or *Day after Tomorrow* (2004), or *Children of Men* (2006).

Obviously, the utopian and dystopian scenarios I have outlined are starkly contrasted, extreme views of what might happen. The likely outcome is probably somewhere in between. This makes clear the disturbing idea that these scenarios are not really opposites. It is quite possible to imagine that a green society could be created but only be available to the rich, while the poor live in a world of toxins, scarcity, and violence. In fact, this is the road we are on right now. Unless our utopian possibilities include equal access to a green future, the powerful may end up inside gated green communities while war and poverty rage outside, but the integrated biosystems of the planet will eventually affect the ability of all human communities to survive, ultimately denying the world-saving ambitions of an elitist environmentalist vision. One would hope that the morality of creating a green future that included everyone would be enough to recommend it, but for those who find that unconvincing, the dystopian scenario must be recognized as a short-term prospect (Hossay 2006). If we want to create a truly sustainable future, we must think about social inequalities as much as we think about environmental problems, and we must understand their interrelations. We will be better off, I believe, working from analytical frameworks that address environmental problems and social inequalities together.

As I have been writing this book, the environmental consequences of global climate change have become more and more obvious and of greater and greater public concern. At the start of my writing, there was widespread skepticism and ignorance about global climate change, especially in the United States, but as I worked on my final draft—during the hot, volatile summer and cold, storm-laden winter of 2007—broad consensus grew that the warming trend is already occurring and that it is caused by human practices. Despite the criticism I will sometimes make in these pages of Al Gore's filmic rhetoric, much of this shift in the United States is clearly due to the work of the Nobel Peace Prize–winner and his Academy Award–winning film, *An Inconvenient Truth* (2006). This perceptual shift demonstrates the power and importance of environmentalist popular culture, in the right context and at the right time. It has also helped that the many critics of the Iraq War have raised public consciousness about the problems of dependency on nonrenewable energy, whether it is in the Global North or in the Global South.[1] The rising price of oil and gas for the Global North, especially the United States (which had been protected for years from the real cost of oil by subsidies), has caused sharp concern and difficult conditions for many people. Suddenly, there is broad support for and a lively interest in alternative energy sources. These twin and related concerns—energy and global climate change—have produced an environmentalist tsunami of positive public opinion and a concomitant flood of green consumer goods and green business initiatives.

All well and good, one might say, and high time. It is an opportunity we cannot afford to miss. But how should we take advantage of it? What kind of environmental renaissance will we have, and what kind of world will result? What kind of environmental and political solutions can we generate that will lead us in a more peaceful, more equitable, and more sustainable direction during the coming storm? I suggest that the environmentalist discourses that appear in popular culture today are not as useful as they could be to help us in seeking to create the understanding we need.

This book traces the varied appearance in the post–cold war era of environmentalist themes in U.S. popular culture and asks critical questions about the implications of these themes for environmentalist politics and social justice. I show that, especially since the 1980s, a mainstream version of environmentalism has become a common narrative framework used to understand and legitimate certain aspects of U.S. consumerism, family values, global military power, and American history. The implications of these popular narratives about nature cut two ways: they become a way of explaining U.S. power and dominant cultural practices; and they become a way of promoting mainstream environmentalisms.

Using a set of critical questions about these narratives of nature, these ways of developing a *politics of the natural*, I try to uncover the implications for environmental, social, and political issues of this traffic across mainstream culture and environmental movements. I do not pretend to have all the solutions, but I will try to show the utility of engaging in what I call a *global feminist environmental justice analysis* as a method of getting to the answers we need. This means using an intersectional approach (seeing at all times an interactive relationship among inequalities of gender, race, sexuality, class, and nation) and revealing the connections between social inequalities and environmental problems to uncover the systems of power that continue to generate the complex problems we face. This also means, as I explain below, critiquing both dualism and naturalization in popular culture.

For several reasons, contemporary U.S. popular culture is a rich arena for developing such a set of questions. First of all, it is an important place to look for dominant cultural narratives, to see the key patterns (as well as the revealing variations) within stories used to explain ourselves to ourselves. Second, U.S. popular culture is a worldwide commodity, exporting "American values" and creating a picture of "America" that is viewed, consumed, copied, and resisted by cultures across the globe. Third, because of its wide impact, U.S. popular culture is an important arena for oppositional activists to enter in order to convince, persuade, and mobilize others to their cause.

The environmentalist themes that begin to appear in almost every arena of popular culture in the post–cold war era are complicated phenomena. They are useful and flexible *tropes* (a phrase, narrative, or image that is used figuratively, for rhetorical effect) that tell powerful stories about who we (in the United States) are, what our history has meant, and what direction we should take in the world. They attempt to explain the United States to the world in a contemporary context of the intense globalization of popular culture, in which new technologies of communication, dissemination, and display operate within international markets of dizzying complexity and variety. In a post–cold war context, the United States has become the only global military superpower, yet new multivalent state and corporate alliances and economic relationships have changed what that might mean.

For the United States, with its long attachment to particular ideas about nature (natural rights, nature as cathedral, nature's nation—ideas that appear throughout this book), the use of discourses about nature and the natural as one way of explaining U.S. character, culture, and intentions should come as no surprise. But we are now in a time when environmentalism has gained an important cultural legitimacy, becoming mainstream, while environmental issues are recognized more and more as global issues: climate change, collapse of fisheries, water depletion and pollution, toxic wastes, environmental illnesses, and so forth. In this situation, it makes sense that U.S. environmentalists use popular narrative tropes to get their message across in ways that they think will be widely effective. But they do not often critically examine what relationship those stories have to the long-standing use of arguments from the natural that have promoted inequality and supported conquest throughout U.S. political and social history. It is crucial, therefore, to examine the negative implications and effects of environmentalist deployment of certain narratives about nature, given that some of those narratives are simultaneously used to uphold troubling ideas about U.S. power, heterosexist and sexist concepts of families and sexuality, and racist ideas about indigenous and Global South peoples. Given the global nature of the environmental problems we face, this critical exercise may be a politically pragmatic endeavor, because problematic tropes about nature may hamper effective alliances with Global South and environmental justice activists. And finally, as I hold throughout this book, if social inequalities and environmental problems are connected such that we cannot solve one set of problems without solving the other, environmentalists need to be more careful about using popular narratives uncritically, not simply because they are wrong or not politically strategic, but because they may prevent us from fully understanding the causes of and solutions to environmental problems.

Contemporary Radical Environmentalisms and Environmental Cultural Studies

Clearly, we have many environmental problems to deal with. What is not as clear is how to deal with them. What are their causes, and how serious a change must we make in our lives, in our economic and political systems, to come up with solutions that are long term, that preserve democracy, and that allow all people and environments to be healthy, sustainable, and productive? There are many kinds of environmentalists who are trying to work on the variety of problems we face, and we will need a combination of many approaches to succeed. No one approach has all the answers. But it is still important to make some distinctions, to clarify the practicality and analytic strength of different approaches.

Environmental historians and theorists of environmental movements have worked hard to try to categorize and analyze different kinds of environmentalisms and the preferred solutions offered by each (Darnovsky 1991; Gottlieb 1993; Guha 1989; Guha and Martínez-Alier 1997; Martínez-Alier 2002; Merchant 1992; Taylor 1997). As I have said, I am particularly persuaded by those environmentalist approaches that argue that solutions to environmental problems will also require solutions to problems of political and social inequality. I call these environmentalisms "contemporary radical environmentalisms," and I include among them environmental feminist, environmental justice, and Global South environmentalist approaches.[2] A recent trend in what is sometimes called the global peace and justice movement is for these three approaches to become increasingly more integrated, hence my choice of the label "global feminist environmental justice" for the analysis I offer here.

Contemporary radical environmentalisms differ from mainstream environmentalisms in that they argue in various ways that there is a relationship between social inequalities and environmental problems. Mainstream environmentalisms do not make such arguments—and this is because they are based on some problematic assumptions. I provide detailed examples throughout this book about why this mainstream (or preservationist, conservationist, or biocentric) approach is not adequate. In brief, however, my argument might be summed up as follows: conceiving of nature and culture as radically separate spheres, presenting humans as a universalized cause of damage to a pristine nonhuman environment, and promoting individualistic solutions to environmental problems without considering the need for structural, economic, or social change does not get at the root of our problems.

Contemporary radical environmentalisms operate from slightly different but related frameworks. *Ecofeminism* is a set of theories and political practices that makes connections between feminisms and environmentalisms. As Karen Warren says, "Ecofeminists begin with gender as a category of analysis. . . . But this is not because gender oppression is more important than other forms of oppression; it is not. It is because a focus on 'women' reveals important features of interconnected systems of human domination" (Warren 2000, 2). Basically, ecofeminism claims that the oppression, inequality, and exploitation of certain groups (people of color, women, poor people, LGBT people, Global South people, animals) are theoretically and structurally related to the degradation and overexploitation of the environment. Theoretically and ideologically, they are related because Western ideological frameworks operate dualistically, separating culture and nature, men and women, white people and people of color, humans and animals, mind and body, rationality and emotion, straight people and queer people. Furthermore, ecofeminists argue, these dualisms are value-hierarchical, with the first term in the previous list assumed to be superior to the second. Thus, the first terms are in closer relation to each other, while the second terms are intimately connected. Thus, if nature is devalued, so are women, people of color, animals, and so forth. Women and nature are also seen as structurally and materially intertwined, as women do most of the domestic work and agricultural work in the world, putting them in integral relation with environmental questions of health, food safety, and water quality. Because most of the world's environmentalist activists are women, examples of ecofeminist activism abound, although sometimes the label of "ecofeminism" is not one the activists themselves would choose (Merchant 1996; Mies and Shiva 1993; Plumwood 1994; Sturgeon 1997; Warren 2000).

Environmental justice advocates most often start with race as their primary category of analysis, and racist dualisms concern them most. Environmental justice operates through a framework in which the primary cause of unrestrained and unhealthy use of the environment is a system of unequal distribution of wealth based on racism and colonialism. In this economic system, people of color are more likely to suffer environmental problems than white people are because the political and economic system is unequal, as a result of previous and present racist structures. Environmental justice activists point to the recent studies that show this effect: more toxic waste plants are built in communities of color, lead paint poisoning is more common among children of color, and the most dangerous uranium mining is done on Native American lands, for example.

These effects are the result of histories of discrimination and economic exploitation that leave people of color more vulnerable and are thus "environmental racism." In this way, negative environmental consequences of our present modes of production and consumption are made invisible to those whose racial privilege protects them from environmental exposure. Many environmental justice activists are women, whose traditional roles of protecting community health and long-term prospects place them at the forefront of these environmental justice struggles (Bullard 2005; Di Chiro 1992; Szasz 1994; Sze 2007; Taylor 1997).

Global South environmentalist theories and movements make similar claims—but they are more likely to focus on specific forms of environmental pollutants and devastation that affect the health and well-being of poor people in the Global South. These activists argue that the forces of colonialism and global capitalism are the primary culprits in creating environmental problems, from the overexploitation of natural resources that are taken from the Global South and used by the Global North to the profit of global corporations, to the environmental pollution visited on poor people in Global South countries. Global South environmentalists, some of them using a non-Western feminist perspective, focus on dualisms that foster the exploitation of "less-developed" countries by the "over-developed" countries as the source of environmental problems, from the lack of environmental regulation in "free enterprise" zones such as the *maquiladoras* in Mexico, to the "biopiracy" of copyrighting indigenous seed stocks for use by agricultural corporations (Gosine 1994; Guha 1989; Martínez-Alier 2002; Shiva 1997, 2005).

Clearly, as these radical environmentalisms develop—in particular, as U.S.–based environmental justice and environmental feminist approaches reach out to Global South feminist and anticolonialist environmentalisms, a process beginning to take place both within the academic arenas I am calling below "cultural environmental studies" and within the global justice movement—these analyses begin to intertwine and enrich each other (Adamson, Evans, and Stein 2002; Pellow and Brulle 2005; Sandler and Pezzullo 2007; Seager 2003; Stein 2004). In this book, the label "global feminist environmental justice" is meant to signal that synthesis.

In working from the integrated insights of these three movements, this book aims to make a small contribution to an important set of challenges, discussions, and debates about these issues that involve activists and scholars all over the world. Through this dialogue, I think we can see a new field of study developing, which I call here *environmental cultural studies*. Environmental cultural studies tries to make connections between scholarship and activism on social justice issues, and scholarship and activism on environmental issues.[3] The varied interdisciplinary approaches that can be characterized as environmental cultural studies add an important emphasis to long-standing analyses of the ways in which culture and power are intertwined historically, by attending to the environment as a factor in these equations. This involves looking at how cultural, political, economic, and social processes influence the use or understanding of the environment, but it also can (though more rarely) involve the converse: examining the way our conceptualization of environmental processes influences cultural, social, and economic practices. In my view, the hallmark of environmental cultural studies is that it moves away from the emphasis on interpretation of texts found in ecocriticism, to use a framework that aims at historically and culturally specific analyses of the intertwining of political economy, cultural production, and ideological representations. One of the things that distinguishes this approach from traditional ecocritical and radical environmental movement traditions is the cultural studies emphasis on a *critique of naturalization*. A critique of naturalization is particularly important when dealing with environmentalist questions, and because this insight is a foundation of my analysis, I briefly look at what a "critique of naturalization" might mean and how it can help us look critically at environmentalism in U.S. popular culture.

Critiquing Dualisms, Critiquing Naturalizations

One of the ways I hope this book will contribute to shaping the new field of environmental cultural studies and the intertwining analyses of radical environmentalisms is via an emphasis on a *critique of naturalization*, analyzing naturalization's use as a tool of power (while keeping in mind the possible strategic uses of arguments from the natural as a potentially oppositional discourse). A critique of naturalization, that is, *a critical approach to any claims to the natural*, is a tool that allows us to get at aspects of environmental and human exploitation that we can miss using only the critique of dualistic constructions of inequality—whether of sexism and heterosexism (emphasized in ecofeminism), environmental racism (emphasized in environmental justice), or environmental colonialism (emphasized in Global South environmentalism)—though I use all three of these methods as well. Critiques of inequality conceived as dualisms of the powerful and the less powerful do not completely articulate all of the structures of power we face and the techniques through which power is maintained and reproduced. In particular, they do not address the *flexibility* of the concept of the natural and the way in which ideas of nature provide a basic but malleable form of justification for social relations in Western culture. Though it is manifested differently in different historical and social contexts, what is persistent in Western cultures is the *naturalization* of social differences and economic systems, the presentation of inequalities and hierarchies as natural orders (especially for the United States). This process of naturalization may deploy or depend on a dualism of gender, race, or national status that assigns certain groups to a more "natural" or inferior status, or it may not. For example, whereas black people were enslaved in the United States through ideologies that painted them as closer to animals, Chinese workers on the western railroads were coded as unnatural "aliens."

If an ideology that justifies inequality does depend on dualistic conceptualizations, it may not necessarily depend on a dualism in which culture is the dominant term. Often, nature is presented as the legitimating force, the source of truth and rational order that supports the construction of the inequality. Alternatively, a dualism may not even be the central logic of an ideological justification of inequality. For instance, if most people believe that our present economic system in the United States (in which profit trumps all other considerations, cost/benefit analyses are the way decisions are made, and economic inequality is assumed to be necessary to the system) is *natural*, the epitome of social evolution, then getting them to imagine other economic arrangements will be difficult. The critique of dualisms (whether of gender, race, or nation), insisting as it does that nature is always relegated to a lesser status than culture, can entirely miss naturalization as a form of legitimation. As I repeatedly argue throughout this book, herein lies a great danger for environmentalists: arguing from or for the natural can support the very relations of power that produce environmental problems.

That ideas of the natural are central to the process of creating hegemonic (dominant) ideologies is an old insight, a founding principle of Marxist, deconstructionist, and feminist analysis. Scholars have long understood that ideology in the West produces itself as though it were a commonsense understanding of the world (Gramsci 1971), presenting the way things are as "natural" in the sense of the way things were meant to be or have always been, that is, a dehistoricized understanding of social relationships. What I want to expand on in this useful and widely used insight is the specific role in U.S. cultural myths played by ideas of the natural *as nature*—in particular, popular stories about biology, evolution, and environment. How do these stories about the natural operate within the process of ideological cultural constructions, and what consequences *for* nature are embedded in hegemonic naturalizations of social inequality and histories of conquest? For contemporary cultural studies critics, myths are not lies, legends, or fairy tales, but the layering of deeply symbolic cultural narratives in such a way that the resulting logic seems natural. As Roland Barthes has written, "We have reached the very principles of myth; it transforms history into nature" ([1956] 1972, 129). That naturalness, especially for U.S. cultural myths, I argue, is not incidental or merely the sign of ideology. It is essential to the particular structure of Western post-Enlightenment ideologies, what Michel Foucault called the rise of "biopower" (Foucault 1980). It is also consequential for environmentalist rhetorics.

Dominant Western cultural myths have presented nature as a foundation of truth while at the same time imagining history as a story of the movement from nature to culture, from "primitivism" to "civilization," from hunter-gathering, to agriculture, to barter, to industrialization, to global capitalism. Western ideology always presents those who are seen as more natural (including natural resources themselves) as ultimately destined to "develop" to become part of a commercial, commodified system. As this process takes place—not incidentally, as the environmental consequences and social suffering of a profoundly unequal economic system built on unchecked growth becomes clear—those who are made to seem closer to nature (while inferior to those who are thought of as "civilized") have often also been given the burden of symbolically representing the tragic aspects of "development," as inhabitants of a lost imaginary Eden. This is an ideological move used to obscure historical contingency and ongoing resistance—justifying power, inequality, and conquest by making those processes of "development" seem inevitable, natural, part of a destined and unstoppable evolution. The tragic Edenic loss of nature to the inevitability of progress is also the ideological birthplace of U.S. environmentalism (Merchant 2004).

Thus, it is not accidental that the embodiment of nature as the source of truth, inspiration, and inevitability develops in some of the same historical and cultural contexts, at least in the United States, that see the rise of a particular form of environmentalism. As I have mentioned, the form of environmentalism that is typically called preservationist or conservationist conceives of nature as separate from humans (and often more sacred and more pure). The nineteenth-century idea of nature as a refuge, a concept that supported the creation of our first national parks and wilderness areas, also contained within it contrasting ideas of urbanization as a site of racial pollution and corrupt effeminacy. More recently, biocentric environmentalist positions (such as deep ecology and Earth First!) that see nature as under attack by human actions can be quite hostile to including radical environmental perspectives, that is, environmental issues that concern the health and well-being of people, especially poor people and people of color (Darnovsky 1991; Guha 1989; Taylor 1997). As a result, the involvement of some forms of environmentalism with dominant notions of nature as truth, purity, and inevitability can be problematic both socially and environmentally.

In the post–cold war era in which we find ourselves, a mainstream environmentalist narrative framework that contains many of these problematic notions about nature appears in various popular culture arenas (as I illuminate in different ways in this book). Despite presenting itself as being about environmental issues, this narrative is also (though perhaps unintentionally) telling stories of legitimation about social and economic inequality. When nature is seen to represent truth, what implication does that have for our efforts to solve problems of nature, of environmental damage and threat? Can we see environmental problems clearly when nature is made to be a repository of ideological narratives, to justify social inequalities? What if, to complicate matters further, those very social inequalities are part of the cause of environmental problems? These are the kind of questions I address in the following pages.

Overview

In the chapters that follow, I try to uncover these intertwined difficulties by using a two-tiered reading strategy within each chapter: first, I examine ideas and stories about nature and the natural used in dominant cultural narratives; second, I look at the use of these same themes in more explicitly environmentalist popular culture. Roughly, I am interested in the twenty-five-year period from the middle 1980s to the first decade of the twenty-first century. Though environmentalism became a powerful contemporary movement in the early 1970s, not until the post–cold war period did environmentalism (at least a mainstream version) became a more or less acceptable narrative frame in U.S. popular culture. Why this should be so and what meanings are generated through this environmentalist framing are discussed in more detail at different points in the book. Primarily, I look at popular culture of this period—U.S. films, television ads, music videos, video games, product catalogs, and magazine ads—to examine how U.S. popular culture reflects and shapes political discourses.

I pose these questions in a number of arenas and following certain differing, though interlocked, narratives of the natural. Chapter 1 is a general discussion of certain patterns found in the conceptualization of nature and the natural found in U.S. culture, using as examples primarily magazine and television ads. I give examples of common themes such as women as Mother Nature; nature as purity; nature as wild, dark, raced; heterosexuality as natural; and indigenous people as closer to nature. Following the strategy of turning to the use of these patterns for explicitly environmentalist purposes, I close the chapter with a look at a Michael Jackson video that uses several of these tropes. This first chapter is meant as an overview of some of the dominant ways of presenting nature and the natural that are critiqued throughout the book. The six following chapters are arranged as couplets within three sections.

The first section, "Naturalizing Frontiers," looks at various uses of the important popular narrative about American character and American history called "the myth of the frontier," in two different cultural and historical contexts. In chapter 2, I analyze certain U.S. movies in the 1980s and 1990s that use environmentalist themes to engage with the history of U.S. genocide and oppression of indigenous peoples, and I examine the rise of the Ecological Indian as a common symbol of a contemporary frontier myth. I close this chapter with a look at the difficulty that the popularity of the Ecological Indian figure presents for indigenous environmentalist activists. Chapter 3 follows the development of the myth of the frontier as it is used in a global and extraterrestrialist framework, examining a U.S. discourse of evolutionary progress that "naturally" ends in space exploration and the ubiquitous use in both popular culture and environmentalist culture of the image of the Earth seen from space.

The second section, "Naturalizing Reproduction," focuses on the ways in which narratives of nature and the natural are used to promote the white U.S. nuclear suburban family form as the only natural family form, analyzing the twinned messages of heteronormativity and racism that are deeply embedded in these messages, as well as the problematic environmental consequences of this normative cultural discourse. Chapter 4 looks at the explosion of environmentalism as a theme in children's movies of the 1980s and 1990s, both as a general framework for moral lessons in kids' films and as specifically environmentalist cultural products. Chapter 5 expands on this analysis by looking at a more recent period, examining the proliferation of penguins as symbols in the popular cultural contest over whether to promote conservative Christian or gay family values, the resulting problematic understanding of the processes of cultural and planetary reproduction, and the ways in which this contest plays out in environmental documentaries and ads in the context of growing concern over global warming.

The final section, "Naturalizing Globalization," builds on the analysis in the preceding chapters to ask pragmatic questions about how we might proceed if we addressed environmental and social questions together within the broader systems of global conflict and the global economy. Chapter 6 suggests some ways that activists in the global peace and justice movement (who share an intertwined anticolonialist, feminist, and environmental justice perspective) might critically analyze militarism and violence. It examines popular cultural versions of genetic determinism that justify violence as inherent in certain versions of masculinity, then uses a set of contemporary films about the U.S. invasion of Iraq as well as war-related video games as a springboard to explore the relationship between war, environmental catastrophe, violence toward women, global economic inequality, and contemporary colonialisms. Chapter 7 is an examination of the popular cultural narratives employed in the spectacular growth of the green, organic, and natural products industries, coupled with a discussion of the ways in which images of racial and sexual purity and discourses of imperialism may play a part in whether this new flourishing of green capitalism can be connected, or not, to sustainable fair trade and labor practices. I conclude with some comments aimed toward ways to implement desirable social change based on the analytical tools generated in the book.

The Politics of the Natural in U.S. History and Popular Culture

Nature plays an important role both materially and ideologically in our culture. Environmental problems, particularly the contemporary concern over global climate change, are crucially important challenges, and we urgently need to be able to think clearly about them. But because "nature" and "natural" have such powerful and complex cultural resonances, the use of these concepts as tropes, metaphors, and dominant cultural narratives has the capacity to confuse and obscure our thinking about environmental policy. In particular, metaphors and narrative frameworks about nature in regard to "human nature"—for example, understandings of human evolution, inherent human capacities for violence and sex, and differences among humans—have often been used to naturalize and therefore justify social inequalities.

There is often quite a gap between how scientists or policy-makers approach questions of nature and environment, and dominant ways of thinking and talking about nature and environment found in popular culture. Nevertheless, the latter provides a framework within which the former is often accomplished. Habits of popular and commonsense thinking can be shaken up by a few simple questions: what are the effects (political, rhetorical, ideological) of calling something "natural"? Does the descriptive term *natural* assume or justify social behaviors and relationships that are actually built on inequity and exploitation? What are the consequences for the environment (the land, animals, water, ecosystems, the biosphere) of these inequitable social arrangements, and how does an

uncritical understanding of "nature" and the "natural" prevent us from seeing these connections?

One of the commonplace assumptions I want to challenge is that nature
and culture, or the natural and the artificial (or "manmade"), are identifiably
and completely separate, and should be so. This is one of the major problems
with popular and mainstream environmentalist discourses. Challenging this
separation goes against the grain for many of us because it troubles the
obviousness or transparency of what we think of as "natural." But we only
have to look at the daily news to see how often ideas of what is natural and
what counts as nature are called into question or called into service to support various claims or positions. Moreover, the lines of separation between
artificial and natural, whether or not they were ever clear, are now becoming more and more blurred. New genetic, agricultural, and reproductive
technologies (such as cloning, stem cell research, in-vitro fertilization, and
genetically modified foods) are serious material challenges to the idea that
nature and culture are or should be separate. And assuming that these two
realms are separate obscures human environmental responsibilities.

Why, when advanced scientific technologies make pinning down
exactly what is meant by the term *natural* harder and harder, does the
designation remain so powerful a tool in important contemporary social
debates? Arguments from nature have long been used to try to justify social
phenomena such as racial and cultural differences in educational outcomes;
different gendered athletic, academic, or work abilities; or the rightness or
wrongness of gay relationships. None of these arguments have proven to
be conclusive, yet attempts to find biological explanations for social differences persist. This is not to say that there are no biological differences
between various groups of people, but the effort to find such differences
has been historically a suspect project.

All of these examples are about people or about "human nature." Things
get even more slippery when we think about the ways in which changing
ideas of nature have affected our conceptions of the environment. Are wilderness areas necessary for preserving "wild nature"? Or are they managed
and commodified leisure resources in which "wild nature" has to be controlled? (For instance, think about the policy of removing "problem" bears in
Yellowstone who have gotten too used to humans and their garbage.) Should
every species be saved from extinction, or should some be allowed to expire
because of "natural selection"? But how would we define "natural selection"
in today's world, when new bacteria are formed in reaction to antibiotics
used for medical purposes and industrial chemicals permeate the biosphere,
possibly affecting our own ability to reproduce? If the bioengineering of a

better tomato means introducing salmon genes into the tomato, does that violate the integrity of both tomato and fish? Are wild salmon superior to farmed salmon if they are basically the same genetic organism, and on what basis are they superior? Are wild salmon preferred because they are valued by a culinary market, because they may taste better? Or are they better for environmental reasons, because the farming of salmon causes a significant amount of pollution? Should wild salmon be valued just because they are authentic, the "original" fish? Or should salmon be preserved because they are sacred beings to several Northwest tribal peoples, who have developed reciprocal relationships to the fish over thousands of years? Obviously, what is "natural" is highly contested and therefore deeply political.

Using Arguments from Nature as a Tool of Power

The arguments and controversies examined in this book, then, are not about the old debate between nature and nurture. I want to move beyond that way of thinking to critically examine the power of the idea of "the natural" and "nature." The persistence of the debate between nature and nurture begs the question about why those divisions (nature/nurture, nature/culture, biology/society, natural/artificial) have such power in certain cultures, especially U.S. culture. The answer is that these distinctions are tools of power. Historically, calling something "natural" places it in an arena of truth, inevitability, and immutability, beyond the reach of social criticism or democratic dialogue. Understanding the history of these ideological uses of the concept of nature and examining the multiple ways in which the politics of the natural affect our social and environmental policies permits us to critically assess various solutions to environmental problems and social inequalities. Under the world-spanning threat of global climate change, such a critical perspective may make the difference in having a world of elite green fortresses in a sea of poverty and war or having an open, equal, and sustainable society.

Those of us who are engaged in and subjected to Western (that is, Anglo-European), especially U.S., dominant cultural and political discourses (encompassing a major part of the world now) are familiar with the idea of nature being invoked to settle arguments or determine policy directions. This is in part because nature has a special place in the founding of Western and particularly U.S. culture. Since the Enlightenment, nature has played the role of foundation, truth, ground—replacing the older European feudal framework of religious order, divine right, and ordained social hierarchy. The overthrow of traditional European monarchies and the establishment of new republican democracies were based on the idea that "natural law" rather than divine law should be the determining source of the rule of law. This radical shift in political arrangements was based on the idea that (some) men were naturally equal and had natural rights inherent in their status as (male) humans and as such were able to rule themselves rather than be ruled by kings and queens.

However, these revolutionary men did not intend to eliminate racial, gender, and class hierarchies that supported their own privilege and power. (This is why I call their understanding of human rights "huMAN" rights.) Some way of justifying the continuance of certain social hierarchies had to logically fit with arguments for natural law. Thus, the idea that some social inequalities were naturally determined developed hand in hand with the idea that freedom and equality were natural rights. In the same period as a series of revolutions brought modern Western democratic politics into being through a celebration of the natural rights of "man," the new modern sciences of botany, biology, anthropology, and primatology were "discovering" a host of "natural" differences that proved the superiority of white European men over European women and certainly over all Africans, Indians, and other subjugated peoples. Thus, while upper-class white European men were freeing themselves of feudal and monarchical structures, they could conveniently argue that others were naturally unfit for the same rights. Those Others included darker-skinned peoples, European women, and in some cases lower-class European men of particular ethnicities such as Irish, Mediterranean, and Slavic peoples (Merchant 1980; Schiebinger 1993). Such logic even allowed slaveholders to see themselves as champions of freedom, given that freedom was understood to be "natural" to white men while slavery was "natural" to Africans (Africans being understood as less "civilized") (Morgan 1975).

The effect of the legitimating function and long historical dominance of this set of contradictory ideas about nature is that Westerners often use the idea of the natural to justify either the way things are or the way we think things should be. To say that some phenomenon is "natural"—for instance, women doing most of the domestic work and child care around the world or men being more likely to use violence—seems to settle the question for many people. Not surprisingly, arguments from the natural often settle the question for those who benefit from the social arrangement in question; tragically, these arguments can sometimes also convince those who suffer from inequality and exploitation to accept their situation.

Arguing that something is natural tends to prevent an examination of whether the situation is just or right or desirable. For example, instead of questioning the conventions of the contemporary gender division of labor, some might argue that women doing most of the domestic work may be unfortunate, but it is part of "nature's plan" (connected to women's biological ability to give birth) and therefore the best arrangement. This argument conveniently obscures the ways in which men can do much domestic and child-care work beyond the actual birthing and breast-feeding that are biologically determined. Women's unequal domestic responsibilities are far from natural, even if they may have been, in specific circumstances, tied to women's biological ability to give birth. Aside from actually giving birth and breast-feeding, other caregiving activities and domestic work have no biological basis for being gendered. Gathering fruits, weeding a field, holding a baby, using a microwave, sewing a shirt, washing a sick elderly person, or driving a kid to day care are not acts determined by nature.

The pattern of seeking a biological or natural basis to justify inequalities of sex, ability, race, and class is not merely located in an origin story of Euro-American democracies—in other words, something that happened a long time ago in the 1600s and 1700s—but is repeated throughout the nineteenth and twentieth centuries, in discursive and institutionalized practices such as eugenics, social Darwinism, Nazism, IQ testing, exclusionary immigration laws, sterilization policies, and certain problematic racialized and gendered projects within employment law, educational policies, and scientific research. Because of this history, those less privileged by "naturalized" social arrangements are rightly suspicious of arguments from nature. Are these "natural" justifications for social inequalities continuing into the twenty-first century? Contemporary debates and trends in popular culture suggest that they are.

But the politics of the natural are complicated. Because of the importance of nature as a legitimating idea, there has been a liberatory possibility in strategically arguing from nature against social norms. Several groups of people originally left out of the Enlightenment social contract have used this liberatory aspect of arguments from nature effectively in many historical cases. For instance, antislavery activists (and later, civil rights activists) argued that if one believed that black people were human, then they must deserve full human rights, since the Declaration of Independence stated that "all men are created equal." Those rights, as the U.S. founding documents state, were meant to be conceived as "natural" rights, inherent in the status of being human (or at least male, according to the founders). A more contemporary example of a liberatory argument from the natural is the strategic power of the insistence by many gay and lesbian activists that sexual orientation is biologically innate and thus unchangeable, "natural" and therefore deserving of social acceptance. This point of view argues against hundreds of years of seeing same-sex practices as "unnatural" and seeks to remove the taint of perversity from same-sex relationships by seeing them as just as "natural" as heterosexual relationships.

Finally, arguments from nature have been used to sustain and inspire numerous environmental struggles. Seeing nature as valuable to human society, or as valuable in itself, has been an important basis for struggling to preserve, protect, and respect animals, plants, ecosystems, and the planet. Environmentalists have had their own complicated debates about what is natural and what is artificial; whether humans should manage nature or leave nature alone; whether environmental decisions should be made based on scientific, cultural, or spiritual grounds. But the shared sense that nature should not be damaged and that entities in their "natural" state are valuable and deserving of our protection—for their own sake, as a touchstone for human understanding, and as the basis for human life—is a core concern of environmentalists and has been a strategically effective and liberatory use of arguments from nature.

Looking over these different uses of arguments from nature, we can see that the contested and illimitable social meaning of the natural means that the same kind of arguments can be and have been used strategically many times for both conservative and progressive ends. One should not always assume that if an argument is being made that some phenomenon is natural, especially a social phenomenon, then it is necessarily an argument meant to prop up social inequality. But one can (and should) be skeptical of such arguments, given their historical uses as justifications for human and environmental exploitation.

In particular, as environmental activists struggle to preserve and support environmental health, integrity, and sustainability, their ways of thinking about and arguing for nature need to be carefully examined for the worrisome possibility that problematic assumptions about nature and the natural that have been used to oppress groups of marginalized peoples are being unintentionally promoted. For example, in 2004, the Sierra Club was thrown into turmoil by some members' attempts to protect against the "natural" increase in population thought to be caused by Latina/o immigrants who "naturally" had more families and thus, in their view, endangered the environment. These members tried to have the Sierra Club promote anti-immigration policies as a way to protect U.S. natural resources, despite the ways these same anti-immigration policies were being used to support racism and the exploitation of immigrant workers (Chea 2004).

Furthermore, some environmentalist discourses about nature may not be the best way to achieve environmental goals, because they may contain unexamined assumptions or justify problematic arrangements that support environmental degradation as well as human exploitation. The Sierra Club example above fits this case as well, since policies that are exploitative of and harmful to immigrant workers and depend on racist attitudes toward those workers, such as the lax restrictions on pesticide use in U.S. agriculture, are environmentally polluting of food, water, and soil.

Asking people to become critical of any claim to the natural, from any position, sometimes creates anxiety that an insistence on the sociality of nature means that one is arguing that nature does not exist for itself; that seeing nature as socially constructed means that we can do whatever we choose with the nonhuman environment; that nonhuman entities and places will therefore have no integrity that must be respected by humans. This conclusion seems extremely problematic to me, and I reject it passionately. A seriously critical position on claims to the natural need not leave us in a state in which "nature" is infinitely flexible, always already socially constructed, immaterial, and endlessly exploitable. To persistently question the status of the natural does not mean that we should reject the materiality, the corporeality, the autonomy, or the agency of the nonhuman (or the human, for that matter) (Haraway 1991, 1992). Nor should we deny out of hand all indications of biological differences, as long as we can ensure that social bias does not affect our understanding of them (which, given the long history of the misuse of arguments from the natural, can be a very difficult thing to determine). Humans are inside, coexisting, and interdependent with nature rather than outside and independent of it. Human biology is responsive to and changed by our environments, just as part of human nature is to change environments; whether those changes are for the better or worse needs to be carefully judged. Thus, the human and nonhuman environment is co-constructed, and there are material (and should be ethical) limits on our interaction with "nature"—whether land, animal, body, water, air, or the planet (Bird 1987; Cuomo 1998; Sandilands 1999). Unless we are willing to recognize the deeply political and ideologically variable status of "nature" in our culture, however, we cannot adequately discuss and decide these important questions about our interaction and use of the environment. So I argue that a relentlessly critical examination of claims to the natural is the best way to learn to respect natural beings and processes (including our own natural status as animal-humans or humanimals).

Patterns of Nature in U.S. Popular Culture

What are the dominant uses of symbols of nature and arguments from the natural in U.S. popular culture? In teaching this material as a class for many years, I have learned a lot about these patterns from my students (to whom I owe a giant debt for their questions and contributions).[1] One of the things I always did with my U.S. students, early in the class, was a wonderful exercise suggested by Carolyn Merchant in her useful book *Radical Ecology* (1992). I recommend that readers try this exercise for themselves. In this exercise, students are asked to reflect, in writing, on their personal histories and the relationship between those histories and their understanding of the environment. They are specifically asked what environmental values, or understanding of nature, arose from their social class, their racial/ethnic identity, their gender, and (an element I added to Merchant's framework) their sexuality.

After the essays were written and students had had a chance to consider the unusual notion that their social locations might influence their conception of nature, I would usually take some of a class period to ask the students to brainstorm about what "nature" meant to them. I would write these words and phrases so that all could see them, and then we would discuss the patterns that developed. Though a wide variety of things could be associated with the idea of "nature," there were, inevitably, consistent patterns that showed up in the U.S. context. This exercise demonstrates that the concept of nature is immensely flexible and variable, yet there are still repeated patterns of meaning that can be discerned, and these patterns are historically as well as culturally specific.

For my U.S. students, one of these patterns was a sharp split between human and nature ("anything 'not us,'" one student offered); another was the idea of nature as a source of purity and regeneration; another was nature as inevitability (a law of nature, an instinct, a dictate of behavior, whether individual, social, or environmental); another (especially for my students from the small farming communities of eastern Washington) was nature as source of food, as site of labor and economic productivity; another was nature as wildness, unpredictability; another was nature as the source of scientific knowledge; and another was nature as the location for play, leisure, and physical action. It was rare to encounter notions of nature as urban, as community, as constructed in interaction with humans, as autonomous agent, or as self.

These patterns could be predicted, given my usual pool of students (primarily but not only white, middle class, from the state of Washington) and the history of Western ideas about nature. In Raymond Williams's wonderful book of cultural and historical definitions, *Keywords* ([1976] 1983), he says, "Nature is perhaps the most complex word in the [English] language" (p. 219) and goes on to declare, "Any full history of the uses of nature would be a history of a large part of human thought" (p. 221). Williams ([1976] 1983, 219) identifies three main senses of "nature":

(i) the essential quality and character *of* something;

(ii) the inherent force which directs either the world or human beings or both;

(iii) the material world itself, taken as including or not including human beings

In these definitions, one can see the likelihood of confusion between the "is" and the "ought" of nature—how Westerners commonly understand nature both as the ways in which things are materially and as the ways in which they are meant to be, instinctually and essentially.

Another scholar of the meaning of the word *nature*, William Cronon, has come up with a list of meanings of nature quite similar to my students' list but also containing some notions rarely found in our brainstorms in class. In his introductory essay to the important collection *Uncommon Ground* (1996, 34–50), Cronon identifies the following versions of nature that arose out of the conversations among the academics who contributed to the volume:

Nature as naïve reality
Nature as moral imperative
Nature as Eden
Nature as artifice, as self-conscious construction (such as parks)
Nature as virtual reality
Nature as commodity
Nature as demonic other, as avenging angel, as the return of the repressed

My students tended to be comfortable with the first three ideas (nature as real, as right, and as good) and the last (the "fury of Mother Nature" cliché, so often used on the Weather Channel). But the idea of nature as artifice, as virtual reality, and as commodity tended to be rejected vehemently. My students wanted their nature to be "real" in some way or another, revealing a strong and common assumption that the natural and the artificial are essentially different (though, as it turns out, any attempt to define the boundaries between the two always generates a lively, unresolvable debate). They also wanted their nature to be untouched by the dictates of the capitalist market economy. Thinking of nature as co-constructing reality with humans meant to them that the force of nature as a location of immutable rules and dictates, a concept in which they were deeply invested, was uncomfortably diluted. My students were often resistant to the idea that nature had a history, both in the sense of being thought of differently at different times and by different cultures and in the sense of being composed of a changing, dynamic set of interrelated entities (including humans) existing in chronological dimensions. Donna Haraway's important concept of "naturecultures" (2004) is meant to encompass these two meanings of nature as a historical entity and, though resisted, ultimately proved a very useful neologism for my students (and, obviously, for me as well).

Although nature is a concept that is essentially contested (that is, it cannot be resolved into one broadly accepted and fixed meaning), as Cronon and many others have pointed out, it is at the same time a powerful force and flexible source of legitimation. Given the diversity and the inconsistency of both Cronon's and my students' lists of meanings for "nature," it is not surprising to see arguments from the natural made from almost any social or political viewpoint to justify widely divergent and even opposing positions. But identifying common patterns, repeated narratives of nature, allows us to analyze serious social and environmental consequences of the deployment of these repeated ideas.

Advertising Natures

As John Fiske (1989) has pointed out, popular culture is a dynamic location where important struggles between those more powerful and privileged and those less powerful and privileged are often carried out. Because it is an arena of intense commodification and because postindustrial global capitalism is always seeking out new niche markets, subcultural oppositional meanings expressed in fashion, food, music, art, and other social practices are constantly being incorporated into dominant expressions of nonoppositional support for buying particular products. At the same time, new oppositional meanings are continually created, sometimes through the very process of consumption itself.

In a chapter called "The Jeaning of America," Fiske describes the process of "excorporation" (subcultural oppositional cultural practice) and "incorporation" (dominant recasting of oppositional meaning into new commodities) as an ongoing dance within the semiotics (or meaning-making practices) of the global economy. Uses of the idea of the "natural" are frequently tokens in this process. His primary example of this process of excorporation and incorporation is jeans, the way in which a garment that at one time referred to the working class in the 1930s and 1940s, was taken up by folk musicians and rockers in the 1950s and 1960s, and was worn torn and faded by young radicals in the 1970s has now become a ubiquitous item of clothing, signaling meanings of youth, status, and high fashion devoid of oppositional content. But even as these meanings changed, Fiske argues, jeans remained symbolic of "naturalness," representing many ideas associated with nature (freedom, comfort, informality, purity, and so forth), thus showing how connections with naturalness can mean many things at the same time that they obscure the sociality and variety of the messages being relayed (Fiske 1989).

Examples from U.S. advertising demonstrate some of the uses of what I have been calling "naturalization." Over the years, my students and I have assembled an archive of hundreds of such ads, only a few of which I can refer to here. These ads exhibit various ways of using images of nature in connection with images of social stereotypes, showing the ubiquitous character of these patterns in U.S. culture. This is not because there is an advertising conspiracy to justify social inequalities with images of nature. Rather, when analyzing ads, you are examining something like a social unconsciousness, since ads are designed to reflect and appeal to our common desires, beliefs, and values. Marita Sturken and Lisa Cartwright (2001, 89) explain,

> Advertising often presents an image of things to be desired, people to be envied, and life as it "should be." As such, it necessarily presents social values and ideologies about what the "good life" is. It is also a central strategy of advertising to invite viewers/consumers to imagine themselves within the world of the advertisement. This is a world that works by abstraction, a potential place or state of being situated not in the present but in an imagined future with the promise to the consumer of things "you" will have, a lifestyle you can take part in.

Because the creators of ads hope to make some powerful symbolic connections with images that will spur people to consume their product, they often draw upon what they assume are widespread commonsense beliefs. Sometimes ads do so in the seemingly opposite approach, by flouting or contradicting widely held assumptions to associate their product with rebellious individualism and freedom from convention. But this move, while often masquerading as resisting conformist attitudes, can still serve to reinforce stereotypes and dominant logics. This might be called "the exception proves the rule" effect; we only notice that something goes against the grain when we accept that there is a grain. Sturken and Cartwright (2001, 206) put it this way: "Advertising uses particular codes and conventions to convey messages quickly and succinctly to viewers. While some ads intend to shock us or capture our attention through their difference, most advertising provides information through the shorthand language of visual and textual conventions. Hence, most ads speak a mixture of familiarity and newness." Ads thus create ideological connections, but often they do so because they reflect preexisting ideological narratives. Because they are designed to appeal to many people, ads are revealing items through which dominant patterns of social meaning in a given cultural context can be ascertained.

A 1994 Discovery Channel ad that tells the viewer to "Explore Your World" (fig. 1) is an image that summarizes many of the patterns addressed in this book. The ad shows six "faces": a Mayan or Aztec sun mask, an Aboriginal man, a Native American man, a jet pilot in a helmet and breathing apparatus, a woman in an obscuring headdress, and a leopard or jaguar. Because the ad exhorts the viewer to "find yourself here," I often begin an analysis of this image by asking my students to see whether they can find themselves in any of the images. Are they a wild cat? An Aborigine? The very few of my students who are Native Americans or Middle Eastern women are clearly not assumed to be the likely audience for this ad. Sometimes I ask my students to find the white man in the picture, and they frequently respond by pointing to the mask of the fighter pilot. In stating that these are "the faces of the world," the Discovery Channel ad presents only one face as the face of technology, of "civilization," and my students are used to associating white men with technology and civilization. The other faces—the vaguely Aztec mask, the Aborigine, the American Indian, the leopard, and the Middle Eastern woman (signified as Muslim by her headdress)—are all placed on the same plane, the natural, "primitive" backdrop to the process of exploration and achievement. The jungle cat is equivalent to the other "natural" faces, all of whom (except the fighter jet pilot) belong to those who have been colonized in the name of "progress" and "discovery." In this way, the colonization and exploitation of nature is made equivalent to the colonization and exploitation of darker-skinned peoples. The statement of the ad, "The faces of Discovery are the faces of the world," tells us that all the "nonmodern" faces are the ones to be discovered; the pilot's mask puts "him" in the position of discovery, given the close connections in U.S. cultural mythology among discovery, space exploration, and militarism. This set of assumptions—that "primitive" peo-

The faces of Discovery are the faces of the world.
When you set your sights on the fascination of real world entertainment, find yourself here.

EXPLORE YOUR WORLD™

1. "The faces of the world" (Discovery Channel 1994)

ples are closer to nature, that there is a natural evolution from "primitive" to "civilized," and that history inevitably involves "progress" defined as a movement toward modernization and industrialization—makes the cost of such "progress," for nature and for particular people, invisible. The fact that the logo of the Discovery Channel is firmly over the mouth of the Muslim woman in effect symbolically silences the one woman present as well.

Another set of dominant patterns visible in late-twentieth- and early-twenty-first-century ads is various associations of gender and sexuality with nature. The representation of women as natural and nature as female is very common. This often places women in an inferior position in relation to men; they are depicted as closer to nature, the "primitive," the animal, the body, and farther from culture, the "civilized," the human, and the mind. Ads frequently portray women as landscapes, as surrounded or subsumed by nature, while men are often shown physically dominating nature, as in many ads depicting men skiing, driving cars, or rock climbing. Men's

2. Flower women (Dolce and Gabbana 2006)

nature is to *control* nature, while women's nature is to *be* nature. (John Berger [1972, 47] made a similar statement on the representation of women in art: "Men act. Women appear.") For instance, you can often see ads that show women (especially white women) as flowers or defined by intense floral or plant-related images. Figure 2 depicts women whose flowery dresses embed them so thoroughly in their leafy background that they can barely be distinguished from nature; it takes us a minute to notice that there are two pairs of identical women in this Dolce and Gabbana ad, their individuality matters so little. By contrast, one rarely, if ever, sees men as flowers.

But what *kind* of woman or man is depicted influences how they are visually associated with nature. There are patterns within patterns here, varying meanings of feminized or masculinized nature articulated by differences of race, class, and sexuality. In a rare image of a man surrounded by and subsumed within nature, from an article entitled "Natural Man" (fig. 3), the man appears to be Latino, with brown skin and carefully coiffed, dark curly hair, offering a coquettish smile while surrounded by fruit. The accompanying article is about Philip Berkovitz, the founder of a line of skin- and hair-care products called PhilipB, and the text assumes a close

NATURAL MAN

Philip B whips up beauty recipes in the kitchen.
By Judy Ellis

Everyone understands that apples and pears, tomatoes and thyme are good for you. Philip Berkovitz, founder of Philip B Botanical Hair and Body Treatment products, wants you to know that they're also good *on* you. "Before there was a beauty industry, people relied on the earth's elements and nature's harvest to nourish and revitalize skin and hair," observes the Los Angeles beauty expert. With his food-based body-care products, Philip redefines this age-old tradition, and the result is a veritable feast for the hair, skin and senses.

Mixed with the purest of ingredients and the highest percentage of essential oil extracts of any products on the market, his line includes such savory-sounding products as White Truffle Oil Shampoo with Hops and Nettle Extract, and Wild Cucumber and Blue Orchid Body Lotion. Claims Philip, "Other botanical products' extracts constitute only 2 percent. Mine run as high as 34 percent."

3. "Natural man" (Mirabella Magazine 1999)

connection between the idea of "natural" products and health. The coiffed hair, the smile, and the association of the word *fruit* as a derogatory word for a gay man assists in this image to convey the idea that if a man (especially a brown man) is portrayed as surrounded by or enmeshed in nature, then he is a feminized man (that is, stereotypically gay). When a man is shown actively engaged in and in control of nature, he is usually depicted as white, straight, and very stereotypically masculine. For example, a Stetson

4. Nature is freedom (Stetson Cologne 1999)

cologne ad (fig. 4) shows a white man in the midst of exuberant exploration, escaping from the dark, claustrophobic city to the "freedom" of the
country. In splashing his way up a river, he epitomizes strength, control,
and manly success.

Another key pattern within a pattern is the association of white women
with nature used to represent purity and health, as in an ad for White Rain
shampoo in which a naked blonde woman ecstatically raises her arms in
supplication to a powerful waterfall (fig. 5). Another version of this asso-

Rain on me.

White Rain shampoo. Pure and simple.

White Rain

Spend time in the rain.

5. Worshipping purity (White Rain 2001)

L'original

6. Mermaid (Evian n.d.)

ciation of white women with nature as purity is the Evian mermaid, who, as part fish, is a sensuous, fabled creature reveling in the purity of water (fig. 6). When a man is used in the complementary Evian ad, he represents "l'original" by symbolizing the "primitive"—he is a brown-skinned man dressed as an Inuit, or Eskimo (to use the colonizer's term for these indigenous people, one that is referenced in figure 7 by the "igloo" the man is making). In this Evian ad, in a common visual association, indigenous

L'original

7. "Eskimo" (Evian n.d.)

people are closer to nature, depicted as more authentic but less "developed" and lower on the chain of evolution than white people—therefore, they are "l'original" people, whose lost purity consumers can capture by using Evian's product.

Unlike the Evian mermaid, most of the images one encounters that associate women with animality are of a more sexualized and aggressive nature. Leopard patterns or leather clothes are often used to convey the

8. Sex, nature, and tanning (Supre 2004)

9. "Dressed to kill" (B-Boots 2002)

"animal" sexuality of women. Figure 8, for example, celebrates a white woman's passionate sexual attraction to the ocean, proposing the medically dubious idea that "natural" tanning products might be healthier for one's skin. The leopard-skin bikini the model is wearing is an advertising cliché, signaling the association of animals and female sexuality.

When women of color are represented as animals, these associations of aggressive sexuality tend to take an even more negative cast. An ad for B-Boots shows a brown woman, dressed in leather, displaying a ferociously clawed and aggressive demeanor (fig. 9). A handbag ad for Bottega Vega

10. "Mix accordingly" (Hennessy n.d.)

compares the leather of the purse with the textured skin of a black woman. And a Moschino ad shows a very dark African American woman displayed on a wall like a trophy animal, dressed in leopard skin.

Some advertising images present lesbians as inherently exhibiting this animal sexuality, as in two women cuddling in leather for Guess jeans. A Hennessy ad combines many of these patterns of naturalization in one image (fig. 10). Here, two women who are to be "mixed accordingly," vaguely hinting at some nefarious same-sex and cross-racial activity to come, have small labels placed above their heads. The white woman, blonde, slim, and dressed in white—all signs of purity—is a "vegetarian," thus refusing to even eat animals let alone be associated with them. In contrast, the Asian woman, dark, dressed in black, applying very dark lipstick to an open mouth, is designated a "man-eater," not merely a voracious animal herself but a man-hater as lesbians (and feminists) are stereotypically assumed to be. This image repeats a long-standing sexist dualism that women are either pure or corrupted, good girls or bad girls, including the racist overlay of the association of good with white and bad with dark skin. But the messages embedded in this image work also to convey other ideas: the association of female sexuality with animality, of women of color as dangerous and abnormal, of same-sex sexuality as "mixing" those that are naturally meant to be kept apart. At the same time, promises the Hennessy ad, all of this danger and perversion is incorporated as pleasurable and erotic, especially for a male viewer who is in proper control of the situation (which seems to mean buying the right cognac).

Another common set of patterns in ads shows nature as heteronormative, that is, supporting the idea that heterosexuality is the only natural, normal and acceptable sexuality. Some examples are images such as a Geo Tracker ad that exhorts the male and female pair to "be two with nature" (fig. 11) and a clothing ad that shows a man and woman together and states, "We're all love junkies. Nature made us that way." A Winston ad foregrounding a mule's head clearly wants us to reject any sexual liaison that is nonreproductive as "unnatural," as it says, "The mule. The offspring of a donkey and a horse. They cannot reproduce. A perfect example of not leaving well enough alone." Thus the idea of purity in tobacco is associated with naturalness, normative sexuality, and health in one move.

Another, very different but pervasive, pattern of naturalization presents nature as something to conquer, to claim, and to control; this pattern is often associated with ideas of nationalism or militarism. The images that use this pattern usually are related to ideas of straight, white masculinity as dominant, hard, powerful, muscular, and competitive. Car ads revel in this imagery, especially those vehicles (such as trucks, SUVs, Jeeps, and Humvees) that are associated with this kind of dominant masculinity. As these tough vehicles bound over a rough, natural landscape, the ads convey a sense of achievement in conquering nature, a thrill of power in being able to penetrate into hidden, desirable, and wild places. These images are often also associated with nationalism as well as masculinism, as in an ad for a ski area that asks, "Should you plant your poles? Or the flag?"

Be two With Nature.

11. "Be two with nature" (Geotracker n.d.)

Images of conquest such as these are also frequently associated with the mythology of the frontier and with associations of Native Americans as nature, as objects of colonization and expropriation. One of the richest images that represent this pattern is not actually an ad but part of a story published in the fashion magazine *W* about the private life of Ralph Lauren, the clothing designer, entitled "Ralph's Teepee" (Reginald n.d.). Apparently, when Ralph wants to get away and relax, he can do so in his very own buffalo-hide teepee on his 14,000-acre ranch in Telluride, Colorado, a teepee he designed himself and filled with trendy furniture and furs. His ability to create a teepee, to expropriate Native American culture and land in the West, is celebrated as a mark of his strength, his success, his independence, his individuality, and his competitive drive. "I don't look at anyone else's teepee. I make my own rules about how I want to live," says Lauren in this story, completely obscuring the costs to others of his "lifestyle choices" and the way in which only his wealth allows him to make his own rules.

All of these patterns of naturalization use ideas of nature, sexuality, animals, the earth, and the natural not only to produce the desire to consume a product (which is the function of advertising) but also to reproduce views that underlie many social inequalities: that nature is female, white women are pure, female sexuality is dangerous, women of color are closer to animals, heterosexuality is more natural than homosexuality, "real" men are competitive and violent conquerors of nature, and indigenous peoples are primitive by being closer to nature or are inherently ecological. Though ad designers seldom consciously intend to support these ideas, they do want to use images that are powerful and bring associations of pleasure, desire, and achievement—dominant associations that may depend on ideas that support unequal social hierarchies. They reveal the degree to which the American psyche remains deeply riddled with prejudices that the ads rely on and reinforce.

Environmentalist Images of Nature

While finding stereotypes in ads may not be surprising, the same kind of problematically naturalizing images that are seen as culturally powerful by advertisers are also widely used in environmentalist messages. Is it troubling to find the same kinds of visual associations for both consumerist and environmentalist messages? Indeed, how are advertisers relying on what appear to be environmentalist images to ease their buyers' minds about the ecological dangers or the "goodness" of the products being sold? Clearly, ads such as the Supre one for tanning lotion promote a common theme that "natural" equals "healthy" and suggest that environmentalism should be seen as positive. The idea that nature is pure or healthy is a longstanding one. But a positive association with environmentalism has only become dominant in the past twenty-five years, as the environmentalist movement has become more accepted—as long as a mainstream version of environmentalism is being referenced. This encourages environmentalist associations to be used even when the content of the ad is by no means ecologically positive. For example, American Spirit cigarettes, the very name of which uses the image of Indians to stand in for a notion of purity, produces an organic line of tobacco. The idea that organic tobacco might be more than marginally healthier to smoke is patently silly (though it might be better for the workers picking the tobacco). Another example is evident in the environmentalist image of the whole Earth that appeared in the series of Humvee television ads that ran in the spring and summer of 2004, combining references to the militaristic origins of the Humvees with the notion that being able to ride roughly over the earth (let alone use the amount of gas the Hummers use) is pleasurable and desirable. These television ads begin with the excitement of driving the vehicles, then inevitably end with the camera panning back until we see the beautiful blue curve of the Earth seen from space.

This image, of the Earth seen from space, is an important one for U.S. culture, as it was first achieved during the cold war and the space race that was supposed to represent the epitome of U.S. ingenuity, technological ability, and competitive spirit (see chap. 3). Yaakov Garb (1990) points out that this beautiful image of the Earth seen from space presents it as an object that can be gazed upon at will, owned, and contained. Garb argues that this is a form of feminization of the Earth, as this kind of gaze is historically a view that maintains masculine power over women as objects. He also argues that the whole Earth image presents the planet as naturally harmonious and pure, allowing us to fantasize that all the occurrences on it are uniform and in balance, without conflict and pollution. Both of these tendencies (dominating the Earth and seeing it as naturally harmonious) inhibit us from understanding the Earth as a dynamic, complex, interrelated set of entities enmeshed in both conflict and cooperation, an Earth in crisis. The whole Earth image allows us to universalize the environmental dangers to the Earth without having to understand the way in which differential power and privilege means that responsibility for environmental devastation is not equally shared (Garb 1990).

For example, a public service message from the Ad Council about recycling shows an image of the whole Earth above the statement "If you're not recycling, you're throwing it all away" (fig. 12). While this is a good message, it gives the false impression that individual recycling is the key to "saving the planet" and that everyone's lack of recycling, no matter who they are and where they fit in the chain of production and consumption, is a cause of the most important damage to the planet—that is, one person could "throw it away." The image is also used positively in a Women, Environment and Development Organization poster, which, under an image of the whole Earth, states, "It's Time for Women to Mother Earth." I have discussed elsewhere (Sturgeon 1997) how this image tries to use the association of women with nature and with maternalism to inspire women to environmentalist actions, but it ends up being a troubling message about women having to do the (house)work of cleaning up environmental damage. In both these cases, the whole Earth image is problematic in that it tends to obscure the underlying causes of environmental problems and encourage superficial solutions. Since, as Joni Seager argues (1993), the biggest environmental polluters and exploiters are governments, militaries, and corporations—all patriarchal institutions in which men have most of the power—and since, as many have pointed out, Global North countries

12. "Throwing it all away" (Ad Council 1988)

use more environmental resources than do Global South countries, images of a whole Earth that obscure these kinds of differentials of power, resource use, and access to decision making do not help us to think more clearly about environmental problems and solutions.

Environmentalist images that depend on the notion of woman as Mother Nature abound. One of the posters for the Fourth World Women's Conference in Beijing shows a woman with an Earth in her womb (fig. 13), and a button about threats to rain forests depicts the forest as a woman (fig. 14). One of my favorite artists, Judith Baca, in her beautiful mural painting *Balance: World Wall* (1990), uses an image of the world as pregnant female. Her written description of the mural does not emphasize nature as feminine but celebrates a balance between male and female: "'Balance' represents the return to a healthy balance between the male and the female, the yin and the yang, the moon and the sun. The central image of the new-born sun is surrounded by the rhythms of the earth and the sky—the cycles of their moon, the rise and the fall of the tides, the planets that, when grown together, replenish the soil."[2] Despite this intention to depict a balance, the overwhelming and moving image of the sun being born at the end of a vagina-like river is clearly an image of nature as female. This image, like all of the ones I have just discussed, is very beautiful, and as environmentalist messages, they can be moving. But the use of the images of a Mother Earth brings us back to dualist notions of culture as male and nature as female that have proven to be destructive for women and for nature.

What we see when we look at these patterns of "natural" images, then, is that even when environmentalists create images of nature, they fall into the trap of stereotyping. Because of the pervasiveness and deep emotional resonance of these tropes, it is very hard to avoid using them and still create powerful environmentalist messages. But the costs of such resonant images may be too high for people and for the environment alike. One final example summarizes many of the patterns of nature just discussed and provides insight into the damaging effects of these images.

The Michael Jackson video *Earth Song* (1995) is a powerful story about the devastation visited on the planet, people, and animals by environmental destruction and war.[3] It is an emotional plea for fighting against these things, using three narrative frames: rain-forest destruction in South America; the poaching of animals, particularly elephants, in Africa; and the ravages of war in Bosnia (all places unnamed but clearly evoked in the film). Intercut with these three narrative frames are images of Michael Jackson, walking through and sometimes dancing in a burnt, smoking, and devastated clearcut forest. In these scenes, despite his torn black and red clothes

13. Giving birth to the whole earth (Beijing UN Conference on Women 1995)

14. Woman as rain forest (button)

of mourning, Jackson is a bright beacon within a dark vision of a dystopian future (or perhaps the present). As he sings, sorrowfully and angrily, Jackson plays the role of both messenger and savior, calling on everyone to be moved to action and to reverse the damages to people and the Earth.

The video opens with several introductions to the three crises featured. In the first, South American indigenous people standing in a group watch as gigantic rain-forest trees are cut down. They are dressed in loincloths, marked thereby as indigenous and thus "naturally" in touch with the forest. While bulldozers rip out huge trees, they stand helplessly by. One member of the tribe, a woman with a beautiful and wise face, stands in the front of the group as though she is their leader.

The second set of images introduces a group of African tribal peoples (in this case, the Maasai, though not identified as such in the video), also dressed in "native" costume and jewelry. The people watch in grief as elephants are killed, their tusks stripped and their carcasses left to rot in the sun.

The third scene is an unidentified Eastern European country, in which the people, dressed in Western clothes, are fleeing from a bombing. One man, who is the focus, seems to be the father of a family, and his little daughter is shown riding a bike. When the bomb hits, we see the girl's bike riderless on the ground, the man's sorrowful eyes, and then his body lying on the ground, his eyes closed.

As Jackson sings out in anger at these events, the sense of desperation and helplessness seems to shift—to anger and a call to action. The Maasai, the indigenous rain-forest tribe, and the Bosnian people fall on their knees and dig their hands into the earth. Jackson stands between blackened stumps of trees, flings out his arms to each side, and, grasping the two trees, begins to proclaim the absolute need to stop the damage and suffering. Clinging to the trees, in the position of Jesus on the cross, Jackson seems to summon up a powerful wind, which we see flowing over the planet seen from space. As he does this, images of the indigenous South American tribe, the Maasai family group, and the Bosnian family are intercut with him. They are all kneeling on the ground, with their hands in the dirt, pulling the earth toward them in supplication. In particular, we see the South American tribal woman over and over, her wonderfully passionate face expressing power and growing hope, as, in rhythm with the pushing and pulling of the dirt, the wind begins to reverse the damage. Literally rewinding the images, the elephants grow back their tusks and rise to their feet, the trees leap into the air and heal their trunks, and the Bosnian man, lying on the ground, opens his eyes, rises to his feet, and walks again.

Despite the power of the images and music, Jackson's environmentalist message, especially in its appropriation of indigenous people as symbolic of animals and nature, supports a widespread but highly questionable notion that environmental problems can be solved only by "returning" to a "primitive" past. The idea is underlined that a hunting-and-gathering culture is the only kind that can truly be in harmony with nature. The strong Christian imagery of Jackson on the cross and the Bosnian man rising again like Lazarus belongs to the already industrialized landscape, one that shows no signs of natural renewal but nevertheless somehow is the location of the power to accomplish change. This mixed, contradictory message may be emotionally moving, but it also produces a sense (given that most viewers believe the idea of a wind that has the power to heal the planet is a fantasy) that the damage has been irreparable and there are no realistic, pragmatic solutions. Only faith or magic or Michael Jackson or some unknown force that would return us to a mythical prehistoric but ecological past can help us. Otherwise, we are doomed to ecological disaster. Furthermore, power remains with the industrialized landscape, and Jackson presents himself as a leader of the entire world (a dubious premise, I think). While Jackson may be lionized by this message, no pragmatic environmentalist practice is offered as an answer, when in fact actual sustainable environmentalist practices have been developed by numerous people, including those in the Global South.

The closing frame of *Earth Song* solicits donations to Jackson's foundation, Healing the World, which had several promising programs focusing on children's well-being around the world but is now pretty much defunct. Like many of Jackson's charitable efforts, it seems to have been started with much fanfare and went on to accomplish various successful but short-term programs before it disappeared through lack of attention or support by the star (Hall 2004). The temptation to see this pattern, like the visual and musical plot of *Earth Song*, as simply about the aggrandizement of Michael Jackson is strong, but there is another interesting aspect in the video's use of images of the natural as pure, primitive, and innocent.

Earth Song's emphasis on saving the rain forest, protecting animals, and ending the suffering caused by war reflects issues of long-standing interest to Jackson. But I think it not accidental that *Earth Song* was produced in 1995, fairly soon after Jackson's short-lived marriage to Lisa Marie Presley, which occurred quite suddenly following the first time Jackson was accused of child molestation. He had also just faced numerous rumors that he had extensive plastic surgery, including efforts to lighten his skin color. Though he strongly denied both of these accusations at the time, one cannot help but speculate that Jackson, in the face of constant gossip about his "unnaturalness," in terms of both his sexuality and his appearance, wished (perhaps unconsciously) to associate himself more closely with nature and the natural. How he (and the director, Nicholas Brandt) accomplished this brings out the dangers of using popular images of nature often chosen to try to raise people's consciousness about environmental problems.

Jackson turned to dominant tropes: nature as female; people of color, especially tribal peoples, as closer to animals and nature; "primitive" cultures as naturally more ecological because they are separated from the corrupt influence of "civilization"; nature as pure and nontechnological; and environmental problems as caused by individual action and individual belief rather than corporate, governmental, or institutional practices. All of these ideas ironically reinforce social inequalities and direct us away from understanding the root causes of environmental destruction or learning about practical environmental solutions. These tropes both support social stereotypes and divisions of labor that underlie social inequalities and point us toward ways of thinking about environmental problems that obscure their systemic corporate and political causes.

Because powerful cultural discourses about what is natural have been involved for so long in arguments about social justice and equality as well as in arguments about how to solve environmental problems, it is past time to look at the intersections of these arguments. The fact that commonplace ideas about what is natural have been implicated in justifying both social inequality and environmental exploitation means that we must make an effort to examine how these areas are linked. We need to entertain the idea that solving environmental problems must also involve eliminating social injustices and vice versa. That we still might want to strategically argue from the natural in opposition to certain social and economic arrangements is a possibility, but we should do so with fuller knowledge of the history and effects of such arguments.

Naturalizing Frontiers

2

Frontiers of Nature

The Ecological Indian in U.S. Film

Some of the patterns in the symbolic use of the natural in U.S. popular culture are the ideas that indigenous people are closer to nature and that "progress" is an inevitable, natural development from the "primitive" to the "civilized," coupled with racist ideas about who is naturally "primitive" and who is naturally "civilized." These ideas are central to a defining American cultural myth, the myth of the frontier, which first legitimized a nation created through invasion, conquest, and settlement, then validated the expansion of U.S. control and influence around the world. The myth of the frontier has remained a flexible but powerful story in U.S. popular culture and has been tied more firmly to an environmentalist framework in the late twentieth and early twenty-first centuries (Nash 2001).

The idea that the frontier was a necessary part of forming an American character and a democratic polity is a long-standing cultural theme. Supporting the myth of the frontier were notions of nature particular to the United States that made this process of conquest seem instead like an inevitable process of natural evolution. The concept of the frontier always assumes a boundary between something called "civilization" and something called "wilderness." In the American imaginary in which the western frontier is the mark of our nation's character, "civilization" is symbolized by the white cowboy, gunfighter, or lawman, while "wilderness" is symbolized by Indians, distinctively western animals such as wolves, wild horses, and buffaloes, and grand natural landscapes. The frontier is often depicted as a male arena, a place to prove a distinctive masculine character, connecting a narrowly defined normative masculinity to violence as an essential aspect of U.S. nationalism.

Looking at a set of movies released during the period from the 1980s to the present that remake the white cowboy as a man who is struggling with the guilt of acknowledging his complicity in genocide and imperialism and that promote the figure of the Ecological Indian (Krech 1999) as a sign of truth, I find in the contemporary frontier myth that redemption comes for the white man through a saving encounter with nature— usually in the form of a close relationship with an indigenous culture and an iconic western animal (though not always together). The repetition of this plot, I argue, shows the way in which an environmentalist narrative is transformed into one that is not about solving environmental problems but about a shallow overcoming of white guilt, particularly that related to post-Vietnam, post–cold war understandings of U.S. history. The film *Dances with Wolves* (1990) is most likely the best-known example of what I am calling the Ecological Indian plot, but numerous other examples exist as well. In these movies, environmentalism is removed from the sphere of politics and materiality and is reduced to a process of symbolic salvation through nature. The problem with the familiarity and repetition of this narrative within popular culture is that indigenous environmental activists and those who care about indigenous cultures have a difficult time making environmentalist arguments that are not eclipsed by this more popular plot. The environmentalist solutions presented by this plot (involving redeemed white men, the efficacy of violence, individualist environmental action, and mystical union with an abstracted nature) are not the environmentalist solutions we need.

What Is the Frontier Myth?

Elements of the frontier myth that supported early Euro-American settlement of the lower part of the North American continent comprise an intertwined set of powerful ideas, some of them myths with their own labels, which together legitimated the process called "progress" by the conquerors and "conquest" by those subjected to it. (The frontier myth is now revised in a global context; see chapter 3.) These ideological notions about nature, evolution, and destiny underlie continued U.S. colonial practices.

Richard Slotkin (1973, 1985, 1992) has argued that the frontier myth is the central myth of American nationalism and that Indians and nature are the most important motifs in that myth. The struggles against Indians and the domestication of the land (involving strenuous encounters with what the Europeans thought of as wilderness) were the intertwined central facts of European life in the New World, and violence was seen as the instrument of survival and success. Slotkin points out, "The first colonists saw in America an opportunity to regenerate their fortunes, their spirits, and the power of their church and nation; but the means to that regeneration ultimately became the means of violence, and the myth of regeneration through violence became the structuring metaphor of the American experience" (1973, 5). He later observes, "Generally speaking, the basic factors in the physical and psychological situation of the colonists were the wildness of the land, its blending of unmitigated harshness and tremendous potential fertility . . . and the eternal presence of the native people of the woods, dark of skin and seemingly dark of mind, mysterious, bloody, cruel, 'devil-worshipping'" (1973, 18).

Taking this aspect a step further, Jane Tompkins has argued that the frontier myth, especially as it is represented in the Western film genre, is centrally about promoting a particular ideal of masculinity that operated as a counterforce against a liberated femininity that arose out of women's social feminist movements of the nineteenth century (including temperance, suffragism, women's education, social welfare for the poor and immigrants, birth control rights, and other issues), which were centered in urban areas. The Western hero, in literature and in the movies, projects a masculinity that is nonverbal, violent, nonemotional, white, strong, effective, rough, and located firmly on the frontier, as against a femininity that is urbanized, verbal, weak, emotional, ineffectual, and nonviolent (Tompkins 1992).

The set of ideas called "the frontier myth" includes the following notions:

- Continued and expanding industrialization and commodification is an inevitable result of "progress," and the concomitant destruction of natural resources and environments is unavoidable (Marx 1964).

- The so-called primitive is (though perhaps noble) inferior to the so-called developed or civilized.

- History is essentially the story of social evolution, seen as "progress," a process paralleling natural evolution (a myth sometimes taking the form called social Darwinism, in which those who are successful in a competitive, socially unequal economic system are believed to be the "fittest").

- White Americans have a divinely ordained mission to "civilize" or "democratize" those (darker peoples) who are believed to be less cultured and more natural, as well as to occupy and "improve" their land (a set of beliefs sometimes called Manifest Destiny).

- Areas that white Americans may occupy in this process of evolutionary progression are in effect empty lands waiting for their use (Merchant 2004; Smith 1950), a concept often accompanied by ideas of the land as female, fertile, rapable, and in need of being tamed (Kolodny 1975, 1984), known as "virgin land."

- American character (democratic, masculine, honorable, hardy, innovative, individualistic, risk taking, competitive) is formed by the challenges of the frontier, as in Frederick Jackson Turner's famous frontier thesis, in which he proposed that the American character was forged out of the evolutionary process of development with first trappers, then traders, settlers, farmers, merchants, and finally city dwellers following one upon the other (Turner [1893] 1996).

- American nature, typically imagined as the mountains, plains, and rivers (often inclusive of the Indians) of the American West, is the prototypical arena necessary to produce American (masculine, competitive, militaristic) character, a point often demonstrated by invoking Theodore Roosevelt's mythos of the Rough Rider cowboy as the prototypical American, coupled with his desire to preserve wilderness areas as arenas where men could free themselves of the feminizing and corrupting influence of cities.

- The vastness of American nature is the necessary condition of the U.S. expansion, which guarantees our democratic institutions. Thomas Jefferson, in particular, believed that the foundation of natural law and the natural bounty of the continental United States were linked and that both were necessary to the creation of a stable democracy. His idea that the United States was "nature's nation" reflects his belief that democratic character was ensured only by providing more and more land for a nation of white, small farmer–citizens (Hausdoerffer 2004).

- Finally, the frontier myth relies on the cultural myth called American exceptionalism, the assumption that the United States is not really imperialist or expansionist, merely a reluctant warrior; in other words, Americans fight only to uphold democracy and protect the weak, never to dominate, exploit, conquer, or control.

Thus, to examine the frontier myth in U.S. popular culture means to examine a central narrative about violence, race, and gender that has constructed the United States' legitimacy as a nation and, later, as a global power. Moreover, to critically examine this myth requires us to carefully analyze the interlocking (and changing) ideas of Indians and of nature that are the heart of this myth.

These cultural narratives have been in place from the beginning of U.S. national history. But after World War II, a new element (one that emphasized the fragility of the Earth in the face of human technologies of war and genocide) entered the cultural fabric. The period of the 1960s and 1970s is a transition to this new inflection of the frontier myth. After the use of the atomic bomb and the full realization of the Holocaust, the successful landing of a man on the moon, the recognition of the misguided imperialism of the Vietnam War, and the challenges to U.S. rhetorics of freedom and equality made by the civil rights, women's, and gay liberation movements, as well as the early success of the environmental movement in the 1970s, a sense of the Earth and its peoples as fragile and endangered developed. In particular, the knowledge of the genocidal practices of the U.S. government in relation to indigenous and darker-skinned peoples (brought out by American Indian activists and scholars, as well as revisionist historians compelled by their opposition to the Vietnam War to challenge the myth of American exceptionalism) clashed with older notions of frontier society as an arena of good against evil, democracy against savagery. The long-standing romantic image of the Noble Savage was welded to the knowledge of the racism of the white conquest at the same time as it was revived by the countercultural sixties "back to nature" movement as a symbol of ecological purity. Post-sixties, post–Red Power, post–atomic bomb, post-Vietnam, the Noble Savage became the Ecological Indian,[1] an icon of redemptive nature, a source of solace from the damage caused by white, militaristic, and environmentally polluting U.S. society. The symbolic frontier became a cultural location in which white American men worked out how to be ethical but still were driven both to regain the violent masculinist character that made them strong and to fight on the side of good.

Whether this turn toward environmental and indigenous salvation of the guilty white man might be a deep enough split from the original frontier myth—whether it is free of racism or sexism or the idea that violence is a solution to social problems—is one issue worth examining. Another is the way in which the ecological twist to the frontier myth continues and strengthens the problematic binary between nature and culture, wilderness and civilization, that is common to mainstream environmentalism, a set of beliefs that prevents adequate solutions to environmental problems.

Changes on the Frontier: The Critical Noble Savage

In the early stages of the European conquest of the North American continent, Indians were often portrayed as wild, violent, immoral, degraded, and even nonhuman. In repeated moments of white aggression, as settlers moved West, the conflict between whites and Indians required a negative view of indigenous people, often accompanied by views of the wilderness as dangerous, untamable, and corrupt (Merchant 2004; Nash 2001; Slotkin 1973). The image of the Wild Savage justified the taking of Indian land, the decimation of numerous tribes, and the rejection of indigenous culture as valuable. Concomitantly (particularly after conquest had been achieved), another view of the Indian began to appear more frequently: the Noble Savage. This idea of Indians—that indigenous people were closer to nature and to a simpler, purer set of values such as courage, honor, and harmony— went hand in hand with the central mythology of American nature as the repository of beauty, spiritual renewal, and grandeur and is part of the founding moment of conservationist or preservationist environmentalism (Nash 2001).

The myth of the Noble Savage, involving the contrasting of good Indians to bad whites and the identification of the Indian with nature, is thus an old plot in American popular culture,[2] perhaps best exemplified by *The Last of the Mohicans* (1826), one of a series of classic novels by James Fenimore Cooper. In these stories, a white man finds friendship and family and gains access to attributes such as courage, strength, and loyalty by becoming as much like an Indian as he can without losing his racially superior status (sometimes he is adopted, sometimes a "half-breed," sometimes completely assimilated into the tribe). But since the Noble Savage was not the only mythological position for Indians in American culture, in most of these stories the figure of the Noble Savage is accompanied by the Wild Savage, or the bad Indian. White men also come in good and bad forms as they engage in the seemingly inexorable forward movement of the frontier, but ultimately, this narrative finds in Native culture (albeit usually when it is stereotyped) a place to critique white society while positing the indigenous culture, a primitive Eden of innocence and good, as ultimately doomed.

For example, *The Last of the Mohicans* is about Hawkeye, a white man adopted into Mohican society as a child who becomes an excellent shot with the long-bore musket (hence his nickname, "Long Rifle"). It contains all of the elements of the myth of the Noble Savage. While native society is depicted as more honest, egalitarian, and closer to nature than white society, racism (closely tied to the need to appeal to white audiences for books to sell) still requires that the hero, who is more brave, intelligent, strong, and heroic than others as well as the best shot, be a white man.

Similarly, U.S. films (particularly the Western) were central cultural products through which the tropes of the Wild Savage and Noble Savage were played out. Prior to World War II, most Westerns portrayed Indians in highly stereotypical ways and promoted the idea of the good white law-man as the hero, protecting white settlers from hostile Indians. Historically or culturally accurate portrayals of Indians were rare to nonexistent, as were Indian actors. If an Indian character was at all important to the plot or portrayed in more complex terms than a simplistic stereotype, the actor was almost always a white person. Starting in the 1950s, as the fight against Nazism promoted a new attachment to ideals of democracy as inherently nonracist, and later, criticism of McCarthyism and rebellion against the repressive culture of suburbia began bubbling up in the artistic subcultures of the period, some Westerns began shifting their depictions of American Indians. Margo Kasdan and Susan Tavernetti (1998, 124) argue,

> Although some silent films, such as D. W. Griffith's *Massacre* (1912) and James Cruze's *Covered Wagon* (1923), conveyed a tolerant view of Indians, the classic Hollywood Western of the 1930s and 1940s reinforced those images and stereotypes that had evolved during the previous century and that relied almost entirely on the figure of the bloodthirsty warrior whose hostile actions and threatening presence impeded the great westward expansion. This conception of American history shifted slightly in the 1950s when a variation arose in the genre. Several directors made B-Westerns that showed the white man's poor treatment of Native Americans: for example, greedy white traders swindling them in Stuart Filmore's *Half Breed* (1952) or hateful cavalry officers provoking them into battle in Sam Fuller's *Run of the Arrow* (1956). Anthony Mann's *Devil's Doorway* (1950), Delmer Daves's *Broken Arrow* (1950), and Robert Aldrich's *Apache* (1954) introduced a different characterization of Indians. Native Americans (albeit played by white actors) are central characters who are honorable and brave, yet targets of racism. The struggle between an admirable Indian and greedy, bigoted whites creates the conflict at the basis of the narrative.

In the post-sixties, post–cold war, post–Vietnam War period, this shift was amplified in revisionist Westerns that were strongly tinged with a critique of the imperialism and racism underlying the history of the frontier; these films made serious efforts to achieve cultural authenticity in their portrayal of Indians (Prats 2002). Though many movies could be discussed as examples of this shift, a few represent the best attempts at achieving culture authenticity and political critique.

The movie that most clearly marks this shift is *Little Big Man* (1970), which used a positive and complex depiction of Cheyenne society to criticize the warlike, corporate, and genocidal practices of white American institutions, especially the U.S. military. As in earlier and later Noble Savage narratives, the protagonist, Little Big Man (played by Dustin Hoffman), is a white man adopted into Indian culture. He witnesses the atrocities of the U.S. Cavalry, especially as directed by General Custer, as well as the overall mendacity and violence of white frontier society. Little Big Man experiences both white and Indian culture; in the end, he chooses the Indian one as superior. In general, the movie goes after the hypocrisy of every leading aspect of U.S. society: religion, conservative sexual morality, business, celebrity, and the military.

Arthur Penn, the director, made an unprecedented effort to depict Cheyenne society authentically, and although he was not consistent in this depiction (see Kasdan and Tavernetti 1998), it is the first film in which Indians are presented as complex, contradictory, and humorous people. That the voice-over provided by the Hoffman character throughout the film calls the Cheyennes by their own term for themselves, *human beings*, provides a constant undermining of racist stereotypes and makes the film groundbreaking in the history of U.S. Westerns.

Post–Vietnam-era, and therefore after the anti–Vietnam War movement challenged the notion of American exceptionalism by making visible U.S. imperialism around the world, the use of Native Americans to leverage a critique of militarism was not always directly made of the U.S. frontier in the standard Western genre format but instead was sometimes made through analogy, referencing U.S. intervention abroad by criticizing the genocidal actions of the British, the French, the Spanish, or the Catholic Church.

The Mission (1986) centers its story on the way in which participating in indigenous societies can redeem white men from the violence of white society. The director, Roland Joffé, had recently completed *The Killing Fields* (1984), which explores the devastation in Cambodia produced by the U.S. invasion. *The Mission* is putatively about a Jesuit mission in 1750 South America that protects the Guarani Indians from Spanish and Portuguese slavers. The central figure, played by Robert DeNiro, is a former slave trader and mercenary who has killed his brother and seeks redemption from his sins by becoming a Jesuit priest and joining a mission (founded by a deeply pacifist priest played by Jeremy Irons) dedicated to serving the Guarani. The DeNiro character renounces his attachment to violence and becomes part of the Indians' Edenic culture. But when the Spanish and Portuguese come to destroy the mission, he takes up arms again, only to see the mission destroyed anyway. The central conflict of the narrative, portrayed as between the greed of capitalist imperialism and the communitarian pacifism of the Jesuits, is clearly (given the mid-1980s context of the making of the movie) meant to be an analogy to the 1980s U.S. military intervention in and support of corporate exploitation of Latin and South America. This allegory is underlined by the appearance in the film (playing the role of a Jesuit priest) of Daniel Berrigan, a radical activist pacifist whose support of Latin American liberation theology played a large role in the popular opposition to U.S. intervention in El Salvador and Nicaragua.

The Guarani Indians in *The Mission* are children of nature—only partially dressed, joyful, peaceful, simple, and loving—serving as a strong counterimage to the warring European conquerors. For the most part, Joffé used South American indigenous people to play the roles of the indigenous people, although the language they spoke was not Guarani. At the end of the movie, all that is left of the Guaranis is a small band of naked children; they take a canoe up the river into the jungle, apparently to begin again from innocence to re-create their culture, while the white men who tried to save them are left dead.

Black Robe (1991; directed by Bruce Beresford) is another tale of Jesuit missionaries, this time during the French colonization of Canada in the 1600s. Father Laforgue is a young Jesuit priest who takes on the task of traveling from Quebec hundreds of miles north to a mission established among the Hurons. A party of Algonquins is delegated to take him up the river. Near their destination, they are captured and tortured by Iroquois. Though most of them are killed, some escape the Iroquois: the priest; his young French follower, Daniel; the head of the Algonquins, Chomina (played with depth by August Schellenberg, a noted Indian actor); and Chomina's daughter, Annuka. After Chomina dies, Daniel and Annuka (who are in love) leave the priest to continue to the Huron mission alone. Father Laforgue finds the mission in complete disrepair, with the Hurons dying of disease and the mission's priest near death. Though the movie ends with Laforgue conducting a mass baptism of the Hurons (who believe it will cure their disease), the concluding captions tell us that fifteen years later, the Hurons are massacred by the Iroquois and the mission is abandoned.

Beresford's film is notable for its strenuous attempts at historical accuracy and realistic depictions of the Indians. Using Native actors, incorporating the real languages of the Hurons, Iroquois, and Algonquins, and giving complex and ambiguous motivations to the Indian characters (as in *The Mission* and *Little Big Man*), *Black Robe* creates a harsh picture of European attempts to conquer the land and the indigenous people. Yet the Indians are not stereotypical Noble Savages, though there are elements of presenting them as more natural, especially in the contrast between the depiction of the Indians' open and animalistic sexuality and the priest's "unnatural" (there are hints that he is attracted to his young follower, Daniel) and repressed sexuality. The overarching impression given is of the almost complete inability of the two cultures to understand each other's basic beliefs and values. The exception in this film is the relationship between Daniel and Annuka, which overcomes cultural incomprehension through heterosexual romance, though not untouched by differences of perspective.

When *The Last of the Mohicans* was made into a movie in 1992 (directed by Michael Mann and starring Daniel Day Lewis as Hawkeye), it stuck fairly closely to Fenimore's narrative but made clear the more contemporary stakes for the Noble Savage as a critic of white society in the penultimate scene when Hawkeye argues with the shaman leader, Ongewasgone, for the lives of the two white women captured by the evil Huron Indian, Magua.[3] Hawkeye presents Ongewasgone with the choice of becoming like white men by murdering the captives or following the "Indian way" by sparing them. (The shaman, more pragmatic or perhaps refusing the cultural dichotomy of the good versus bad Indian, like Solomon chooses both ways.) Inserted into the movie where it does not occur in the book, Hawkeye's speech underlines the moral that the Indian society is less violent and more just than the genocidal white society.[4] The presence of two Indian actors who first became famous in the Red Power movement, Russell Means (Chingachgook) and Dennis Banks (Ongewasgone), further emphasizes the lesson of the movie that Indian society is better than white society.[5]

These movies are representative of the rise of the critical revisionist Western and (except for *Black Robe*, which uses the stereotype much less) rely heavily on the stereotype of the Noble Savage. For the most part, they engage in a serious attempt to present Indians as culturally specific, complicated, and equal to white people (if not clearly superior, as in *The Mission* and *Little Big Man*). They present critical versions of the conquest of Indian people and land by white societies. This form of revisionism represents major progress in popular cultural depictions of Indians and serious critiques of the frontier myth. Yet in continuing the stereotype of the Noble Savage, these movies still limit viewers' ability to understand Indians as fully human.

Jacquelyn Kilpatrick (1999), in discussing the more sympathetic depiction of Indians in U.S. films of the 1980s and 1990s, argues that the pressure of the Native American civil rights movement, especially in criticizing the popular culture stereotypes of Native Americans circulating in the use of Indian mascots and filmic representations, was largely responsible for a turn toward a more positive depiction. One of the clearest signs of this influence on these revisionist films is the attempt to produce cultural authenticity, using real Native languages, dress, and Indian actors (though less commonly actors from the actual tribe depicted). This aspect of the newer revisionist films directly responds to Native activists' complaints that the history of Native Americans in films depended on images that eliminated tribal differences and thus reduced the cultural complexity of distinct tribal cultures into a narrow stereotype (usually of Plains Indians, who are the iconic Western representatives).

However, Kilpatrick does not note the way in which, in the late 1980s and 1990s, such revisionism depended more and more heavily on the myth of the Ecological Indian, trapping dominant understandings of indigenous people more securely in the limited role of the Noble Savage by more explicitly tying representations of Indians to the function of portraying an ecological moral. Thus we should recognize the influence of mainstream environmental ideas on these moviemakers, as well as the influence of the Red Power movement. Despite admirable attempts at cultural authenticity, the overlay of the Ecological Indian returns depictions of Indians in film to the limits of the earlier Noble Savage stereotype. In the context of the growing acceptance of environmentalism in the 1980s, ecological plots become a way to transplant the critique of white society into a supposedly authentic indigenous perspective, undermining the effort to avoid stereotypes of Indian culture. David Ingram (2000, 46) observes,

> That a society based on non-industrial technologies may damage the environment less than one based on industrialism is a plausible hypothesis. But the idealization of Native cultures as living in a pristine, unfallen Eden is more a product of white liberal guilt and wishful thinking than of such considerations. . . . [T]he prelapsarian Noble Savage serves as a figure of moral absolution for the bad conscience of the industrial world, attesting to the continuing need of some white liberal Americans to construct a pure, original Other that embodies absent values of authenticity and community, and thereby transcends the alienations of modernity.

The clearly ecological motifs of the movies I discuss below, then, are not primarily about environmentalism, in the sense of being focused on environmental problems and solutions, but a revival of the Noble Savage stereotype transplanted into the revisionist Western. Such a narrative move is reductionist in terms of portraying environmental problems, let alone Indians; it reconstitutes the frontier myth on a different plane, by reifying the divide between (white) culture and (Indian) nature and implying that "real" Indians are already extinct or at least endangered species.

The Ecological Indian

As previously noted, the use of the Noble Savage as a critic of white society has carried an ecological twist throughout its history. For instance, in *Little Big Man*, the revered Cheyenne chief Old Lodge Skins speaks of the way the white man "does not know where the center of the earth is," and Little Big Man emphasizes the sacredness of the treaties made with whites because they are based on how long "the rivers flow, the grass grows and the sky is blue." But this ecological narrative thread, in movies and in other popular culture arenas, became much more explicit after the advent of the modern environmental movement in the 1970s.

Very important to the rise of the mainstream environmental movement was the image of the "Indian" actor, Iron Eyes Cody,[6] in a famous antilittering commercial aired on the second Earth Day in 1971. This ad, which marks the decisive entry of the Ecological Indian onto the contemporary popular cultural stage, was the opening salvo of an antilittering and antipollution group called Keep America Beautiful. The campaign, supported by "Lady Bird" Johnson (President Lyndon B. Johnson's wife), was carried on through television, magazine, and newspaper advertisements, local signage on highways, and both local and national antilittering legislation. A comprehensive effort, antilittering was one of the earliest successful environmental campaigns (along with the anti-DDT campaign started by Rachel Carson's 1962 book, *Silent Spring*). The 1971 television ad featuring Iron Eyes Cody caught most people's attention (certainly it is a vivid personal memory of mine). In the ad, Cody, dressed in buckskin leggings and fringed shirt, with a tall eagle feather in his long hair, is seen paddling a canoe in a stream. As he continues on the river, he passes floating garbage in the water and industrial stacks spewing smoke into the air. Pulling up on a bank covered with litter, he stares at a crowded interstate highway. A male voice-over says, "Some people have a deep abiding respect for the natural beauty that was once this country. Some people don't." At this point, a person in a car is shown throwing a bag of fast-food garbage that spatters Iron Eyes Cody's moccasins. As the camera pans tightly to his beautiful, seamed, wise face, a single tear courses from his sad eyes down his cheek, and the voice-over comments, "People start pollution. People can stop it."

The powerful image of the crying Indian convinced many that littering was wrong, that environmentalism was important (and not too radical), and, not incidentally, that Indians were natural ecologists. At the same time, Indians (like nature: "the beauty that was once this country") were represented as vanished and anachronistic—in a canoe rather than a car, Iron Eyes Cody is like a ghost visiting his devastated homeland. The ad also was typical of the mainstream environmental movement in that it proposed individual solutions to the problem of pollution, rather than addressing corporate responsibility. The focus was on people throwing litter in the street, not on the corporate smokestacks polluting the air. Though appearing in the first year of the U.S. mainstream environmental movement, the crying Indian image as a recurring presence in U.S. popular culture—not least in the form of many parodies (including one in *The Simpsons* animated television series) but also as re-created in another Keep America Beautiful ad in 1998—demonstrates the strength and longevity of the connection between the disappeared Noble Savage and an ecological popular consciousness.[7]

Another iconic Ecological Indian in popular culture is Chief Seattle (or Seaathl, a leader of the Suquamish and Duwamish tribes in western Washington in the middle 1800s). Once again emphasizing the set of ideas outlined above, the popular speech attributed to Chief Seattle was actually written by a white scriptwriter named Ted Perry in 1971.[8] The purported speech began by asking "How can you buy or sell the sky, the warmth of the land?" and continued,

> The idea is strange to us. If we do not own the freshness of the air and the sparkle of the water, how can you buy them?
>
> Every part of the Earth is sacred to my people. Every shining pine needle, every sandy shore, every mist in the dark woods, every clear and humming insect is holy in the memory and experience of my people. . . . We are part of the Earth and it is part of us. The perfumed flowers are our sisters, the deer, the horse, the great eagle, these are our brothers. The rocky crests, the juices in the meadows, the body heat of the pony, and the man, all belong to the same family.
>
> So, when the Great Chief in Washington sends word that he wishes to buy our land, he asks much of us. . . . For this land is sacred to us. . . . This we know—the Earth does not belong to man—man belongs to the Earth. This we know. All things are connected like the blood which unites one family. All things are connected. Whatever

befalls the Earth—befalls the sons of the Earth. Man did not weave the web of life—he is merely a strand in it. Whatever he does to the web, he does to himself. (Perry 1971)

This "message of Chief Seattle" caught the dominant popular cultural imagination and has had a long and varied life despite its questionable origins. A popular poster in the 1970s, it was used by the counterculture as an emblem of a new approach to nature. Joseph Campbell, the influential scholar of myth, referenced the message apparently without knowing of its spurious origin, in a 1988 book and television documentary written with Bill Moyers. Campbell (1988, 33) holds up the message as an exemplary position for human society and the Ecological Indian as the source of that wisdom:

> Moyers: No one embodies that ethic [nature as an interconnected web] to me more clearly in the works you have collected than Chief Seattle.
> Campbell: Chief Seattle was one of the last spokesmen of the Paleolithic moral order. In about 1852, the U.S. Government inquired about buying the tribal lands for the arriving people of the United States, and Chief Seattle wrote a marvelous letter in reply. His letter expresses the moral, really, of our whole discussion.

The "message of Chief Seattle" was adapted in 1991 as the subtitle for an award-winning children's book by Susan Jeffers entitled *Brother Eagle, Sister Sky*.[9] The book, which remains popular today, is criticized (by indigenous as well as white reviewers) for its use of Plains Indians to represent the Pacific Northwest origins of Chief Seattle. The cover shows an Indian man in a buffalo headdress (the buffalo is not native to the coastal Northwest) with his hand protectively placed on a white boy's shoulder, while the boy looks rapturously at a dragonfly on his hand. Doris Seale (n.d.) points out the various levels of inauthenticity in Jeffers's book:

> As she has changed the words to suit herself, so Jeffers has drawn pictures that, with the exception of what may possibly be a carved canoe on the title page, have nothing at all to do with any aspect of Northwest coast life. In a letter of reply to Dooley's review (*School Library Journal*, November 1991), Jeffers indignantly states that her research for the book was "extensive," and that "Mag La Que, Miyaca, Mahto-Topah and Bear Woman—all Lakota Sioux—edited the text and sat for portraits."
> That. Is. Not. The. Point.
> Native nations are *not* interchangeable. All the research in the world doesn't mean squat, if it isn't about the right people!

The powerful statement of "Chief Seattle's message," in all of its mutable inauthenticity, criticized the degradation of the environment by modern industrial development and consumerism but also fixed the idea of the disappeared Indian in the popular cultural imagination. It is a clear example that the position of critique given to the Ecological Indian relied on racist depictions of Native peoples as interchangeable despite their different tribal cultures, vanished in the past, outside of and different from white society. The stereotype of the Ecological Indian was leveraged by white environmental activists as an ecological critique of dominant culture through attaching the notions that Indians were closer to nature, more attuned to ecological practices, and uncontaminated by industrialized economies. This image of Indians fit nicely with the hippie imitation of what was conceived as the more ecological and socially egalitarian ways of indigenous peoples: long hair, beads, feathers, moccasins, leather clothes, pagan spirituality, and subsistence agriculture. The appropriation of Indians for these uses by the counterculture in the 1970s continued into the 1980s and can be seen in the present in the New Age movement's appropriation of what it claims to be Native spiritual practices (Smith 1991). The close fit between ecological practices and romanticized images of Indians thus suffuses the culture from the 1970s to the present.

Ecological Indians and Saving Animals in Contemporary U.S. Film

With the increased adulation of the Ecological Indian, nature and the indigenous as redemptive forces were deployed together in the late 1980s in numerous movies as a means to purify the guilt of white men and, as Megan Stern (1993) points out, "remasculinize" them on new cultural terrain. Given the instrumental function of new frontier narratives to mitigate white guilt over the violence of conquest, combining the critical Noble Savage image, the Ecological Indian, and some living agent of nature allowed white male characters to unproblematically access the power of the traditional masculinist association of violence with moral righteousness, of might with right. Composing this story within an environmentalist framework increased its moral fiber.

The rise of the "green" movie was not simply spontaneous but actively encouraged by environmental advocacy organizations formed by media activists. According to David Ingram (2000, 20–21), the Environmental Media Association (EMA) was formed in the late 1980s by "a group of Hollywood producers, directors, actors, and agents, including television producer Norman Lear and Disney chief executive Michael Eisner, and . . . actors such as Christopher Reeves, Lindsay Wagner, and Billy Crystal."

The EMA sought to promote both environmental narratives in the movies and environmentally friendly film production practices. Such organized promotion of the greening of U.S. film also reflected the general sense in the 1980s that environmentalist stories could reflect positive moral values and thus be an attractive narrative framework (see also chapter 4 of the present volume). Though some environmentalist-themed films had been made earlier—for example, *Silent Running* (1972) and *Soylent Green* (1973)—many more environmental films appeared in the late 1980s and 1990s. Several combined the Ecological Indian stereotype with the saving action of animals.[10]

Perhaps the earliest glimpse of this developing plot structure is the remake of *King Kong* (1976). An early example of a strongly explicit environmentalist film, the movie changes the original plot of *King Kong* (1933) by positing a corrupt oil executive rather than an out-of-control movie director as the bad guy who steals Kong from his island paradise. Although the racial structure here is white against black, the island natives and Kong are the essence of "primitive" (indeed, their close relation to each other secures the idea that the "primitive" is one step above the "animal"). But the environmentalist overlay creates an association of Kong with the Noble Savage. He is explicitly "the last of his kind" and, although too lustful and violent for "civilized" tastes, is portrayed sympathetically as kind, loyal, and fighting a just cause against the destruction of his island paradise by antiecological corporate forces. This is quite a different character portrayal than the terrifying beast of the original *King Kong*.

The Emerald Forest (1985; directed by John Boorman) is another example of a specifically environmentalist film, clearly attached to the narrative framework of the critical revisionist frontier story but using the Ecological Indian plot. Set in the Amazon, it follows the story of an engineer who brings his family to the rain forest to build a dam (which will cause untoward ecological destruction). During one of his first visits to the forest, the engineer's young son (played by Boorman's son, Charley Boorman) is stolen by a tribe of indigenous people and brought up as their own. Despite the little matter of child stealing that first introduces us to them, the members of this tribe are the good, light-skinned, ecological Indians (called the "Invisible People") in contrast to the bad, darker-skinned Indians (designated the "Fierce People") who assist the white men in their dam-building project. In a scene making clear the extensive ecological knowledge of the good Indians, the light-skinned Indian adoptive father of the white boy teaches him the ways of the animals in order to hunt, while stressing the necessity not to kill animals heedlessly or without paying attention to the animals' own need for survival. In the midst of this pedagogical hunt, the two hear a strange grunting and hooting, then see a group of the bad, black Indians moving through the jungle with apelike halting, brutish movements. These nasty Indians later are seen drinking and threatening to rape the Indian love interest of the boy.

Boorman made a serious attempt to achieve cultural authenticity. Traveling to the Brazilian rain forest, he spent three weeks in a Xingu village called Kamaira. In his version of a white man becoming indigenous, he lived in the shaman's dwelling and accompanied the Kamaira villagers on religious and hunting excursions into the forest. According to a reporter writing about the genesis of the movie, Boorman went through a personal transformation: "[He] saw the boredom of repetitive daily tasks transform itself for him into a kind of beauty in the knowledge of permanency. . . . 'Increasingly,' Mr. Boorman says, 'I felt Takuma [the shaman] was in possession of a knowledge, a consciousness, that far surpassed my own. I can't imagine ever seeing things quite the same again'" (Noble 1985). Not wanting to disrupt the Kamaira villagers' lives, Boorman used Indian actors from Brazilian urban areas and taught them Xingu rituals, dress, and dance.

Though this attempt at authenticity is commendable and far outstrips the efforts of most Hollywood moviemakers to respect indigenous peoples, the story Boorman created relies heavily on frontier stereotypes of the Ecological Indian and Noble Savage contrasted with the Wild Savage (for example, in his outrageous depiction of the Fierce People). The white boy gone native, Tommé, is shown as unredeemably savage and animal-like (he is intensely white skinned but is dressed in a leather breechcloth and adorned with feathers and tattoos), especially in the scene where he goes to the city to seek his father's help. After finding the multistory apartment building where his father lives, Tommé scales the outside of the building, in a shot copying similar scenes from the *King Kong* movies where the giant ape climbs skyscrapers (perhaps this was Boorman's homage to the ecological moral of the Dino de Laurentis/John Guillermin 1976 remake of *King Kong*).

The film's plot was based on a true story, in which the young son of a white engineer was taken by a South American forest tribe and found years later after many years of searching by his father, who decided to allow him to remain in the tribe. The ecological overlay to the story, in which the building of the dam is criticized and the dam is ultimately destroyed by the combination of the white man's action and Native magic in tune with nature, was entirely Boorman and his scriptwriter's invention (Noble 1985). This need to firmly associate indigenous people with nature undermines

Boorman's attempt at truthfully portraying the Kamaira villagers, though it fits the narrative seamlessly into dominant U.S. cultural expectations. Ultimately, both depictions of the Invisible and the Fierce People are thus made culturally inauthentic and problematically stereotypical.

When the boy, on behalf of his adopted tribe and the rain-forest animals, seeks out his father to plead for the dam building to stop, his father first rejects his argument. But the father begins to doubt his decision as he encounters the beauty, peacefulness, and innocence of the good Indian tribe. The primitive ecological example of the tribe shows the father not only the way to redeem his guilt as the tool of industrial development but also an avenue to reclaim his place in his son's affections (at the price of letting his son return to the tribal state of nature).

In a strange, mystical scene closing the movie, the father-engineer sets dynamite to blow up the dam just before completion. But the explosion fails to break the dam. Nevertheless, as result of the Invisible People's rituals, a huge rainstorm has arisen, accompanied by an overwhelming chorus of tree frogs (there is a South American rain-forest amphibian called the emerald forest frog). The frogs swarm onto the dam and it bursts. Like most of these specifically environmentalist films, encounters with indigenous peoples are not enough to achieve redemption; animals also function as tools for an ecological saving grace.

Another clear depiction of the use of the intertwined ideas of indigenous ecological and animal redemption of white male guilt is Kevin Costner's *Dances with Wolves* (1990). This is the story of a white soldier named John Dunbar (played by Costner), morally sickened by his part in the Civil War, who is deployed in the West to man an isolated outpost in Lakota territory. His voice-over claims that he sought this post so that he could "see the frontier before it is gone forever." Lonely and sad, he befriends a wolf, which he names Two Socks, that keeps him company in the desolate plains. After a time, Dunbar meets a Lakota warrior, Kicking Bird (Graham Greene), who brings Dunbar to his tribe and slowly teaches the white soldier the language and customs of the Lakota people, naming him "Dances with Wolves" after seeing him playing with Two Socks. An adopted white woman is already part of the tribe; she first becomes Dunbar's interpreter, then his love interest. Though treated with suspicion by some of the Lakota people, especially the warrior Wind in His Hair (Rodney Grant), Dunbar proves his worth in a buffalo hunt by saving a young Indian man from a wounded buffalo's charge. After he eats the heart of the buffalo, he is confirmed as a member of the Lakota people. Because he chooses to fight on the Indian side when they are attacked by U.S. troops (who are aided by "bad" Indians), the troops shoot Two Socks and Dunbar, mistaken for a "real" Indian, is captured. Refusing to betray the Lakotas and rejecting his white identity, he loses his new family and his tribal paradise forever.

One of the crucial scenes in the movie is the buffalo hunt, which amplifies the ecological moral of the narrative. The Lakotas and Dunbar come upon a massive slaughter of buffaloes, with hundreds of the animals' corpses dotting the plains, stripped of their hides and left to rot. Dunbar recognizes that the culprits "could only be white hunters." The power of this scene, with the Native people walking past the dead and mutilated animals with tears in their eyes, confirms the antienvironmental nature of white society and foretells the notion that the Indian people are, like the buffalo, doomed to slaughter and extinction.

The makers of *Dances with Wolves*, as with the other critical revisionist Westerns I have discussed, insisted on authentic portrayals of the Lakota people. Costner, who as director, producer, and lead actor clearly saw the project as his personal mission, found speakers of Lakota to teach the actors the language (though apparently they used only the feminine form, so the male Indian actors sounded like women), hired many Indian actors as well as Lakota people as extras, and consulted tribal historians to make sure to present the actors in culturally accurate costumes and activities. All this commendable use of present-day Lakota knowledge and people belies the film's strong message that the Lakotas were extinct, their culture gone and their existence firmly in the past. Their harmonious, ecological way of living could only exist, the film implies, in a premodern state. The film ends with the following caption: "Thirteen years later, their homes destroyed, their buffalo gone, the last band of free Sioux submitted to white authority at Fort Robinson, Nebraska. The great horse culture of the plain was gone and the American Frontier was about to pass into history" (Costner 1990). Nothing is added about the actual survival of Lakota culture, despite the appearance of contemporary Lakotas in the film and mentions of their assistance in the credits. Similarly, the idea that the frontier "has passed into history" elides the ongoing strength of the myth and the institutions it creates as it continues to justify U.S. expansion and structures the lives of indigenous peoples and the descendants of white settlers within the nation.

This narrative of redemption for a white man who becomes conscious of the genocidal and antiecological character of his society follows the formula found in most of these revisionist frontier narratives: the white man becomes Indian (or sometimes is already partly Indian) and through contact with indigenous society (often facilitated by an animal) engages in an act of rejection of his own history and becomes accountable to ideas of justice and equality. But this story is a narrow and limited avenue to true responsibility, a dead end for real change that would create social justice and environmentally sound practices. *Dances with Wolves* is a tragedy— placed in an unreachable past, it takes for granted that the Indians will disappear. They are the losers of history. The drama of redemption is internal, involving personal, not social change: the advertising tagline for *Dances with Wolves* was "Inside everyone is a frontier waiting to be discovered."[11]

The Ecological Indian Goes Global

The Ecological Indian plot can also be used to justify U.S. conquest abroad. For example, an interesting twist on the formula can be found in the film *Hidalgo* (2004), starring Viggo Mortensen, fresh from his star turn as Aragorn in *The Lord of the Rings* (2001–2003). In *Hidalgo*, released a year after the U.S. invasion of Iraq, the Ecological Indian plot takes place on a global scale, moving the scene of the frontier from the United States to the sands of the Iraqi deserts. Advertised as based on true events, *Hidalgo* is the story of Frank Hopkins (Mortensen), a man whose life story encapsulates the tragic fall and heroic rise of the frontier myth but on a global stage. A superlative horseman who served an important role as a Pony Express rider and a messenger to the U.S. military during the Indian wars in the West during the late 1870s, Hopkins was also famous for endurance racing, always with his preferred "wild Indian" (mustang) horses. A tall tale–teller who was rumored to be part Indian, Hopkins was a larger-than-life figure about whom there is a fair amount of controversy.[12] In the movie, working as an army messenger, Hopkins delivers the fateful order to the U.S. commander of the troops at Wounded Knee on December 29, 1890. The troops, as in real life, massacred many unarmed and unsuspecting Indians, including women and children.

The movie makes clear that Hopkins is part Indian, though ambivalent about his identity. At Wounded Knee, an Indian woman calls him by his Sioux name (the movie does not distinguish between the different tribes historically incorporated under the name Sioux), "Blue Child," and he clearly knows some of the members of the tribe by name. After the massacre, we see Hopkins next in a drunken state as a member of Buffalo Bill's Wild West show, with his friends Calamity Jane and a Sioux elder, Chief Eagle Horn (played by the eminent Dakota actor Floyd Red Crow Westerman, a musician and activist for Indian rights and the environment). In a scene set in the train moving the troupe from place to place, Eagle Horn asks Hopkins, whom he calls "Long Rider," to translate for him in a conversation with Buffalo Bill. The scene serves to demonstrate Hopkins's Indian identity (he speaks the tribal language and stumbles over saying the tribe's concerns are his own), as well as the idea that the wild horses, the mustangs, are disappearing in concert with the tribe. Hopkins translates, "Chief Eagle Horn says our, his, nation's hoop has been broken and scattered and the buffalo herds have been destroyed, the elk and deer are gone and now the government is rounding up our wild horses and they plan to shoot them before the first snows." The horses, like the Indians, are being confined to reservation-like land and murdered.

The movie then moves on to its main plot: Hopkins is challenged by Bedouin sheikhs to enter an ancient three-thousand-mile-long race, the "Ocean of Fire," traditionally involving only purebred Arabian horses, which ends on the shore of Iraq (despite the fact that Iraq as a name of a particular country dates only to World War I, when it was created out of separate regions by European treaties—which of course begs the question of why the scriptwriters wanted to use the name). Three motifs run through the action: the Bedouins are a warrior horse culture, "primitive" and close to nature, like the Sioux; the "mixed-blood" status of both Hidalgo (*mustang* comes from the Spanish *mixteño*, "mixed-blood") and Hopkins is a threat to racial purity for both the English and Bedouin characters, marking "American" as mixed-race but stronger for it and locating racism only in the non-American characters; and the romance of the frontier myth (cowboys, Indians, Western tales, the Colt pistol) is an attractive narrative to those (like the Bedouins) who value masculinism, honor, courage, persistence, and violence. The love of Colt pistols, Westerns, and horses creates a strong tie of friendship between Hopkins and the Bedouin sheikh, played by Omar Sharif. The film—in which, of course, the impure mustang and his mixed-blood cowboy-Indian rider triumph by winning the race—is a fable of U.S./Arab bonding over the mutually held values and symbols of the frontier, deeply ironic given the movie's release in the year following the U.S. invasion of Iraq.

Hidalgo is a strong example of the Ecological Indian narrative. The part-Indian, part-white Hopkins is tormented by his guilt over the genocidal and environmentally destructive practices of the United States, and he redeems himself through honorable violence with the assistance of an animal and an encounter with indigenous spirituality (he is also a feminist, on top of everything, as he supports the desires of the Bedouin sheikh's daughter to ride horses as a man does and to decide on her own husband). In the crisis of the race, with a wounded Hidalgo prone on the desert sand and Hopkins exhausted, delirious, and dehydrated, Hopkins cries out in his Indian language for help. As he begins to sing an Indian song, the shimmering desert heat forms into Native dancers, who sing with him and implore the sky for assistance. He also sees an image of his Indian mother, holding the hand of a boy meant to be himself as Blue Child. This mystical intervention inspires Hidalgo to suddenly rise from his almost-dead state and to carry his rider faster than the last two Arabian horses in the race, to win. As Hopkins celebrates, his Kurdish assistant brings to him his flag— the sacred red, black, white, and yellow circle of many Native American cultures, the flag of his "nation." Thus Hopkins can simultaneously be indigenous and American; cowboy and Indian; U.S. victor over the Arabs while culturally sensitive friend to the sheikh; masculinist man and feminist ally to women. What he is most of all is an ecological warrior; at the end of the film, Hopkins uses his prize money to buy the mustangs their freedom on the Blackjack Mountain range in Oklahoma.

The historical setting of *Hidalgo* is the same 1870s–1890s time period of *Dances with Wolves*, *The Last Samurai* (2003), and several other "frontier" movies, a popular time period with filmmakers because it stands for the last gasp of the frontier and the tragic "disappearance" of both Indians and the "true" West.[13] All of these movies use the Noble Savage myth to depict good white American military men as able to reverse or at least mitigate the devastating consequences of U.S. militarism and imperialism. But ultimately, the Ecological Indian motif in *Hidalgo* does not help us to understand the intertwining of environmental and social problems caused by militarism in ways that could point us to rejecting the forces that cause these problems; rather, the expression of regret, guilt, and sadness is relegated to a past we cannot change, while the combination of valor, loyalty, violence, and code of honor of military men is still upheld as the preferred character of honorable Americans. Meanwhile, the ideas of the frontier myth—that Americans are on the side of good, truth, and justice in fighting barbarous, incomprehensible, inhuman enemies—continues to be available as an ideology to justify war and invasion.

Ecological Indians and Environmentalist Indians

A somewhat different and therefore revealing use of the Ecological Indian narrative can be found in the 1992 film *Thunderheart*. In this film, a "white" FBI agent, Ray Levoi (Val Kilmer), who has long denied his Indian ancestry because his Lakota father was an alcoholic, is sent to an unnamed reservation in search of an outlaw (Jimmy Looks Twice, played by an American Indian Movement activist and former chairman of AIM, the poet and musician John Trudell) who is alleged to have murdered two FBI agents. On the reservation, Levoi meets an elder, Grandpa Sam Reaches (Chief Ted Thin Elk), who quietly insists on Levoi's coming to terms with his ancestry. In doing so, he also is able to solve the mystery of the murder, which is the responsibility of the conspiracy between corrupt Indian leaders with the FBI and white corporate owners to keep the pollution of an illegal uranium mining operation from coming to light.

As Levoi interacts with the Indians, he begins to have visions that draw him into identification with his Indian background. The crucial scene, in which his new indigenous vision becomes so strong that he changes sides to the Indian point of view, occurs while he is staking out the house of Grandpa Sam Reaches late at night in his car. It is four o'clock in the morning, still dark. Grandpa Sam Reaches is standing outside his trailer, his arms uplifted, singing a traditional song to the coming dawn. Levoi is sleepily spying on him from the front seat of the car. As the camera pans back to focus on Levoi's face, we see that next to him on the front seat is a dog, a rough-looking "Indian" dog. This is the first appearance of the dog in the movie, and his presence is never explained then or later. As we see the dog, we hear a hawk's cry. Almost unconsciously, Levoi begins to hum along to Grandpa Reaches's song. The dog also begins to sing. At that moment, Levoi has a vision connected to the U.S. massacre of Indians at Wounded Knee, which took place in 1890 on the Lakota reservation (and is also central to *Hidalgo* and *The Last Samurai*). He sees the reservation graveyard and the monument that lists the names of the dead. The camera quickly pans the list of names, so that the viewer almost misses one that says "White America." Levoi's vision is interrupted suddenly by the end of Grandpa Reaches's song, as he bends to pick up a heavy container. Reluctantly, Levoi starts to get out of the car to help, and because of this, he just misses getting hit by a gunshot that shatters his windshield. We never see what happens to the dog. He has served his function, integrating Levoi into a Native perspective by his presence and participation in the song. Nature and the Indian have touched Levoi's soul and saved his life.

In the same year, the director of *Thunderheart*, Michael Apted, also released a respected documentary called *Incident at Oglala* (1992). The documentary examines the 1973 Wounded Knee controversy in which the FBI, with the complicity of the corrupt Lakota leader Dick Wilson, pinned two murders on the Indian activist Leonard Peltier (who remains in prison today through a legal process many consider unjust). This involvement in real-life, contemporary Indian struggles gave Apted a much better grasp of the politics of moviemaking using narratives about Native peoples. Unlike the other two recent movies, *Hidalgo* and *The Last Samurai*, which use the 1890 Wounded Knee episode as their moral center, Apted makes clear in *Thunderheart* that indigenous people face issues of colonialism and violence in the present; by using the more contemporary 1973 Wounded Knee episode as his setting, he emphasizes their ongoing struggle to fight back. Perhaps given this unusually deep understanding of the issues facing the Lakota people, *Thunderheart* avoids almost all of the worst aspects of the narrative of the Ecological Indian in several ways. The Indian characters are real, complex, and willing to make fun of their strategic participation in Indian stereotypes. Traditional values (spirituality, community as priority, respect for elders) are integrated into modern ways of living (trailers, cars, television, jobs). The Indians in *Thunderheart* are a specific, distinct tribal people living in a present-day context, with political problems particular to their land and history, and are deeply involved in continuing processes of cultural negotiation that are effective and vital. Neither the people nor their culture is portrayed as disappeared, defeated, irrelevant, or tragic. The ecological issues are not described in vague, sweeping references to the disappearance of a pristine Edenic wilderness or an iconic animal such as the buffalo or the mustang but are presented as concrete issues of corporate exploitation of natural resources in the context of complicated structures of sovereignty, ownership of land, and political corruption on both Indian and white sides—in this case, involving uranium mining. Most important, the issues are portrayed as not easily resolved by individual action or violence.

Yet despite this admirable attempt at presenting an engaging story of the realistic environmental issues that present-day indigenous people face, Apted could not tell the story without certain elements of the Ecological Indian narrative. His part-white, part-Indian narrator must "become" Indian to take action. Levoi cannot do this without encountering a redemptive nature, in this case through the strange and unexplained appearance of the symbolic Indian dog, to assist his transformation. Indians and nature, interwoven permanently and mystically together, provide the only effective avenue toward successful environmental political action.

What are the consequences of this persistent narrative for environmental activists, especially indigenous environmental activists? How can indigenous activists promote a more sustainable, respectful, integrated view of nature without being heard as Ecological Indians, mystical (and therefore unrealistic), historically irrelevant, beautifully and tragically vanished? It is interesting that the few movies in which some authorial or directorial control is in the hands of indigenous artists, in which primarily Native

American actors appear, and which have been distributed by mainstream film companies and thus seen by significant numbers of people often spend quite a bit of time poking fun at the stereotype of the Ecological Indian. Examples include *Pow-Wow Highway* (1989; written by Native American author David Seals and distributed by Warner Brothers) and *Smoke Signals* (1998; written by Sherman Alexie and directed by Chris Eyre, both Native Americans, and distributed by Miramax). These films either forgo or satirize the motif of the Ecological Indian, even when environmental issues (as in *Pow-Wow Highway*) are part of the plot.

Environmentalism for indigenous activists is part of an interlocking set of concerns involving sovereignty, economic independence, community health, and cultural preservation. When Indian environmentalists use the kind of language the dominant culture associates with the Ecological Indian stereotype, they are strategically referencing the importance of seeing humans as interdependent with the land (the opposite of seeing nature as separate from culture), making sustainable decisions about the use of natural resources, and valuing cultural traditions associated with sacred spaces. Depending on the context, these goals may or may not lead them to make decisions that white mainstream environmentalists would necessarily support. In general, indigenous environmentalists do not want to associate their (differing) intertwined ecological, political, economic and cultural values with the idea of their tribal people as disappeared, vanished, primitive, or more natural (that is, less human) and simple (that is, less culturally developed) than white people. For white and non-Indian people, distinguishing indigenous environmentalist rhetoric from Ecological Indian stereotypes involves carefully listening to numerous Native activists and developing a critical approach to mainstream environmentalism. Zoltan Grossman (1995, 47) points out, in an article describing the work of the Indigenous Environmental Network (IEN), that

> IEN conferences are not a typical environmental gathering. First, there is a complete absence of the concept of "wilderness"—or the idea of nature devoid of human beings. Instead, humans are presented as an integral part of different natural regions, acting within them to gather their sustenance. Second, the human race is not seen as the inherent collective enemy of ecosystems. Instead, the corporate and governmental forces that destroy the environment are clearly identified. Third, animals are never presented as cute or fuzzy, but as sacred parts of Native cultures, economic subsistence, and clan systems. Indeed, if any single-issue animal rights activists accidentally wandered into the Hunting, Fishing, and Gathering workshop, it would

have sent chills up their spines. The right to gather the bounties of nature is put on the same level as the protection of the resources from corporate polluters.

The Ecological Indian stereotype insists that actual indigenous people conform to certain prescribed behaviors and values to be deemed proper environmentalists. Allowing tribes to decide how to use their own natural resources or how to define environmental issues on their own terms is made impossible or invisible by the overlay of the stereotype. There is a whole subset of criticism examining the idea of whether Indians were or were not ecological actors before European conquest (Krech 1999; Vecsey and Venables 1980). Annette Kolodny (2007) makes the important point that Indians used the Ecological Indian stereotype strategically to argue for treaty rights, distinguish their cultural norms from those of whites, and promote their own cultural traditions in contexts where they were under attack. She describes the ambivalence articulated by her American Indian students upon encountering Krech's deconstruction of the Ecological Indian stereotype:

> For them, Native cultures, however imperfectly, *had* once given rise to communities that do "not waste or despoil, exhaust or extinguish." These students see the Ecological Indian as an exaggeration invented and appropriated by the White Man, but not as a symbol wholly devoid of truth. And yet, at the same time, these students also stated that they were relieved at being unburdened by the responsibility for representing what Krech terms "ecological sainthood". . . . Arguing for a more pragmatic view, several other Native American student activists said they accepted the continuing political usefulness of the Ecological Indian as another tool (in addition to legislation and litigation) for addressing the ongoing environmental despoliation of Native homelands. (Kolodny 2007, 3)

Regardless of whether preconquest Indian tribes always behaved ecologically and whether they might now strategically articulate ecological ideals to assist them in their political goals, the Ecological Indian stereotype carries the danger of constricting their image as fully equal and complex human beings. Krech (1999, 216) points out, "The connections between Indians and nature have been so tightly drawn over five hundred years, and especially in the last quarter of the twentieth century, that many non-Indians expect indigenous people to walk softly in their moccasins as conservationists and even (in Muir's sense) preservationists. When they have not, they have at times eagerly been condemned, accused of not acting as Indians should, and held to standards that they and their accusers have seldom met."

Finally, while it might have the positive result of encouraging non-Indians to look to indigenous peoples for environmental guidance, the imposition of the Ecological Indian stereotype could prevent non-Indian environmentalists from learning the complex details about how Indians are approaching environmentalist issues today and from understanding how their struggle for cultural continuity, tribal sovereignty, healthy communities, and adequate economic benefits for all is thoroughly intertwined with environmental goals. The close connection between social justice issues and environmental issues offered by many Indian activists could teach us all quite a bit about practical and sustainable environmental solutions, if we do not restrict our attention to narrow expectations of their beliefs and preferred policies. As I note in chapter 5, indigenous understandings of the interrelationships between human, animal, and ecological practices and needs are often portrayed as mystical (and thus impractical or unscientific) understandings of "the web of life." Instead, the dominant culture might learn from indigenous environmentalists and scientists a more practical approach to seeing ourselves as interacting with, and responsible to, a world that is not separate from us. Attention to this work, freed from stereotypical expectations, might inspire a wider and more effective effort to achieve social and environmental justice together.

"Forever New Frontiers"

Extraterrestrialism and U.S. Militarism in Space

On January 14, 2004, under the tagline "A renewed spirit of discovery," U.S. president George W. Bush announced his vision for further space exploration. Stating his intentions to create permanent living spaces on space stations and the moon's surface, as well as manned missions to Mars, Bush clearly hoped to generate the public enthusiasm produced by former U.S. president John F. Kennedy's famous 1961 challenge to land a man on the moon (Kennedy 1961). To stimulate this response, Bush's speech explicitly articulated a new expansion of the space program with the frontier myth that continues to sustain U.S. expansionist ambitions:

> Two centuries ago, Meriwether Lewis and William Clark left St. Louis to explore the new lands acquired in the Louisiana Purchase. They made that journey in the spirit of discovery, to learn the potential of vast new territory, and to chart a way for others to follow. America has ventured forth into space for the same reasons. We have undertaken space travel because the desire to explore and understand is part of our character. . . . Mankind is drawn to the heavens for the same reason we were once drawn into unknown lands and across the open sea. We choose to explore space because doing so improves our lives, and lifts our national spirit. So let us continue the journey. (Bush 2004)

Bush is not alone in this dream. The resurgence of an older frontier myth via the expansion of militarism into space is a recurring motif in the post–World War II world order, whether it is the new frontier (President

Kennedy's slogan in the 1960s), the high frontier (the name of both a 1976 book on space colonization by G. K. O'Neill and a right-wing missile defense organization), the final frontier (made famous by *Star Trek*'s Captain James T. Kirk of the USS *Enterprise* in the 1970s), or as the aircraft and space technology company Boeing puts it in a twenty-first-century ad campaign, "Forever New Frontiers." We also see the use of related symbols and narrative frames in worthwhile environmentalist efforts such as Al Gore's documentary, *An Inconvenient Truth* (2006), and the efforts of an environmentalist, labor, and business coalition called the Apollo Alliance. Are there potential dangers of linking the frontier myth to environmentalist purposes, via the extraterrestrialist trope? As Zoë Sofia (1984) has pointed out, extraterrestrialism often functions within the dominant culture as a new "safety valve" in outer space that enables avoidance of environmental and social problems. In other words, more than identifying just another territory to explore, this taken-for-granted linkage between the frontier myth and outer space within the United States is revealing about past, present, and emergent environmental and social relations in the twenty-first century.

To map the cultural politics at stake in the articulation and perpetuation of this discourse, or what I call the *extraterrestrialist global frontier myth*, I assemble a range of popular media texts. What is the special status of "nature" in the process of constructing the extraterrestrialist global frontier myth—for upholding not only systems of power between people but also between people and the environment?[1]

This map of the extraterrestrialist global frontier myth consists of four layers:

- The post–World War II frontier myth relies on a notion of space exploration as an evolutionary pinnacle, naturalizing and justifying U.S. militarism on and off the planet

- This myth also attempts to ease cultural anxieties about environmental problems, problematically importing a justification for U.S. imperialism and superpower status into environmentalist rhetorics

- Space-related militarism results in environmental damage disproportionately visited on poor and indigenous people both domestically and globally

- The seemingly innocuous imagining of the Earth as a unitary, abstract object seen from space, though common in environmentalist popular culture, should be rejected in favor of a view that sees people as part of the planet in situated and responsible ways

The Final Frontier: Space Exploration
as Evolutionary Imperative

The cultural narratives making up the frontier myth have been in place from the beginning of U.S. national history (see chapter 2). The central idea of the frontier myth is that continued American conquest is a form of natural progress, supported by the assumption that there is an evolutionary drive to develop pristine nature and civilize "savage" peoples (Knobloch 1996; Slotkin 1973, 1985, 1992). The layering of symbolic cultural narratives that make up the frontier myth legitimized early Euro-American settlement of the lower half of the North American continent and involved an intertwined set of powerful ideas, some of them myths with their own labels—such as "virgin land," Manifest Destiny, Frederick Jackson Turner's "frontier thesis," and American exceptionalism. Together these myths legitimated the process of settlement called "progress" by the conquerors and "conquest" by those subjected to it, even as the United States moved its pattern of imperialist conquest past the North American continent.

As the United States became involved in projecting its power beyond its initial national borders—including places such as Hawai'i, Cuba, the Philippines, Latin America, Vietnam, Iraq, and others—elements of the frontier myth were extended to apply to Third World peoples and natural resources. Seeing Third World peoples as primitive populations or cheap labor rather than complex cultures, conceptualizing natural resources in the Global South as available for "development" and presenting ideologies of the "free market" as a narrative of inevitable and desired evolutionary progress are all ways of expanding the frontier myth to have global relevance. The appearance of "developed" and "underdeveloped" countries is thus imagined as a natural process resulting from some countries being incidentally "ahead" of others on a biologically determined trajectory of progress, rather than being understood as a process of uneven socioeconomic changes occurring as a result of histories marked by colonial power, military coercion, decisions made by economic elites, and deliberate state or international policies. Slowly, after the cold war, the United States emerged from this context as the world's primary superpower.

Yet as the myth of the frontier expanded after World War II, domestic unrest also began to gain increased traction. The civil rights, anti–Vietnam War, women's, and gay liberation movements challenged U.S. rhetorics of freedom and equality. Together, these social and environmental movements produced a growing sense of the Earth and its peoples as fragile and endangered. This disturbed, to some extent, older ways of legitimating U.S. militarism and imperialism.

Within this emerging context of domestic and international social change, the frontier myth became increasingly linked with the next "new frontier": outer space.[2] Beyond the iconic image of the first man on the moon planting a U.S. flag in 1969, linkages between expanding U.S. frontiers, U.S. global power, the exploration of space, and a growing environmental awareness began to permeate popular culture. The motif that emerges from this process emphasizes that the push to "conquer" outer space, to engage in the "high" or "final" frontier, is a natural, evolutionary drive (particularly for white men) that can potentially evade environmental problems. Three examples are particularly apropos illustrations of the characteristics of this extraterrestrialist global frontier myth as a narrative of power and control: a segment of the popular movie 2001: A Space Odyssey (1968); Boeing's ad campaign "Forever New Frontiers"; and several Web sites connected with the organization High Frontier.

A famous cultural representation of the idea that conquest is a natural, evolutionary drive that leads us into space as its ultimate culmination occurs in the movie 2001: A Space Odyssey, in a sequence that depicts the dramatic transition between the segment called "The Dawn of Man" (in the book, "Primeval Night") and the future space age of 2001. In this segment, apelike prehumans are living hand-to-mouth in desert caves, when, through the apparent intervention of the mystical extraterrestrial black monolith, one of them, a male ape/human, gets the idea of the first tool: a large animal bone. First, he uses this new tool to kill an animal for meat; then, in another conceptual leap, he uses it to kill another ape/human. As the dominant ape/human male glories in his first political kill, he throws the murder weapon, the bone, up into the air, where it transforms itself into an orbiting space object—a satellite? a station? a ship? a weapon? This sequence is gorgeously set in slow motion to the stirring music of Richard Strauss's "Thus Spake Zarathustra." Once we are in space, watching the ballet of space vehicles and weapons against the beautiful blue orbs of the planets, the music of Johann Strauss's "Blue Danube Waltz" fills our senses with peace, beauty, glory, and awe as we see the Earth floating in space.

In this narrative, we are presented with a leap into space and the vision of an orbiting spaceship or space-based nuclear weapon as the desired and celebrated end result of a naturalized discourse of male violence: the logical evolutionary extension of masculine invention and ingenuity. This example is particularly compelling for its emphasis not simply on space but on how the need for more space is predicated on our species' evolutionary impulses to improve the quality of "our" lives (as President Bush asserts in the speech quoted at the beginning of this essay). Though we are led to think of this dependence on violence as the basis for progress as natural, alternative narratives are available. Imagine the different evolutionary moral that could be drawn if the story of the "first tool" was about the basket rather than the weapon. The basket (or other containers such as pots or slings)—necessary for successful foraging, water transport, and storage—was at least as important as the weapon for early human survival, as well as necessary to the development of agriculture (Haraway 1989; Zihlman 1985). Not incidental to the reasons why this alternative story is not the dominant one is the fact that the basket or pot traditionally is a woman's tool, quite likely connected to the invention of devices to carry children. Containers such as baskets were used for the gathering of the mainstays of the early human diet, whereas hunting meat was more of an occasional (though important) nutritional supplement. Ursula K. LeGuin wrote a famous literary essay entitled "The Carrier Bag Theory of Fiction," in which, with serious humor, she points to the way in which masculinist narratives of heroism and adventure depend on the idea that the weapon is a more important tool than the basket. In doing so, she specifically references the scene in 2001: A Space Odyssey discussed above:

> If you haven't got something to put it in, food will escape you—even something as uncombative and unresourceful as an oat. You put as many as you can into your stomach while they are handy, that being the primary container; but what about tomorrow morning when you wake up and it's cold and raining and wouldn't it be good to have just a few handfuls of oats to chew on and give little Oom to make her shut up, but how do you get more than one stomachful and one handful home? So you get up and go to the damned soggy oat patch in the rain, and wouldn't it be a good thing if you had something to put Baby Oo Oo in so that you could pick the oats with both hands? A leaf a gourd a shell a net a bag a sling a sack a bottle a pot a box a container. A holder. A recipient.
>
> "The first cultural device was probably a recipient. . . . Many theorizers feel that the earliest cultural invention must have been a container to hold gathered products and some kind of sling or net carrier." So says Elizabeth Fisher in *Women's Creation* (McGraw-Hill, 1975). But no, this cannot be. Where is that wonderful, big, long, hard thing, a bone, I believe, that that Ape Man first bashed somebody with in the movie and then, grunting with ecstasy at having achieved the first proper murder, flung up into the sky, and whirling there it became a space ship thrusting its way into the cosmos to

fertilize it and produce at the end of the movie a lovely fetus, a boy of course, drifting around the Milky Way without (oddly enough) any womb, any matrix at all? (LeGuin 1989, 168–69)

The 2001 example shows us that, on the one hand, extraterrestrialism is simply another variation of the frontier myth, the legitimization of expansion into space and domination over the whole world. On the other hand, it is particular to a post-1960s myth of escaping the Earth to control it—the kind of logic that Nancy Hartsock (1983) identified as peculiar to late-twentieth-century white hegemonic masculinity, especially in the context of normative ideals of the suburban family. Hartsock argues that under conditions in which men, as commuting breadwinners, are absent from the family, do not participate in childrearing in intimate, daily ways, and still have economic and personal dominance within the home, gender roles for boys and girls are differentiated by the requirement that the boy identify with an abstract masculinity, while the girl identifies with a real person involved in her everyday care. The boy must strenuously reject the set of characteristics (nurturance, daily housework, intimacy) that are identified with femininity, even though those may be more real to him than the characteristics associated with the masculine role (competition, willingness to use violence, control). The underlying logic of extraterrestrialism is separating from the mother, claiming independence from her, putatively admiring her from a distance but in reality violently rejecting any possibility of identification with femininity and its connection to the body, the earth, and the messy, unpredictable qualities of the basics of reproductive work. Extraterrestrialism is thus deeply connected to the desire for control of nature (and women), particularly the promotion of violence (as LeGuin points out) as an adventurous, heroic, and necessary aspect of human evolution and achievement (Garb 1990; Litfin 1997; Sofia 1984).

This latter implication is evident in a recent ad campaign by Boeing, begun in 2000 and entitled "Forever New Frontiers" (Boeing 2000). This ad campaign embodies several representational logics but fundamentally relies on the notion that an evolutionary drive toward space exploration and the earth-spanning information technologies that such exploration enables is innocently connected to control of nature and to U.S. military domination of the globe.

Boeing deliberately uses as the base of its ad slogan the phrase "New Frontier," introduced as a campaign theme by President Kennedy in 1960. Deploying a variety of frontier tropes, JFK spoke passionately of the need to militarily face down communists and of his expectation that Americans in the 1960s were ready to work and sacrifice for a glorious destiny, as white pioneers had done before them. These themes were stressed again in Kennedy's first major policy statement to Congress in 1961. Along with several new military initiatives, in 1962, he also announced the major push behind the space program that resulted in the first moon landing eight years later (Kennedy 1961, 1962). He set out three goals for the space program: to serve as a symbol of U.S. military strength, to enable space exploration, and to put satellites in place for communications and weather information.

These three intertwined goals—militarism, space exploration, and surveillance of the globe—became Boeing's bread and butter, and the company's ads are masterful at interweaving these three ambitions as though they are naturally equivalent. In fact, a 1997 Boeing commercial serves as a kind of backstory about Boeing's involvement in space being part of a heroic national destiny that depends on the valorization of militarism. We first hear former U.S. president Ronald Reagan, then U.S. civil rights leader Martin Luther King, then Kennedy, and finally Reagan again, speaking in various ways about America's destiny to reach the highest of our goals, while we see a rapid montage of clips of "the American century." Cynically combining visuals of war heroism with images of the civil rights, antiwar, and gay liberation movements (all in reality opposed to militarism and sometimes critics of Boeing itself), the ad serves to obscure the company's war profiteering by connecting militarism to the drive for human rights. The commercial ends with an image of a spectacular rise above the Earth into space. This jump into space, with the Earth seen as a lovely blue circle against the black of space along with an orbiting Boeing-produced satellite to keep it company, appears as the final or penultimate image in almost every one of the "Forever New Frontiers" television ads (and, of course, recalls the famous segment from 2001 discussed earlier).[3]

The first "Forever New Frontiers" ad, which I have labeled "Farmers" (2000), illustrates how the theme of Third World peoples as natural resources is coupled with notions of militarism, industrialism, and progress, with extraterrestrialism as the final achievement of an evolutionary narrative. "Farmers" begins with images of Third World peoples harvesting crops, implying that the Boeing satellites are helping them with agricultural or marketing information (the titles flashed across the screen say, "A farmer's guide / from outer space / it flies at 1,000 feet"). Exciting shots of sea-based missiles, military jets, rockets taking off, and planes swooping across the skies follow, intercut with faces from various "traditional" cultures. The ad ends with several stunning images of the Earth seen from space, with space vehicles and space-suited astronauts in the foreground. As other scholars have pointed out,[4] this creates the sense that Boeing products bring cultures together without conflict and that profiting from decades of militarism is a human achievement, a pinnacle of our experience, allowing astronauts to float in space above the beautiful blue marble. As in the Discovery Channel ad discussed in chapter 1, the implication is that the Earth is the site of "primitive" cultures, while space is the natural home of those wielding advanced technologies. Thus, military uses are embedded in peaceful uses of this space-bound technology; indeed, for Boeing, there is no distinction between the two.

Along with Boeing, many other corporations and organizations that wanted to connect space exploration with the militarization of space greeted with glee Bush's 2004 space policy statement and his willingness to pull out of the 1972 Anti–Ballistic Missile Treaty (which opened the door to the increasing militarization of space). In particular, the members of an organization called High Frontier were very enthusiastic, given that their two reasons for existing were the realization of actual space colonization and the creation of an antiballistic defense/offense system. In the first ambition, the founders of High Frontier were following the vision outlined by G. K. O'Neill, a Princeton physics professor whose 1976 book, *The High Frontier*, contains a detailed description of permanent space stations. O'Neill's book presents space colonization as a necessary step in human evolution, since he believed that overpopulation of the Earth would cause ecological disaster. Space colonization, in small decentralized groups relatively free of government oversight (like Thomas Jefferson's vision of "nature's nation"), would in his view re-create the conditions of the old U.S. frontier society, conditions necessary to allow social and technological innovation to flourish. As a blurb by a representative of the National Aeronautics and Space Administration (NASA) says about the book, "*The High Frontier* provides a lucid description of the next phase in biological evolution." Similarly, the Space Frontier Foundation (2005), an organization dedicated to the private development and colonization of space, says, "The next step to growing up is going up."[5]

The two ambitions of militarizing space and colonizing space are brought together in a High Frontier project called, appropriately enough given my argument here, Jamestown on the Moon (Jamestown was the first permanent English settlement on the North American continent, in what is now Virginia). This project of High Frontier's has spawned conferences exploring the possibility of creating condominiums on the moon that would establish a moonbase of operations both entrepreneurial and military. As stated on the first page of the site, "With the President's renewed commitment to a return to the Moon, this time to stay, the people of the United States are setting out—once more—to open and explore the frontiers of space for all mankind—bearing the flag of Freedom and Enterprise."[6]

In all three examples just discussed, the seamless interweaving of space-based "weapons for peace" with more-peaceful uses of space technologies obscures the dangerous militarization of terrestrial and extraterrestrial environments. Thus, it is ironic that one of the post–World War II particularities of an extraterrestrialist global frontier myth is the recurring idea that space exploration is one way to achieve solutions to environmental problems; also ironic is the frequent use of the Earth seen from space as an environmentalist icon.

All "We" Need Is a Little Elbow Room: Space as a Solution to Environmental Problems

Demonstrating that environmentalist desires animate a particular post–World War II version of an extraterrestrialist global frontier myth (such that the connection between environmentalism and space is ubiquitous in post-sixties U.S. popular culture) are several popular culture examples, including a segment of the children's television show *Schoolhouse Rock*, various science fiction movies, and some contemporary environmentalist rhetorics and images. Within these examples, besides the assumption that space exploration contains avenues for environmentalist solutions, the ideology of the frontier myth is hitched, problematically, to environmentalist yearnings.

Schoolhouse Rock was an educational children's television series that ran on ABC in the mornings from 1973 to 1985. Lauded as one of the most successful and effective versions of educational children's programming ever produced and seen by as many U.S. children at the time as *Sesame Street* (if not more), *Schoolhouse Rock* featured catchy rock tunes and goofy cartoon characters teaching the basics of math, grammar, science, and U.S. history. Though it stopped major production in 1985, the videos continue to be used in elementary and middle school classrooms (in fact, my son told me he was shown a *Schoolhouse Rock* segment in his eighth-grade class in 2004, albeit with critical commentary from his teacher). The segment I discuss here, "Elbow Room," was parodied by Michael Moore in his movie *Bowling for Columbine* (2002) as quintessential nationalist propaganda.[7]

"Elbow Room," first shown in the year of the U.S. bicentennial, is described by the *Schoolhouse Rock* Web site as providing an explanation of

Manifest Destiny and the settling of the continent.[8] The video, narrated by a lively pop song, begins with the assertion that it is natural that when you are living with other people, you will need to find a way to expand your personal space. "Everybody needs a little elbow room," the song explains, trivializing and individualizing the bloody and difficult process of invasion and settlement of the continental United States by white European colonists. The phrase "needing a little elbow room" is visualized as a colonial couple (tri-cornered hat and Revolutionary-era overcoat on the man, bonnet and long dress on the woman) learning how to get through a narrow door together, jostling each other, then smiling in pleasure and affection with their faces in close proximity when they finally make it out of doors. Thus, the idea that needing "elbow room" is natural is underlined by a "natural" moment of heterosexual romance; the implication is that the pressure of increasing population, pictured here as the result of pleasant romance as well as continued English immigration to America, is natural (that is, biologically determined), inevitable, and, indeed, a happy outcome.

As the video continues, it shows an inexorable and seemingly unresisted conquest of the continent by white European-American settlers. It illustrates the need to first overcome the restriction on settlement west of the Mississippi (solved, in the video, by Thomas Jefferson's purchase of the Louisiana Territory—as the song glibly says, "without a fuss"); then it dramatizes Lewis and Clark's journey to the Pacific Ocean, in which they find, in the words of the video's musical narrative, "the most elbow room we've ever had."

There are two important things to notice about this particular visualization of exploration and conquest: the apparent emptiness of the land before any of the white people arrive there (the "virgin land" myth), and the notion of "we" as thoroughly and unquestioningly white (the idea that conquest is white people's Manifest Destiny). Sacagawea, in the narration, is described as "hired" by Lewis and Clark, and in one of the more stunning visual segments of the video, she stands in the prow of their boat with her one arm uplifted, pointing west, literally carving the land out of empty white space, creating a colorful river of mountains, animals, and plants flowing from the stern of the Lewis and Clark canoe. Besides Sacagawea, the only other indication of the original indigenous inhabitants of the land is a single arrow shot through the hat of a white male settler (his wife is holding a Bible); of the other inhabitants of multiple origins (Spanish, Mexican, Russian, French) of the period there is no indication at all. It seems likely that someone responsible for the video had read or heard of Frederick Jackson Turner's famous essay on the frontier, for the process of settlement follows his evolutionary gloss, with the linear appearance in the video of trappers, traders, peddlers, and politicians echoing Turner's notion of the natural evolution of settlement (Turner [1893] 1996).

After the video celebrates "our" finally having room from "sea to shining sea," it speculates that if we ever feel "crowded up together" and need a little more "elbow room," we can just "go to the moon." The image of two astronauts dancing their way into a rocket, which blasts off to the moon, is accompanied by the verse "It's the moon or bust, in God We Trust, it's a new land up there," and the video closes on the final image of the Earth seen from space melding with the moon.

Here we can see how the extraterrestrialist moment, in which people are launched into space, fits an environmentalist logic into the story of the frontier myth. If needing "elbow room" is "natural" (especially because of overpopulation), then continued expansion onto the moon and into outer space is the logical answer, for where else can we go? In this narrative, the function of the myth of the frontier is to disappear the violence that is part of imperial conquest, including the conquest by European settlers of Native Americans and the wholesale slaughtering of animals (such as buffalo) or destroying environments as techniques of invasion. In this way, the violence of genocide and environmental destruction are naturalized, suggesting that evolution and progress require—indeed depend upon—white masculinist domination of others, including the Earth.

Furthermore, this leap into space specifically connects the U.S. expansion of the past to the U.S. domination of space in the future, legitimized by the need to solve environmental problems. The ease with which the "Elbow Room" segment suggests Americans can just "go to the moon" demonstrates the way in which the United States is assumed to be the natural owners of space. Surely, if a moon colony did exist, it would have to be "ours"—after all, weren't we "first" on the moon? Didn't we plant our flag there?[9] The leap into space at the end of the video and the idea that if "we" run out of land to conquer, "we" can just "go to the moon," presents space as the logical outcome of a supposedly evolutionary drive to violently acquire not just more room for everyone but specifically U.S. territory. HuMAN nature is described as reaching its ultimate goal in the conquest of space, and U.S. astronauts are the epitome of this evolutionary process.

While the myth of the extraterrestrialist frontier assumes that we can leave our planet and all of its problems behind, this is often not a triumphal moment in these popular cultural imaginings; the fragility of the planet is the central point and the loss of the Earth a tragedy. Anxiety about the dangers produced by militaristic projects or resource-depleting corporations runs deeply in U.S. popular culture, especially engaging the extrater-restrialist imaginary in science fiction movies. The original *Planet of the Apes* (1968) depicts an Earth destroyed by nuclear war, in which apes dominate humans, our present evolutionary order frighteningly overturned by human warmongering. The movie *Silent Running* (1972) is about the sending into space of the last of Earth's plants as a way to protect them from the ecologi-cal collapse of the planet, and the movie evokes the sadness of destroying the environment as a price for human corporate industrialization. More than twenty years later, *Gattaca* (1997) is about a man's desire to go into space as a way to escape a planet where natural birth is eliminated in favor of genetic engineering (both movies have male heroes named Freeman).

These repeated patterns, displaying anxieties about space being a place where we have had to go because we have destroyed the planet or disrupted nature, show the underside of the extraterrestrial myth. But there is also an important thematic thread in U.S. culture in which environmental dan-gers usefully bring the world together, overcome historical differences and conflicts, and produce a healthy, peaceful world. Whether in the form of a military weapon used unwisely, as in *The Core* (2003), or a human-produced ecological disaster, as in *The Day after Tomorrow* (2004), the possibility of global annihilation is portrayed as the only means of bringing the world together in the popular science-fictional imagination. This is also a cher-ished environmental belief: what threatens the whole Earth will bring all of the world's peoples and nations together in collective problem solving, overcoming (without resolving) national competitions, ethnic hatreds, and social inequalities.

Despite this apparent desire for universal peace, the dominant popular imagination often finds the solution to threats to the whole Earth to be another form of the problem—that is, cowboy militarism, U.S. go-it-alone leadership, and risky technoscience. In *Independence Day* (1996), a movie poised between the 1991 Gulf War and the 9/11 terrorist attacks on New York in 2001, an invasion by implacably hostile aliens revives the U.S. mili-tary (especially Vietnam jet-pilot veterans) as heroes of the world, leaders of an international strike force that defeats the aliens against impossible odds. The president of the United States (played by the ultimate nice guy, Bill Pullman) is a George Bush the First character, a Vietnam veteran thought of as a too-reluctant warrior, a demasculinized sensitive wimp. But by the end of the movie, he has shown his willingness to strike at the aliens and regain his stature as a real man by being willing to kill. His stirring speech to the ragtag bunch of jet pilots assembled all around the world symbol-izes the end of several historical conflicts (we are shown a series of paired pilots listening to the speech: Israeli and Iraqi, British and Russian, Chinese and Japanese), brought about by the common threat to the planet. In his speech, the president reclaims the U.S. national holiday of July Fourth as an Independence Day for all of "mankind." But, says the president, it is America that will naturally lead the way. So while the threat of alien invasion and destruction of the whole Earth presents an opportunity to dream of international peace, the dominant cultural imaginary can only picture U.S. militarism and white male leadership as the means of achieving this deeply desired end. As in the Ecological Indian plots of chapter 2, the only imagined solution to violence is violence, especially if it is the violence of naturally good white men.

Commendable mainstream environmentalist efforts in the real world also turn to the rhetoric and ideology of space exploration and the extraterrestrialist view of a threatened Earth to inspire activists and produce the appearance of a solution to our environmental problems. For example, the environmentalist-labor-business coalition called the Apollo Alliance is so named because it claims to be inspired by the "can-do" spirit of the Apollo moon missions, noting in its "Agenda for Action" that "Americans have always pulled together during tough times to accomplish great missions. We can do it again. This time we need a moonshot for energy independence and good jobs" (www.apolloalliance.org). On the section of its Web site entitled "Why Do We Call It the Apollo Alliance," the alliance reprints the 1962 speech by JFK in which he announced his plan to land a man on the moon, using the rhetorics of American exceptionalism (that the United States engages in conquest not for reasons of exploitation or power but for the common good, and that, as in the president's speech in *Independence Day*, the United States is the natural leader of the world) as well as the language of the frontier myth and its assumption that exploration is an evolutionary technology:

> This country was conquered by those who moved forward—and so will space.
>
> William Bradford, speaking in 1630 of the founding of the Plymouth Bay Colony, said that all great and honorable actions are accompanied with great difficulties, and both must be enterprised and overcome with answerable courage.
>
> If this capsule history of our progress teaches us anything, it is that man, in his quest for knowledge and progress, is determined and cannot be deterred. The exploration of space will go ahead, whether we join in it or not, and it is one of the great adventures of all time, and no nation which expects to be the leader of other nations can expect to stay behind in the race for space.

Those who came before us made certain that this country rode the first waves of the industrial revolutions, the first waves of modern invention, and the first wave of nuclear power, and this generation does not intend to founder in the backwash of the coming age of space. We mean to be a part of it—we mean to lead it. For the eyes of the world now look into space, to the moon and to the planets beyond, and we have vowed that we shall not see it governed by a hostile flag of conquest, but by a banner of freedom and peace. We have vowed that we shall not see space filled with weapons of mass destruction, but with instruments of knowledge and understanding.

Yet the vows of this Nation can only be fulfilled if we in this Nation are first, and, therefore, we intend to be first. In short, our leadership in science and in industry, our hopes for peace and security, our obligations to ourselves as well as others, all require us to make this effort, to solve these mysteries, to solve them for the good of all men, and to become the world's leading space-faring nation.[10]

The Apollo Alliance's motto is "Three Million New Jobs, Freedom from Foreign Oil," putting together the need for high-paying jobs for Americans with an attack on dependency on nonrenewable fuels motivated by a fear of reliance on Arab oil sources. The environmentalist vision supported by this effort is a needed and praiseworthy effort to support alternative energy and "green-collar" job formation. It is a rare example of a mainstream environmental organization attentive to questions of racial and economic equality as part of its green agenda. Its president, Jerome Ringo, is an African American who worked for the petrochemical industry before becoming alarmed at the consequences of oil development—cancer and pollution—for the African American communities in Louisiana. The board of the Apollo Alliance includes Van Jones, an experienced African American activist who is attentive to questions of environmental justice as well as the need for jobs for urban communities. But as a big tent organization, the Apollo Alliance also includes business and labor leaders not previously supportive of environmental issues, as well as Carl Pope, president of the Sierra Club but (more worrisome) also president of the anti-immigrant and anti–population growth organization Zero Population Growth (see chapter 5). The agenda of the Apollo Alliance is focused on passing federal and state bills to support job growth through clean energy development, a practical and important set of interlocked goals. But locked into the nationalistic and protectionist rhetoric of the extraterrestrialist frontier myth, such an agenda is meant to serve only the needs of the United States and to promote U.S. global leadership; it is not designed to consider global inequities as part of its vision. The space race as an analogy to the effort to conquer the pressing issues of global environmental problems dangerously assumes that the United States is an unproblematic leader for a world threatened not only by environmental problems but also by U.S. power and militarism.

Another example of the wistful desire that a threat to the whole Earth will overcome divisions of culture, history, religion, and power is Al Gore's popular documentary, *An Inconvenient Truth* (2006). Bringing home the urgency of addressing global warming as a threat to our present way of life, this documentary presents powerful images of the devastating consequences of the warming trend in climate change caused by industrial pollution. Gore and his film, respectively winners of the Nobel Peace Prize and an Academy Award, are rightly credited with moving the United States forward on the issue of global climate change and with creating widespread support for action on the issue. However, the entire documentary is framed by the extraterrestrialist imagery of the Earth seen from space, as well as constant references to the importance of seeing the Earth as one unitary object, attributed by Gore as a benefit of space exploration. Like the Apollo Alliance, Gore deploys the U.S. space program as an inspiration; echoing JFK's desire to emulate the pioneers, Gore emphasizes that if the United States could go to the moon, then it is capable of addressing the challenges of global climate change.

Both of these efforts (the Apollo Alliance and *An Inconvenient Truth*) are commendable and important attempts to come up with real, immediate, and desperately needed solutions to environmental problems. The Apollo Alliance, at least, is also sensitive to the necessity of addressing social inequalities of race and class along with environmental problems. Given the importance of addressing environmental issues and the need to inspire coalitional partnerships and the commitment of significant resources, it makes sense that activists would turn to the historical example of the major mobilization required to accomplish the U.S. landing on the moon. The danger of this extraterrestrialist environmentalist rhetoric is that it ignores the problematic connections between the frontier myth, space exploration, militarism, and environmental damage. It sidesteps an environmental justice analysis of our problems and workable solutions, because it assumes, through extraterrestrialist imagery, that differences of power can be ignored or easily overcome (Garb 1990). Such mainstream environmentalist rhetoric implies that frontiers are innocent and that metaphors of conquest are appropriate inspirations for projects of peace. Instead, white U.S. environmentalists in particular need to be mindful that any reliance on extraterrestrialist frontier rhetorics may present a barrier to coalitions with Global South environmentalists and environmental justice activists.

Zones of Sacrifice to Militarism: Wastelands in Space, Wastelands on Earth

The image of the Earth seen from space is a common environmentalist icon. However, the image we are used to seeing, the one used in Gore's documentary as well as hundreds of other environmentalist cultural products, let alone consumer ads and Boeing commercials, is a beautiful globe turning in empty space. In reality, the Earth is surrounded by hundreds of thousands of items discarded by years of space technology: defunct military, communications, and data-gathering satellites; junked space vehicles; bits and pieces broken off from these objects; residues of explosions in space; and even human garbage jettisoned from living quarters. Rather than images of a clear blue marble, we might instead look at a NASA image of space debris (www.windows.ucar.edu), in which space garbage creates a crowded field around the Earth. Peter Spotts (2003) writes, "Within 1,200 miles of Earth, some 2,200 tons of debris orbits." Although for objects in low orbit, debris can be directed toward the atmosphere and safely burned up as it reenters, debris in the upper orbit will circulate for thousands of years. Its existence represents the results of an attitude toward space not unlike the attitude displayed toward "wastelands" on the ground—space is an "empty" environment into which garbage can be jettisoned with no harm. Following hundreds of years of historical frontier logic, space is "virgin land" that can be filled at will.

We should not be surprised by this attitude toward space environments, since militarization on Earth has proceeded by using similarly skewed assumptions about the environmental and social consequences of military activity, closely tied, of course, to U.S. expansionism. Both the nuclear weapons industry and the anti–ballistic missile defense program (dubbed in its Reagan years as "Star Wars") have relied on testing in the Marshall Islands at the Kwajalein Missile Range, now renamed the Ronald Reagan Ballistic Missile Test Site. Missiles shot from Vandenberg Air Force Base in central California land with regularity on or near this atoll in the Marshalls, close to the site of Bikini Atoll, where the hydrogen bomb was tested in 1954. During that test, code-named Bravo, fallout fell on three inhabited islands. The exposure of the Marshallese produced widespread thyroid disease; reproductive impacts such as deformities, stillbirths, and miscarriages; and significant long-term disruption of indigenous liveli-hoods and culture (Cronkite, Conrad, and Bond 1997, 176, 185).

A similar set of circumstances exists in other heavily militarized areas of the United States and the wider world: areas of land, frequently those inhabited by indigenous people, are in effect designated as areas suitable to be sacrificed to the needs of the development and testing of military weapons and technologies, as well as the waste of "peaceful" nuclear power plants. There are particularly dangerous health and environmental effects associated, of course, with nuclear military and energy programs, but there are also environmental and health effects from non-nuclear military tech-nologies and testing (pollution of landscapes, water, and air; sound pol-lution; harmful effects on animals and plants), as well as the taking of the use of the land from indigenous inhabitants and the imposition of regimes of secrecy and expertise used to protect the military and its scientific and corporate dependents from oversight and control by citizens. Indeed, Val-erie Kuletz (1998) has pointed out that huge areas of the U.S. Southwest interdesert region (stretching from California to New Mexico, Utah to Texas, and including most of Nevada) are designated as "zones of sacrifice" required by U.S. militarism.

Clearly, the creation of these militarized "wastelands" is an extension of the history of colonization and racism supported by the frontier myth. These lands were seen as "empty" of worthwhile inhabitants—the "virgin land" assumption (Kolodny 1975; Merchant 2004; Smith 1950)—and des-ert landscapes were assumed to be preferable environments for the kind of exploitation that renders them sterile and poisoned. For example, these indigenous desert homelands are offered as appropriate repositories for nuclear waste (Yucca Mountain in Nevada, a sacred site to the Western Shoshone, has been designated a national nuclear waste depository despite questions about its geologic suitability—the controversy is still unresolved as of this writing). The language of the military and science "pioneers" of these areas of "national sacrifice" frequently compares them to empty, lifeless extraterrestrial environments, "moonscapes" on the Earth, while to their indigenous inhabitants, they are fertile landscapes, sacred and life-sustaining (Kuletz 1998).

I cannot resist illustrating the connection between the colonialist use of indigenous lands and the space race by retelling an amusing story told by Peter MacDonald, former chairman of the Navajo Nation. In 1971, NASA asked to use a portion of the Navajo reservation to practice for the upcom-ing Apollo 15 moon mission, because the terrain was so like the moonscape they would encounter. As the astronauts, Jim Urwin and David Scott, were working in their helmets and suits in the mock space capsule and landing area, an "old Navajo medicine man" came by. He asked MacDonald what the astronauts were doing there, and upon hearing that they were planning a trip to the moon, he recalled a legend that the Navajos once stopped by the moon on their way to the sun. He asked if the astronauts would be willing to take a message to the moon in case some Navajos from this older trip were still there. The astronauts were happy to agree, and they told the old man to write down his message. MacDonald informed them that Navajo was not a written language, so they produced a tape recorder and recorded the old man's message. After the old man left, they asked to play it back but of course could not understand the language. "What's he saying?" they asked MacDonald. "He says, beware of these two fellows, they will want to make a treaty with you" (MacDonald 1980, 163–64).

The wastelands of space and the wastelands of Earth will continue to be connected to each other and both firmly connected to militarism by present space development policies. Despite the heroic sense of pure scientific exploration fostered by NASA, Boeing, and space-positive narratives in mainstream environmentalist discourses such as those of the Apollo Alliance and *An Inconvenient Truth*, the space program is dependent on military projects, dreams of star wars, space lasers, and killer satellites. Warfighting has been one of the major motivations behind exploring the "frontiers" of space. "Weaponizing" (that is, putting weapons into space, forbidden by the 1967 Outer Space Treaty) is understood as legally different than "militarizing" (that is, developing satellites and other space technologies that provide military support).[11] For example, in the 1991 Gulf War and in the 2003 invasion of Iraq, satellites assisted in the deployment and targeting of guided missiles on the ground and in providing tactical information to be used by troops. At least two of Boeing's "Forever New Frontiers" ads, "Mission" (July 2004) and "Bigger Picture" (April 2005), refer to the role of Boeing satellites in "protecting" the U.S. military during the invasion of Iraq (or, in more pointed language, assisting in the destruction of Iraqi troops and the later "insurgents," civilians, and environments).

However, even the ban against the direct weaponizing of space is likely to soon be breached. Beginning with Reagan's support for the Strategic Defense Initiative (SDI, more popularly known as "Star Wars"), the U.S. military began to seek ways to put weapons in space. In 2002, the Bush administration withdrew from the 1972 ABM Treaty, allowing it to propose situating weapons in space that would be able to shoot down incoming nuclear ballistic missiles (though to the date of this writing, the testing of these weapons has been mostly a spectacular failure). And plans for other kinds of weapons have been proceeding apace. According to the *New York Times* (May 18, 2005), the U.S. Air Force has spent billions of dollars developing space-based weapons systems. These include bombs ("Common Aero Vehicles," contracted to Boeing, incidentally) lifted into space on military space planes and designed to penetrate bunkers or hit moving targets on the ground; hypervelocity metal rods (revealingly nicknamed "Rods from God") designed to strike moving targets and to penetrate deeply into the earth; and laser weapons of all kinds, intended to either illuminate or directly strike ground targets.

The Yearning for the Whole Earth and the Need for Global Feminist Environmental Justice

Because of its connection to militarized wastelands on Earth, the creation of militarized wastelands and colonies in space is an environmental justice issue; that is, it requires an analysis that puts the effects of racism, colonization, and resulting political and economic inequalities at the center of our thinking. Granted, not every impulse toward discovery is colonialist; nor is the desire to achieve more knowledge, to develop better technology, to boldly seek out new experiences, new understandings, new worlds even, somehow always imperialist, militarist, and patriarchal. As a child of science fiction (perhaps more than most, even in my baby-boomer science fictional generation), I could never completely deny or reject that heady mix of science and adventure, anthropological curiosity and creative audacity, that accompanies the desire to find out new things, to go beyond the bend, to be immersed in other cultures, to live in other environments.

Nevertheless, contemporary space programs depend on the continuation and acceleration of the creation of toxic landscapes in areas of "national sacrifice" inhabited by indigenous peoples, as well as the increased violence of environmentally destructive wars partially directed from space that will be suffered disproportionately by poor people and peoples of the Global South, whether they are soldiers or civilians. As projects presently justified by frontier rhetorics, stories of masculinist adventure, and evolutionary determination, space colonization and militarization are extraterrestrialist ventures with terrifying consequences. For environmentalists who treasure the fragile image of the whole Earth, such rhetorics should give one pause.

So far, the abstracting of the Earth through the universalizing view from space has not produced encouraging results. Karen Litfin (1997, 38) writes,

In an unequal world, globalism—including global science—is all too likely to mean white, affluent men universalizing their own experiences. Global problems are amenable to large data banks, to Big Science, to grand managerial schemes. . . . [T]he view from space renders human beings invisible, both as agents and as victims of environmental destruction. It also erases difference, lending itself to a totalizing vision. The "global view" cannot adequately depict environmental problems because the impacts of these problems vary with class, gender, age and race. . . . [T]he global view removes problems from the realm of immediacy where meaningful action is possible and most likely to be effective.

Seeing the Earth from space as an object to be saved puts the viewer in a godlike position separated from the Earth, rather than the more humble and pragmatic position of being integrated into local and global ecological and social systems of which we are a part and to which we are responsible. Furthermore, the socially useful capabilities of extraterrestrial technologies will only live up to their promise if inequalities on the Earth are addressed. For example, the ability to foresee the disasters of the Indian Ocean tsunami in December 2004 and Hurricane Katrina in August 2005 was to a great extent created by our technological development of space. Had the poor countries ringing the Indian Ocean been able to afford them, devices called tsunameters could have warned of the devastating wave by beaming a signal to a satellite. Instead, more than 110,000 people were killed. Similarly, weather satellites clearly tracked the birth, growth, and trajectory of Hurricane Katrina. For days beforehand, television news programs were filled with the dramatic satellite pictures of Katrina's growing strength. But despite the evacuation order given as a result of this space-based information, those who were too poor to leave were abandoned in New Orleans to face the devastation alone and without help. The fact that most of the poor were black was compelling visual evidence of America's institutional racism. Both of these "natural" disasters are environmental justice issues because, on this actual Earth, how badly someone is hurt by a disaster depends on how many resources he or she has and whether those in power value that particular life.

Rather than a god's-eye view empowering a small elite, the extraterrestrialist view of Earth seen from space has to be firmly connected to realities of power on the ground. Unless we correct social inequalities, unless we think of planetary security as crucial to us as national security, unless we portray adventures in global justice as exciting as adventures in space, we doom ourselves to a world fatally dominated by the idea of "Forever New Frontiers."

PART II

Naturalizing Reproduction

"The Power Is Yours, Planeteers!"

Race, Gender, and Sexuality in Children's Environmentalist Popular Culture

Many of the patterns of symbolic nature discussed in the previous chapters deal with naturalizing gender and sexuality. These patterns may be important in terms of upholding gender, race, and sexual stereotypes, but they also have consequences for our understanding of environmental problems, especially when they appear in environmentalist popular culture. These gendered, raced, and sexed stories, particularly the promotion of certain kinds of family forms and reproductive practices as "natural," may be problematic environmentally. A broader understanding of human reproduction, one that includes social and economic aspects, is fundamental to a notion of global reproductive justice that more responsibly embeds our reproductive practices in global environmental and political systems, not just as individuals or families but as societies and integrated natural entities.

In a post–cold war context, environmentalism became a new moral framework for children's popular culture. But we should not rush to celebrate this, because the messages contained in these environmentalist stories are often counter to what environmental justice, ecofeminist, and Global South environmentalist activists are fighting for. Instead of the recognition central to these radical environmental justice positions that social equality and environmental sustainability are interconnected, these stories contain habits of thinking that naturalize social inequality and disconnect environmental problems from their corporate causes. Promoting ideas about what constitutes "natural" men and women, "natural" families, "natural" racial/ethnic identities, and "natural" sexuality might have a toxic effect. Those of us who support global environmental justice efforts should be wary of underlying messages in these mainstream environmentalist stories that contradict their moderately progressive surface. We need to be aware of how these dominant cultural messages may undermine the understanding of environmental justice issues we want to promote. Though doing so may sometimes go against our own unquestioned assumptions, we must be very careful of fostering cultural arguments or movement practices that accept the "naturalization" of gender and sexual relations, or racial/ethnic identities; in these children's stories as well as other dominant cultural products, these three aspects (sexism, heterosexism and racism) often reinforce one another.

Two particularly problematic themes in these environmentalist popular culture stories for kids are the association created between homosexuality, evil, and environmental destruction, coupled with an anxiety about the successful reproduction of white middle-class nuclear families; and the "naturalizing" of racial and ethnic differences in the gender-balanced multicultural kids' teams that successfully deal with environmental problems. In these stories, the white, middle-class, nuclear family form is presented as "normal" and "natural," without any critique of its complicity in the overconsumption of corporate products in an environmentally destructive system in which the toxins, waste, pollution, and radiation produced are visited on the poor, people of color, and the tribal peoples of the world. The patriarchal white middle-class nuclear family, organized in the 1950s specifically as a unit of increasing post–World War II consumption situated in environmentally problematic suburbs, was presented at the time as the antithesis to the extended or non-nuclear families located in the inner cities, rural close-knit communities, or tribal reservations (May 1999). The insistence in these children's films that this nuclear family form is natural, normal, and the best for the planet goes against the argument of most environmental justice activists that healthy empowered communities, strong extended families, tribal sovereignty, participatory democratic politics, and interconnections with the land through sustainable practices (such as increasing public forms of transportation and decreasing long-distance travel for food) are the social and economic forms we will need to create social justice and environmental health. Thus, what I call in this chapter the "heterosexist" family is meant to point to a particular emphasis of these stories on the "normal," "natural" status of a specific kind of white, middle-class, suburban nuclear family in which men often have most of the power. I am certainly not against families per se—even small families formed of one man, one woman, and one or two kids living in their own house, with a yard and a garage for their car, outside urban areas (a family that looks a lot like my own at the moment, incidentally). But this family structure, held up as an ideal and a pinnacle of natural evolutionary development, is built on environmentally consequential economic, geographic, racial, class, and gender policies and institutions that we should be able to critically examine if we want to solve environmental and social problems. Doing so becomes difficult when we think of this kind of family as "natural," without historical and social origins.

Additionally, racial and ethnic differences are "naturalized" through the idea that environmentalism is best achieved through the work of gender-balanced, multicultural kids' teams—such as those of *The Animorphs* (Applegate 1997) and the Planeteers of the television cartoon series *Captain Planet* (1990–93)—which present all cultures as equally responsible for environmental problems; their enemies are never corporations or the military or governments. Furthermore, despite the superficial evenhandedness of these racially balanced environmentalist kids' groups, white, male, and middle-class characters have the most power, while people of color, especially women of color, are seen as closer to nature and less powerful. The predominant intertwining in children's popular culture of environmentalism coupled with a certain promotion of liberal racial equality could serve to raise concerns about the role of inequality in creating environmental problems; instead, the logic of these stories ends up "naturalizing" white middle-class values and economic practices.

Bringing Up Baby to Reduce, Reuse, and Recycle: Environmentalism as a Post–Cold War Framework

How and why did environmentalism become such a common framework for children's culture? As a new parent in the early 1990s, I was exposed suddenly and rather overwhelmingly to U.S. kinderculture. One of the things I was struck by was the importance of environmentalism as a theme in nearly every aspect of my son's life. This environmental emphasis popped up everywhere: on unbreakable plastic plates and fast-food containers, on T-shirts and backpacks, in books and museum exhibits, in elementary science curricula and field trips—and above all in movies and television shows such as those I concentrate on in this chapter.

The appearance of this emphasis in my son's and other U.S. children's lives, however, should not be simply accepted as the positive influence of environmentalism; rather, it should be approached with a critical eye, in hopes that these cultural products can be improved. Of course, as Susan

Davis (1996), among others, points out, there is a long-standing Western middle-class practice of using images from nature to educate children (Davis 1996).[1] But the thematic narratives encountered by U.S. children in the 1990s and afterwards, especially from those from three to ten years of age, were about saving nature, not just identifying with Moles who like to boat and Toads who like to drive automobiles (as in the classic 1908 children's story, *The Wind in the Willows* by Kenneth Grahame [1983]). Something new was going on; what did it signify?

Certainly, environmentalism was not a dominant theme in my childhood in the 1960s and 1970s. In my recollection, I moved without any memorable cognitive dissonance from Fran and Ollie and Captain Kangaroo to *Mad Magazine* and Bullwinkle, to the Beatles and then Jimi Hendrix. Though my family background definitely has some eccentricities, I think I partook in standard U.S. children's popular culture, which, while dominated by white middle-class liberal ideas and values, was definitely mass culture and thus broadly experienced by my cohorts in many different race and class locations. We were taught to save the world, yes, but not necessarily to save the planet. Aside from Shel Silverstein's *Giving Tree* (1964), Dr. Seuss's *Lorax* (1971), and Bill Peet's *Wump World* (1970)—all produced in the 1960s and early 1970s, during the emergence of the mainstream U.S. environmentalist movement—moral tales for children about greed and sharing, good guys and bad guys, were told not through an environmentalist lens but through an anticommunist lens. Additionally, the civil rights movement, with its emphasis on social equality and democratic participation, provided many of us with a different moral framework of right and wrong.

But for children today, environmentalist stories of protecting endangered species and saving forests are the ones that are most frequently coupled with lessons about how to treat others, how to fight against greed and corruption, and how to maintain family values.[2] The appearance of the threat of global climate change in these children's lives makes the environmentalist framework even more pertinent. It also encourages an emphasis on global environmental issues that has the potential to both "bring the world together" and obscure differences of power and resources that underly our problems. Globalizing environmentalisms are ambiguous political initiatives, holding out the possibility of comprehensive solutions but also the imposition of policies and practices on the less powerful.

One of the pervasive qualities of the environmentalist material and popular children's culture is the peculiarly American stories about nature that are being told (similar to the frontier myth examined in chapter 3). The parochial status of these tropes about nature does not, however, make them incidental or marginal to processes of globalization. Rather, these U.S.-inflected children's cultural forms, sold and consumed around the world, are frequently tales about a global world, a U.S. dream of a common planet and an undifferentiated childhood experience. This is particularly true of the movies and television shows I concentrate on here; these objects travel cross-culturally more easily than do environmentalist museum exhibits or primary school practices. So in a strong but not totalizing way, I want to emphasize that these cultural objects reflect and reinforce a project of U.S. cultural hegemony that aims to assist the opening of global markets and the imposition on other cultures of the equation between liberal democracy, postindustrial economies, and free-market ideologies.[3] These are exactly the kinds of messages that global environmental justice activists might seek to counter. Like the discourse of anticommunism that in 1950s and 1960s popular culture pitted American apple-pie democracy against godless evil communists, the hegemonic discourse of globalizing environmentalisms too often turns out to be about good-guy U.S. scientists and ecologists against bad-guy foreign polluters and poor brown people squandering resources. Surely the fact that environmentalism has become so accepted a value in our society today is a clear mark of success for environmentalist movements even as it belies the movement's claims that environmentalist values are incompatible with ideologies of growth, exploitation of labor, and militarism.

Environmentalism was pervasive in post–cold war children's culture; it was often used as a frame for the action even when it was not necessary to the plot, thereby providing an important logic for moral adventures of good and evil, similar to the way in which earlier cold war–era children's stories of good and evil centered on tropes of world domination, the revealing of central national secrets, doomsday weapons, and invasion by dark alien hordes.[4] In this respect, the original *Star Wars* trilogy (1977, 1980, 1983) is interesting as a transitional narrative between saving the world cold war style or environmentalist style, in that it moves from the Second Cold War ideology of Reaganism, which promoted can-do white male fighter pilots against the communistic "evil empire," in the first movie to a saving encounter with the Luddite animal/human tribe of furry Ewoks in the third movie. Movies such as *Babe* (1995), the *Jurassic Park* movies (1993, 1997, 2001), *Open Season* (2006), and *Over the Hedge* (2006) also depend on an environmentalist frame to tell their stories. In television shows such as *Teenage Mutant Ninja Turtles* (1987–93) and *Mighty Morphin Power Rangers* (1993–96), even though the heroes were not specifically environmentalists, the evil in the world was antienvironmentalist. The Turtles' mutation was the result of a toxic poisoning of some kind, and the Power Rangers fought against figures such as Ivan Ooze, who planned to cover the globe with mucky stuff very like toxic waste.

There are also plenty of examples of deliberately environmentalist movies and television shows, which have as their animating purpose raising children's consciousness about the destruction of nature through telling entertaining and adventuresome stories that kids will identify with and love. In this category are films including *Ferngully: The Last Rainforest* (1992), *Once upon a Forest* (1993), *Free Willy* (1993, 1995, 1997), *Happy Feet* (2006), *The Simpsons Movie* (2007), and the television cartoon show that inspired part of the title for this chapter, *Captain Planet* (1990–93).

Given the status of these objects as carriers of dominant raced, gendered, classed, sexed, and naturalized stories that are part of global contests for cultural, political, and economic hegemony, it is crucially important to examine what stories are being told, what values are being promoted, which actors get to have agency, and what solutions are being offered. What lessons are being learned, and what kind of environmentalism has become the medium of these messages? What connections are made for children between environmentalism and social justice, between nature and morality? How will children use these frameworks as adults faced with the seriousness of such issues as global climate change?

Saving the Planet Is Saving the Family

One of my favorite examples of the theme of offering the nuclear family as the answer to environmental disruption is in *White Fang 2* (1994). The ending of this 1994 movie neatly encapsulates several themes that I want to discuss. The main character, a young white man named Henry Casey, comes from a broken family, travels to the Alaskan wilderness, and ends up fighting against greedy miners (who are environmentally destructive) on behalf of what appear to be Northwest Coast Indians, along with his animal sidekick, the wolf White Fang. At the end, after the miners have been defeated, one of the young women of the tribe (who also happens to have, coincidentally, a female wolf sidekick) declares her love for the young white man, her willingness to form a family with him. The touching scene in which this happens shows her calling him as he walks away (supposedly leaving forever); in classic Hollywood style, the two are then shown running slowly toward each other for a heartfelt (but relatively chaste, given the PG rating) kiss. At the same time, intercut comically and ludicrously with the two human lovers, the two wolves also run together and kiss. The movie closes with a charming scene in which the female wolf has puppies, and White Fang is, in very unwolflike ways, behaving like a proud daddy.

Some of the themes found in this movie we could easily predict, given their long-standing involvement in the U.S. cultural imaginary: two main ones are the figure of feminized nature and natural femininity, especially in its maternal form; and the naturally Ecological Noble Savage (see chapter 2). In the historical inflection of these children's films, these aspects are almost always combined, as represented in *White Fang 2* by the Northwest Coast Indian woman and in *Pocahontas* (1995) by the title character. Earth Mothers are almost inevitably brown women, especially indigenous women, thus ensuring that nature and natural wisdom are feminized and raced simultaneously (while white mothers, as discussed below, are almost entirely absent). These movies began to be made after civil rights and women's movements challenged many cultural stereotypes, and their makers, generally liberal-minded folks, clearly want to do the right thing. Post-feminist and post–civil rights–era inflections mean that these figures are also presented as tribally specific, independent, choosing beings, even if their romantic choices are still narrowed to nice white guys (such as Henry Casey in *White Fang 2* and Captain John Smith in *Pocahontas*).

This female Ecological Indian trope does not prevent, however, the bad guys in these stories from being sometimes imagined as racialized (on occasion orientalized) others. But more frequently the bad guy is a sexualized other, a nonreproductive, unnatural upper-class twit, the kind of campy, limp-wristed, unpatriotic male closet queen long seen as subversive to the naturalized patriarchal American nuclear family, the only legitimate reproductive unit in the cold war era. Figures such as Scar in *The Lion King* (1994) and Governor Ratcliff in *Pocahontas* represent the deeply problematic idea that gay men in particular are threatening to the "natural" family.

Starting in the middle 1980s, as part of what was a major conservative move to gain political power, the U.S. religious right wing was anxiously arguing that civil rights, feminism, and gay liberation movements had supposedly destroyed the suburban cold war family unit. Though the liberal makers of many of the environmentalist cultural items I am talking about here may reject this conservative position, a similar anxious message about the collapse of the "traditional" nuclear family (ignoring the limited historical, raced, and classed characteristics of this family form) is strongly promulgated throughout these children's stories. Those cultural, economic, and social factors that "threaten" nuclear families also involved challenges to masculinist power within the family and to images of white normality and superiority. Clearly in reaction to achievements of the women's movement in the 1970s, the instability of the nuclear family is thus presented by these stories as a crisis, one that can be solved only by reinstating a "natural" order. Over and over, the plots of these movies involve nature in the task of saving young white boys (and more rarely, white girls) from "broken" family circumstances. In particular, mothers are peculiarly absent; if an alien came down and watched kids' films from 1990 to 2005, she would be convinced that there was a 95 percent chance of a kid's mother (especially if the child was white) having met a fatal accident around the time the child was seven or eight (an incomplete list of recent popular U.S. children's films in which the mother has died, or the child is completely orphaned, would include *Alaska, Free Willy, Finding Nemo, Fly Away Home, Beauty and the Beast, The Lion King, James and the Giant Peach, Anastasia, Once upon a Forest, Harry Potter, Spiderman, Jurassic Park II, Star Wars, Batman, X-Men, Aladdin, The Black Stallion, Babe, Ice Age,* and *A Little Princess*).

As a response to this postfeminist absence of the "good maternal woman," nature is deployed again and again in many of these films to reconstitute the heterosexist patriarchal family, in movies including *Alaska* and *Free Willy, Fly Away Home* and *Wild America, White Fang 2* and *Homeward Bound, The Emerald Forest* and *Jungle 2 Jungle.* Sometimes the nature that accomplishes this healing of the broken family is an animal, such as the geese in *Fly Away Home* (1996) that teach the young girl who has lost her mother to accept a new family with her father and stepmother, or the orphaned bear cub in *Alaska* (1996) that helps bring two kids together with their missing dad. But equally often (and again utilizing the Ecological Indian motif discussed in chapter 2), the nature that accomplishes this reconstitution of the nuclear family is a combination of a indigenous figure and an animal, as with *Free Willy*'s Indian character, Randolph, who along with Willy the whale helps the white boy Jesse accept his foster family, or in *Jungle 2 Jungle* (1997), in which the white boy has "gone native" and, with the help of a friendly tarantula, instructs his wayward father in how to get back together with his mother, or in the example from *White Fang 2* mentioned above. A figure related to White Fang and Willy the whale is the baboon–African shaman character Rafiki in *The Lion King,* who reinscribes the lion-cub Simba properly into the patriarchal legacy he initially rejects and thereby recovers the (environmentally sound) circle of life from its dangerous and deadly nonreproductive state.

In equating the restoration of natural harmony with the restoration of the two-parent, suburban family, then, this kind of environmentalism naturalizes the nuclear family. In perfect symmetry to this dominant message of mainstream environmentalist popular culture that protected and valued nature equals white heterosexist reproduction (meant on both biological and social levels), the figure of the evil male homosexual often inhabits the ecovillains of these films. One of the best illustrations of this figure is the character Scar, the evil uncle in *The Lion King*, voiced by Jeremy Irons, who depends on his past history of playing sexually perverse, socially dangerous male characters to animate his depiction of Scar. This is clearly evidenced in a famous interchange with the lion cub Simba, in which, when Simba says, "You're so weird, Uncle Scar," Scar replies, "You have no idea," the exact same line that Irons spoke in the exact same plummy overtones as the sexually ambivalent Claus von Bülow in the film *Reversal of Fortune* (1990), with enough style to win an Oscar nomination.

A segment from *The Lion King* chillingly demonstrates the way in which racialized, sexualized, and ableist identities inhabit the depiction of environmental villainy (Ingram 2000, 22). In this scene, the nasty hyenas, voiced by Whoopi Goldberg and Cheech Marin to lend them the proper "ghetto" feel, are given a demonstration of Scar's desire to become king in Simba's father's place. Scar's musical number begins with a thoroughly campy intro, in which he prances about in classic drag queen style, and ends disturbingly with a scene of goose-stepping hyenas worshipping him, borrowed almost frame by frame from Leni Riefenstahl's film promoting Hitler, *Triumph of the Will* (1935). Scar is figured here first as an evil homosexual, then as a Hitler worshiped by hyenas either marked as people of color by their voices or presented as mentally disabled.[5] My narrative description of this scene does nothing to convey the emotional power of these images and sounds for kids and their accompanying parents, carried by the high production values of these movies. The audacity of the use of the Riefenstahl images to depict a campy gay male figure as a Hitler in league with untrustworthy and moronic people of color is appalling. Here, Hitler as the embodiment of evil is equated with Scar's "unnatural" sexuality and his antinature power politics—quite contrary to the history of the Nazis' deadly combination of racism and the slaughter of Jewish, gay, and disabled peoples, along with their celebration of heterosexist reproductive family forms and their deep love of nature.[6]

In case the importance of this evil gay male figure seems exaggerated in my argument, I can point to other examples. For instance, in the film *Ferngully* (subtitled *The Last Rainforest* and a specifically pro-environmentalist film), there is the evil character Hexxus, voiced by another sexually ambivalent actor, Tim Curry, best known and most well-loved as the actor who played the "sweet transvestite from Transylvania," Dr. Frankenfurter, in *The Rocky Horror Picture Show* (1975). Hexxus is not merely campy and creepy; he is very, very black, both in color and in his mutable features. In his signature musical number, "Toxic Love" (the title alone gives away the sensibility), Hexxus oozes dangerous and nasty dark sexuality, tied to a stomping rock beat. Once again, the high quality of the music and images makes this movie, like *The Lion King*, a product that is intensely pleasurable; try to watch those two scenes from a critical perspective, without tapping your feet. Another of these evil gay male figures appears in *Pocahontas* in the form of the nasty imperialist Governor Ratcliffe, who is more concerned about the state of his hair than the people he callously orders to be killed as "savages." Ratcliffe carries a little dog around with him on a velvet pillow, and his valet is always close behind with a mirror.

As discussed in chapter 2, that people of color, particularly indigenous people, should be exploited as natural resources for white environmentalism is an old story in U.S. environmentalist history, a story the environmental justice and Global South environmentalist movements are determined to disrupt. But the persistence of combining this story with the notion that part of restoring natural balance involves promoting heterosexist patriarchal family forms as the only means to healthy reproduction (of white people in particular) points to our dominant culture's constant confusion between "nature" and the naturalization of social inequality. In fact, successful environmental strategies may require us to rethink entire modes of production and reproduction that are presently built on this nuclear family form. But our children, particularly U.S. white male children like my son who will grow up privileged in multiple ways, will not learn to think through these connections between environmental destruction, middle-class consumerism, and racism if all they have are these environmentalist stories to go on. We need instead stories of other kinds of reproduction (see chapter 5) that do not depend on these heterosexist, racist, and naturalized tropes.[7]

One could see the movie *Babe* (1995), for instance, as a counterexample to most of the messages of these other films. In *Babe*, the story of a pig who wants to be a sheepdog—an argument against naturalizing political orders, "racial" identities, or social roles—is clearly, charmingly, and humorously presented. In an environmentalist plot containing strong statements against the exploitation of animals as workers or as meat as well as the importance of certain participatory democratic practices, the story has Babe accept as a "mother" the dog Fly, in a cross-species complication of naturalizing families. In an important scene in which Babe is asked by the farmer to show his sheepdog abilities by rounding up some sheep in a pen, he at first encounters failure as the sheep just laugh at his attempts to intimidate them. Fly, his sheepdog mother, tells Babe to take power over the sheep: "You have to dominate them . . . You're treating them like equals. They're sheep, they're inferiors." Babe protests, "Oh no, they're not." Fly continues, "Of course they are, we are their masters . . . Make them feel inferior. Abuse them, insult them, bite them! Whatever it takes, bend them to your will." As Babe trots off to try this method, which fails miserably, the male sheepdog, Rex, who does not approve of Fly's attempt to teach Babe sheepdog methods, reprimands her with a speech that knits together the rationale for violence and power with strong racialized overtones: "You and I," he tells Fly, "are descended from the great sheepdogs. We carry the bloodline of the great Bahoo. And today I watched in shame as all that was betrayed." Babe achieves success with the sheep only when he rejects the "natural" tendencies of sheepdogs to use violence, by treating the sheep as equals and asking for their consent to be herded out of the pen. As the lead ewe says to him, "No need for all this wolf nonsense. All a nice little pig like you need do is ask." This rejection of naturalized bodies, violence, families, racial roles, and hierarchies could serve as one example of a different way of imagining the connection between environmentalism and social equality that does not naturalize the dominant order.[8]

In most of these films, however, not only is the white nuclear family naturalized, but also kids are given the responsibility to fight environmental problems on their own without adults (Dauer 2004). Often, they do this work in racially balanced, gender-equal kids' teams. What kind of environmental and social messages are contained in promoting multicultural kids' teams as the ultimate ecowarriors?

Combining Powers: Liberal Multiculturalism or Environmental Justice?

Of course, my criticisms are likely to come as a shock to the producers of much of this environmental children's culture, for they clearly want to create liberal messages about racial and gender equality (though less attention is paid to equality for those who challenge sexual norms, until perhaps *Happy Feet* [2006], discussed in chapter 5). Everywhere in this material, there is an insistence on a certain notion of easily achievable multiculturalism and gender equality, a diversity just as naturally achieved as biodiversity is imagined to be. Yet as environmental justice activists know, achieving collaboration across racial differences in U.S. society is no easy task for coalition politics.

In popular culture texts, this racial and gender diversity is often represented by groups of five or six teenagers, with particular patterns that unfortunately ensure the reinstantiation of white middle-class men in the position of leadership. Thus, the Animorphs (characters in a 1990s book series and a less popular television show) are teenagers who are given the power to acquire animal DNA and morph into animals to fight against the invasion of mind-controlling sluglike communards called Yeerks. Like the Power Rangers, the Animorphs group consists of two white boys, one white girl, one boy of color, and one girl of color. This is a liberal form of multiculturalism, of course, in which racial differences are seen as naturally necessary to an effective team, like certain notions of ecosystems in stasis, in which differences never reflect competing interests or signal histories of genocide, slavery, rape, or exploitation but instead are brought into accord as examples of good managerial theory.[9] Just as static notions of biodiversity (sometimes found in mainstream environmentalism) only make sense within depictions of ecosystems as closed, circular, in-balance, and without history, so too does the easy necessity of racial and gender diversity of these kids' teams exist within a homogenous middle-class existence in which the favorite place for the kids to meet is the suburban mall (a kind of closed ecosystem in itself).

These discourses of mainstream environmentalism and liberal multiculturalism effectively combine in these children's stories to eviscerate power-laden histories of socially constructed difference. For example, in the *Animorphs* books, Cassie, the African American girl on the team, is figured as closer to nature by her ability to befriend animals (both of her parents are veterinarians) and by her comfort with her body (she is the most controlled and graceful morpher, given her natural affinity with animals). These associations follow long-standing U.S. cultural patterns of portraying African Americans as closer to animals. However, when faced with the Animorphs' risky attempt to free two members of the enslaved alien species Hork-Bajir, which are almost always defined in the books by the adjective *enslaved*, Cassie responds not by referencing abolitionist discourses one would assume to be easily deployed by a fourteen-year-old African American girl. Instead, Cassie passionately wants to save them because they are a breeding pair of an endangered species (Applegate 1997, 72).

This form of liberal multiculturalism serves a more distinctively post–cold war purpose in the service of a globalizing environmentalism in the *Captain Planet* television series. Here the five teenagers of the group hew pretty much to the pattern mentioned above (one white U.S. guy, one black African guy, one brown South American guy, one white Russian girl, and one generically Asian girl), but this pattern of biodiversity is very much about globally significant cultural diversity, a quasi-U.N. version of multiculturalism (Dauer 2004).

Despite (or rather, through) this cultural diversity, the Planeteers are a United Nations clearly led by the United States, while dependent on the work, body, and knowledge of a brown woman. Gaia, voiced in the first Captain Planet by the distinctive tones of Whoopi Goldberg, is a brown woman who is the spirit of Earth and serves as the source of the Planeteers' abilities. Once again, the Mother Earth figure is a woman of color. But for the animating life-force of Earth personified, Gaia is curiously powerless, dependent on the work of the five teenagers she gives rings to so that they can call up the powers of fire, water, earth, wind, and the fifth element, heart (Dauer 2004). Of course, the U.S. alpha male, the white Wheeler, has the power of fire; the African male, Kwame, naturally has the power of earth; and the geopolitically marginal brown male, the South American Ma-Ti, is given the feminized power of heart.

When the Planeteers are in deep trouble, they combine their powers and call up a real superhero, Captain Planet, who, despite his blue skin and green hair, is a typical wisecracking suburban white guy straight out of sitcom-land. For example, when faced with a mutant giant octopus created by toxic dumping off Japanese coastal waters, Captain Planet says, "I've got to stop that super-squid before it turns the city into sushi!" And zipping into the sky, he calls out, "Calamari, dudes!" The character Captain Planet, to quote from the "Mission to Save Planet Earth" section of the show's Web page,[10] is meant to be "a metaphor for that which can be accomplished by teamwork," and thus he "symbolizes that the whole is indeed greater than the sum of its parts." But this particular whole created by the unification of the "world's cultures and ethnic diversity" is—far from being anything like the "sum of its parts"—nothing more than a good old American white male adolescent superhero. The notion of the world's cultures "combining powers" may seem like a nice metaphor for political coalition, but not if its purpose is creating a unity that looks and acts just like a white Southern California surfer dude with body paint.

In some ways, it may seem supercritical to pick on *Captain Planet*, which is a thoroughly self-conscious environmentalist cultural product—and a very successful one, garnering several media and educational awards and reaching over 7 million people a week in the United States alone, while being distributed in over sixty countries during its heyday in the mid-1990s, according to its promotional material.[11] *Captain Planet* is unusual and commendable as a media product in its effort to provide action-oriented information, political inspiration, and organizational linkages. More children's cultural products should emulate this. At the end of every episode is a thirty-second bit called "Planeteer Alert," which focuses on a specific problem (for instance, the safe disposal of household wastes) and gives kids tips on how they can be environmentally conscious consumers and citizens.[12]

Turner Enterprises, the creator of *Captain Planet*, through its Captain Planet Foundation (http://captainplanetfoundation.org) also set up several links with other institutions in a position to influence kids and their parents, a process the producers call "combining powers" (which is what the Planeteers do when they summon Captain Planet). The Captain Planet Foundation makes the shows available to teachers for classroom use and has collaborated with such organizations as the American Public Transit Association, the Environmental Protection Agency, Microsoft, Whole Foods, the Weather Channel, Coca-Cola, and the U.S. Fish and Wildlife Service. (With the latter, it has held a program called "Earth Day with the Braves," neatly combining Ted Turner's environmentalism with his love of baseball, while ignoring the Atlanta Braves' use of Native American stereotypes.) The Captain Planet Foundation also funds numerous children's grassroots environmental efforts.[13]

So why pick on *Captain Planet*? After all, wouldn't we rather have environmental messages than non-environmental ones? Messages of multiculturalism rather than messages of bigotry? Messages in which women play important roles rather than ones in which they are powerless or invisible? Messages that allow agency to non-Western peoples rather than ones that assume the only teenagers with power are middle-class U.S. suburbanites? Yes, of course. But its very status as the most radical example of children's environmentalist popular culture shows the deep dependence of these stories on problematic tropes of powerless (but protofeminist) brown indigenous women, exoticized pure nature such as Gaia's Hope Island, and individuals characterized by naturalized differences operating in conflict-free teams.

Captain Planet's attempt to produce a liberal message is also beholden to certain assumptions about the necessity to preserve corporate America's good reputation. The producers explain,

> The use of villains to delineate good and evil is common in action-adventure series. However, given that we deal with real life issues, we were concerned [that] children might come to the conclusion that if their parents worked in a polluting industry they were somehow villains. Although our show is basically realistic, our eco-villains are intentionally exaggerated so that they are clearly operating outside of the law. They are symbolic of the environmental problems rather

than representative of the actions of individuals. We are careful not to be critical of business/industry, but to encourage responsible business practices and a balance between the needs of people, environment/ wildlife, and industry.[14]

Like every other one of the environmentalist objects of children's popular and material culture that I have encountered, then, *Captain Planet* presents solutions that are almost entirely restricted to individual lifestyle changes, to legitimating the rule of law rather than challenging business as usual. In the world of *Captain Planet*, environmental catastrophes always happen "outside the law" rather than exhibiting the reality in which legal parameters often protect polluting corporations or governments. Ecovillains are nasty male queens, dark spirits, long-haired men with accents, brittle and demented white female scientists, or mutant human/animal paranoids with delusions of grandeur.[15] Though children get the notion that trees are cut down and animals killed because of greedy behavior, it is almost always the greedy behavior of a single ecovillain. Never are the ecovillains corporations or militaries or governments or white patriarchal science—the real ecovillains on our planet, the ones the global environmental justice movement is presently confronting. Gaia lives on a pure tropical island far away from the many urban sites of environmental struggle. As discussed in chapter 2, solutions that romanticize ecological Noble Savages lock both nature and people of color in an imagined preindustrial past, but they are almost the only solutions offered, along with the idea that recycling and disposing of toxic waste "properly" (rather than identifying the source of the waste and preventing it from being made) are important tasks for children.[16]

Who's Got the Power?

In a story such as *Captain Planet* (which, like other examples of children's environmentalist popular culture, wants to equate environmentalism with social equality), how do we evaluate the notion that "the power is yours"? There are a number of ways to read this phrase and to speculate about its likely results as an internalized message. We might start by thinking about who gets to be a Planeteer, which individuals most easily can imagine themselves as global citizens, empowered to combine powers with others on a planetwide scale. That this story might be most invested in addressing or interpellating privileged Western children comes as no surprise. And it may be an appropriate strategy, given the inordinate amount of the world's resources these children will consume over their lifetime. So perhaps this message will have unforeseen radical results. After all, some of the important demographic actors in the sixties movements were privileged children like myself, who, having been brought up on the notion that we were empowered to promote Truth, Justice, and the American Way, realized with a shock that it was up to us to follow the lead of those less privileged and to force our country and our parents to correct deeply held hypocrisies. Perhaps the Planeteers of tomorrow will someday rebel against the corporate forces that are destroying the planet and causing suffering for so many of the world's peoples. Perhaps the megamedia empires, such as Turner Enterprises, will take responsibility for the misleading stories they are promoting, in which environmental damage can be cured by constructing a suburban nuclear middle-class family or by promoting superficial multiculturalism. This is perhaps a utopian hope, but maybe one day the multinationals will wish that they had never told these kids "the power is yours," allowing the liberal, superficial, and individualistic solutions presently offered to be rejected for collective, social, and revolutionary action.

But another, more pessimistic reading of this message is possible. Clearly, the dominance of the environmentalist theme is not centrally about environmentalism at all but about producing morally uplifting and privilege-maintaining stories that legitimate the notion that especially for white middle-class children, the power is theirs to do what they will with the world. Like the idea of easy multicultural kids' teams, the "environment" appears to be a safe issue when freed from questions of power, privilege, and history. Given the Planeteers' superpowers, their incapacity for wrongdoing, and the overwhelming priority of saving an otherwise doomed nature over other social problems, the privileged kids who identify with the Planeteers might feel fully justified in imposing putatively environmentalist solutions undemocratically on less powerful non-Planeteers.

And what about the kids who do not readily identify as Planeteers? Certainly the kids being poisoned by lead in the cities, the kids who are malnourished by corporately produced salinification and erosion, the kids who are drinking pesticide-laced water at migrant farmworkers camps, the kids who are living on uranium tailings on Navajo land—are Captain Planet's producers worried about whether *they* will start holding *their* parents responsible for "polluting industries"? Will these kids be satisfied with the idea that nature will be restored if they all form happy, consumption-oriented nuclear families? It is less likely that these kids, in a postfeminist, post–civil rights environmental justice era, will be unaware of the shape and character of the real ecovillains. These kids cannot wait—and in fact are not waiting—for an awakened force of white middle-class Planeteers to take on the combined problems of environmental destruction and social inequalities.

Looking critically at environmentalist children's popular culture underscores the difficulty of telling stories about saving nature from the point of view of dominant U.S. culture without engaging in problematic stories about social difference, which depend on the naturalization of social inequalities, via the invocation of the "natural order," nature as truth, foundation, all that is right and valuable. These themes are particular to our present historical and political context, showing the traces of recent social movement critiques while transposing them onto justifications of white, male, straight, liberal capitalist hegemony—that is, they tend to be postfeminist, post–civil rights stories about environmentalist new world orders. But even when apparently promoting the kind of environmentalist values shared by environmental justice activists (for instance, struggling against toxic waste in poor communities of color or against uranium and coal mining on Indian lands), these stories often portray people of color or gay people either stereotypically or as the villains. Even more disturbingly, they combine homophobic and racist portrayals in ways that distract audiences from remembering that the ecovillains of the real world are corporations, militaries, and governments (Seager 1993).

Rather than thinking that the power is yours or ours or theirs or the planet's, we must think about powers that arise out of struggle and contest, which are justified on the basis of participatory democratic practices rather than what is natural. Rather than look to superpowered teams that naturalize U.S. white male middle-class leadership, we need to think about combining powers in political coalitions that go against the present "natural" order. And this is what the global environmental justice movement, in its refusal to depend only on biocentric environmentalist arguments about saving a "pure" nature, has the potential to do.

The intertwining of naturalizing "family values" discourses with environmentalism does not only occur in children's popular culture. In the next chapter, we will look at some more adult examples, and engage the question of what concepts of reproduction are most useful for constructing a global feminist environmental justice framework.

5
_____

Penguin Family Values

The Nature of Planetary Environmental
Reproductive Justice

In 2005, a nature documentary entitled *The March of the Penguins* was a surprise hit, winning an Academy Award in 2006 for best documentary. The
beautifully filmed story of the improbable but gorgeous Antarctic emperor
penguins and their incredible effort to produce and nurture their babies
was a tale of terrific difficulties overcome with amazing persistence. In
an interesting twist, and to the astonishment of the director, Luc Jacquet,
right-wing fundamentalist Christians in the United States adopted the film
as an inspiring example of monogamy, traditional Christian family values,
and intelligent design. At around the same time, apparently unbeknownst
to those same fundamentalist Christians, penguins had become a symbol
of the naturalness of gay marriage.

Meanwhile, in other political and cultural discourses, penguins (along
with polar bears) became popular symbols of what we would lose to global
warming. Relatively invisible in the public cultural arena, in contrast, were
the growing effects of the pollution of our atmosphere, which are visited
unequally on marginalized human beings, such as indigenous peoples in
the Arctic regions, who are struggling to preserve their culture and societies in the face of rapid climate change. Instead of these issues, penguins
have become the newest terrain on which to fight culture wars over human
reproduction, while at the same time they have become the latest environmentalist icons. What is the connection between these popular cultural
trends? Does it matter in terms of environmental consequences what kind
of familial and sexual arrangements we make?[1]

The Nature of Reproduction

Familial and sexual arrangements are clearly important to environmental issues (see chapter 4). Reproduction (involving questions of sexuality as well as gender and race) is an important political issue in our culture, a contested topic in almost every arena of our life. Here, I propose a broader notion of reproduction than is customary, using the concept of environmental reproductive justice as a way of connecting environmental issues with social justice issues. In doing so, I am building on the insights of feminists, especially feminists of color and Global South feminists, who have argued for framing analyses in terms of reproductive justice, as opposed to reproductive rights. The term *reproductive justice* refers to more than the mainstream conception of reproductive rights (that is, access to abortion, birth control, the morning-after pill, and so forth), attempting to address the need for equal access to the means of supporting and nurturing children (including child care, health care, prenatal care, freedom from coerced sterilization, healthy environments, clean air, food, and water, and adequate housing), not merely allowing individual women to control whether they become pregnant. The critique of the narrower term *reproductive rights*, including the emphasis that more-privileged feminists place on reproductive choice, should be recognized as part of the effort to develop a global feminist environmental justice analysis (Silliman et al. 2004; Silliman and King 1999; Smith 2005). Giovanna Di Chiro argues for a similar perspective, conceptualizing reproduction as necessarily about the intertwined reproduction of the environment, communities, and individuals, which she calls "living environmentalism." Di Chiro (2008) shows how women environmental justice activists consistently challenge a division between reproductive issues and environmental issues in their efforts to sustain healthy communities and control the means of social reproduction.

Trying to think differently and clearly about these interrelated questions is important, but it is complicated by the fact that how we reproduce—whether we are reproducing people, families, cultures, societies, or the planet—is politicized in several layered and contradictory ways. Ironically, given the extreme consequences of certain human models of reproduction for the environment, appeals to the natural are one of the standard ways in which this politicization of reproduction is obscured. Embedded in contemporary appeals to the natural status of reproduction are deep attachments to political positions with serious economic and environmental consequences: to dominance of the Global North over the Global South, to sexism, to heterosexism, and to unfettered exploitation of environmental resources by corporations and social elites. Those attachments need to be brought out and analyzed for us to be able to properly understand and to critically examine current political discourses around reproduction, including those of environmental activists. Yet gender and sexuality are often ignored as part of explanatory schemes used to analyze contemporary political and economic arrangements.

For example, Thomas Frank (in his book *What's the Matter with Kansas?* [2004]) perceptively explores the contradiction embedded in the recent right-wing dominance of U.S. politics, examining how an alliance between far-right conservatives and traditional pro-business Republicans has been able to mobilize lower-income people on its side even though the political and economic policies that working-class people are asked to support are contrary to their class interests. Though his analysis is insightful in many ways, he pays little or no attention to the way in which changes in gender roles and reproductive labor have been an essential part of this story. Though Frank does not note this, the wedge issues that he portrays being used to whip up feelings of anger, oppression, and fear among those who support the extreme right wing—abortion, "vulgarity" in popular culture, homosexuality, family values, and so forth—are all centrally about beleaguered gender expectations, driven by changes in economic practices in a globalizing economy. Thus, the recent right-wing coalition that has done so much damage to environmental agendas has been deeply driven by issues of gender and sexuality.

In short, the politics of gender often combine the politics of reproduction with the politics of production—the intertwined ways in which people produce more people; manage bringing up children; figure out how to do the work at home at the same time as the work that brings in a paycheck; decide how and where to buy food, clothing, shelter, and transportation; take care of elders; and create and maintain all of the social institutions that surround this work. All of this is central to whether our ways of living cause environmental degradation. The politics of reproduction—of people, families, economies, and environments—center on gendered arrangements of work and sexuality. Recognizing this is important to coming up with solutions to social and environmental problems, let alone being able to resist manipulative political discourses.

Furthermore, these social arrangements are heteronormative, naturalized by assumptions about human relationships—sexual, affective, generational, economic, and institutional—built on a foundation of a particular family form, which is embedded within a romance plot involving narrow views of male and female attraction, differentiated gender and work roles, and unequal power relations. Yet we are encouraged to think of these sexual/social arrangements as "only" personal, a matter of individual choice (in the liberal version) or of natural/divine determination (in the conservative version). To the contrary, such a heteronormative, patriarchal foundation is not merely about family and personal relationships; rather, it structures understandings of and consent to matters of citizenship, market relations, nationhood, and foreign policy. As Lauren Berlant and Michael Warner (1998, 553) have put it,

> Heterosexual culture achieves much of its metacultural intelligibility through the ideologies and institutions of intimacy. . . . First, its conventional spaces presuppose a structural differentiation of "personal life" from work, politics and the public sphere. Second, the normativity of heterosexual culture links intimacy only to the institutions of personal life, making them the privileged institutions of social reproduction, the accumulation and transfer of capital, and self-development. . . . Intimate life is the endlessly cited elsewhere of political public discourse, a promised haven that distracts citizens from the unequal conditions of their political and economic lives, consoles them for the damaged humanity of mass society, and shames them for any divergence between their lives and the intimate sphere that is alleged to be simple personhood.

Though one could argue that such a use of intimacy to evade the realities of unequal social and economic arrangements could be based on any form of sexual relationship, this would miss the way in which social and economic structures are presently based on a tight insistence on the connection between normative heterosexuality (in other words, socially sanctioned, limited versions of only some kinds of heterosexual behaviors, intimacies, and relationships) and "acceptable" ("natural") reproduction.

Heterosexist arguments commonly conceptualize human sexuality as strictly binary (homosexuality versus heterosexuality; "opposites attract"; "men are from Mars, women from Venus") and normative (heterosexuality is assumed to be better, that is, more natural, more moral, more normal, more wholesome, better for parenting children). Such assumptions structure social institutions in such a way that heterosexuality is privileged— not simply heterosexual sexual practices but dominant notions about what a family should look like; who should do the domestic work; how women and men should look, act, and behave; and how life should be maintained (what is called heteronormativity). The assumption that heterosexuality is the only form of sexuality that is biologically reproductive underlies heterosexism and gives it its persuasive force. Normative heterosexuality is seen as natural and therefore right because it is a form of sexuality that is reproductive. When more closely examined, this logic is not persuasive; sex is not simply about human reproduction in the sense of having babies. After all, given contemporary reproductive technologies and practices, as well as the fact that sexual desire is far more complex and motivated by far more than the potential for pregnancy, actual heterosexual sex is not so closely connected to reproduction as these arguments about its naturalness want us to believe. Otherwise, no heterosexual would have sex unless he or she intended to conceive a child, and no heterosexual would have any kind of sex other than sex that would produce a child. Rather, these heterosexist arguments are usually about preserving and reproducing particular forms of family, social power, and economic practices.

For example, one could argue that the importance of the "pro-life, pro-family" perspective on reproductive rights issues is not motivated simply by a desire to prevent abortions but is centrally about the reproduction of a certain historically and culturally specific idealized family form—a father who is the authority, a mother who is the helpmate and chief child care provider, and several children living in a framework that is Christian, religious, patriarchal, heterosexual, nationalistic, U.S., and "nuclear"—that is, politically right wing. Roger N. Lancaster (2003, 336) argues that "the family is to act as a miniature welfare state, modulating consumption, curbing excess desires, improvising child care, and providing social security—in the absence of a Keynesian or social-democratic regulatory state . . . it is the dreamworld conveyed in the . . . 'serious' media . . . where the conservative variant of the neoliberal utopia is attributed to the biologically fixed 'nature' of desire."

One of the fears mobilized to support opposition to reproductive rights, emphasized especially in antiabortion rhetoric, is that allowing women (especially young women) to decide about their own sexuality and pregnancies flies in the face of what are seen as normal, natural relationships of control and decision making underlying what is believed to be a normal, natural family structure (often articulated as a worry about the apparent reduction of parental rights or fathers' rights entailed in women's access to abortion). This fear also concurrently appeals to an underlying racism and classism that wants to prevent women of color and poor women in particular from having access to choices and support for their reproductive decisions and thus forming other kinds of families than the kind imagined to be the model blessed by the (right-wing) Christian God. Thus, a central belief of right-wing Christians (and some other conservative religious perspectives) is that the heterosexual, patriarchal family is divinely created. But there is a close relationship between God and nature in the logic of this position, because the other foundational assumption is that such a family is the only normal and natural one. In fact, this slide between normal, natural, and divine is what allows right-wing Christian arguments to sound persuasive to a broader public that may be less invested in this specific religious-based family structure but remains uncritical of such implied connections between this family form and nature (a dynamic that is clearly in play in the public debate over gay marriage).

What Lancaster (and many other feminist and queer theorists commenting on the use of essentialist ideas of nature to legitimate a conservative form of family values) overlooks is that this family form, especially when located within a suburban, consumer economy dependent on extremes of global inequality, might be an important origin of our present environmental problems—and that environmental health is an aspect centrally important to reproduction and production. When such heteronormative family forms are bound up in environmentally dangerous social and economic practices, we have a situation in which we are promoting environmental damage by naturalizing heteronormative patriarchy, preventing us from imagining and putting in place alternative ways of living more lightly on the Earth. In the present contemporary U.S. context, the suburban American family that is most frequently portrayed in our popular culture and our political arguments as "natural" depends on women's unpaid domestic labor, particularly in the areas of child care and elder care; the use of nonrenewable fuel–intensive transportation such as cars and long-distance shipping of consumer products; and the promotion of women as "shoppers" who buy all of their food, clothes and consumer goods in stores that are involved in globalized production and distribution chains dependent on the exploitation of the labor of the poor, often in the Global South, often women. Painting particular reproductive arrangements as natural in one way or another is an important tool in controlling political debates about these reproductive and productive arrangements. The burden that is implicitly placed on the Western suburban heteronormative family form to guarantee human survival in the face of environmental degradation of the biosphere is based on a dangerous contradiction. Thus, resisting and critically evaluating claims to the natural are essential methods of enabling people to consciously create better, more environmentally sound, and more socially just arrangements of work and life.

This chapter examines the relationship between various heterosexist, patriarchal, and colonialist discourses about the family and reproduction, including those found in environmentalist rhetoric. Though the focus in this chapter is on how discourses of the natural are deployed in popular culture depictions of hetero- and homosexuality, as well as overpopulation, these are only some examples of the many popular cultural discourses about reproduction that depend on problematic assumptions about what is natural and that can lead us astray in trying to solve political, economic, and environmental problems.[2] The overall point I wish to make is that reproduction is a materialist and a planetary issue—that is, all reproduction comes with consequences for the global environment, economies, and social practices. If we take the term *reproduction* in its broadest sense, what are the socioeconomic and sociopolitical arrangements best suited for successful and sustainable reproduction, on the biological, social, and environmental levels? What happens to our understanding of reproductive politics if we take a wider view, always thinking about the environmental consequences of those social, economic, and political practices we presently engage in? What happens if we refuse to separate human fertility and the fertility of the earth, not by promoting an ancient pagan set of practices and beliefs but in terms of examining the reciprocal relationship between the reproductive capacities of humans and what gets called "the environment" (that is, animals, plants, "nature")? For instance, what are the reproductive consequences for human mothers and fathers of toxic environments?[3] And how is the effort to find sustainable and just practices of living with planetary implications challenged by the forces of economic globalization, changing gender roles, militarism, natural resource depletion, and environmental pollution? Various stories about reproduction found (or conversely, made invisible) in contemporary popular culture illuminate how our accepted ideas about the nature of babies, families, marriage, populations, genes, and parenting intertwine with and influence our understanding of environmental issues, or what might be called planetary reproduction, an approach that could be labeled "environmental reproductive justice."

Penguin Family Values: Sexuality in Nature

Popular versions of what might be called "penguin family values" (that is, the use of the sexual and mating habits of penguins) have been adopted as tokens in the culture wars over the naturalness of heterosexuality or homosexuality. The Academy Award–winning 2005 nature documentary *The March of the Penguins* drew a surprise fan base: Christian fundamentalist evangelicals. According to the *New York Times*, some conservative religious ministries encouraged their families to attend *The March of the*

Penguins together and to write about their spiritual responses according to prompts provided by their pastor. The conservative film critic and radio host Michael Medved was quoted as saying that *The March of the Penguins* "passionately affirms traditional norms like monogamy, sacrifice and child rearing. . . . This is the first movie [traditional Christian audiences] have enjoyed since 'The Passion of the Christ.' This is 'The Passion of the Penguins'" (Miller 2006).

Particularly odd about this promotion of the penguin family as the ideal Christian family was the equal gender division of labor depicted in the film. Though conservative Christians claim that traditional family values involve a complementary appreciation of women's work and men's work, each having a valued and necessary place in the family, the patriarchal framework of the husband acting as Christ to the wife as his domestic helpmate belies true equality.[4] Unlike the idealized patriarchal division of labor that fundamentalist Christians espouse, the division of domestic labor by the penguins is not complementary but rather more strictly equal. After the egg is laid, the male penguin takes care of it by balancing it on his feet, while the female penguin is the first of the pair to make the arduous seventy-mile trek back to the water to get food for the incubating chick. When the females return, the males transfer the newly hatched chick to them for care, feeding, and warmth while males make their trek to the ocean in turn. Both leave to forage for food, and both care for offspring. This arrangement is very unlike the historically specific (beginning in the 1950s) white middle-class suburban division of labor by gender so frequently thought of as "traditional" by U.S. conservatives, in which the man is the breadwinner and the woman the domestic worker. Interestingly, the penguin's domestic arrangement is closer to the arrangement required by the transformation of the economy by globalization and modernization in the 1990s, a transformation that has caused real anxiety in the U.S. working and middle class and prompted a conservative backlash against feminist promotions of domestic and economic equality, which conservatives believe is undermining family values (Coontz 1992; May 1999).

One possible way to understand the right-wing Christian fondness for the penguin's arrangement of sharing domestic labor, so unlike what they usually promote, is the effect of the heroic way in which the males are portrayed, daddies suffering collectively to protect their young against the brutal cold and blinding snowstorms. Clearly, this is how patriarchs should protect their families, with complete commitment and at risk to themselves. The female penguins in the movie, though also sacrificing their health and well-being for their babies, somehow are not as moving in their long arduous walk as the huddled mass of penguin dads toughing it out together through the arctic night; neither is their equally long wait for the males to return an important part of the narrative. Such a heroic portrayal may also be a way of unconsciously taking out the sting of the material reality that under the conditions of postindustrial global capitalism, women are often co-breadwinners and men may have to do more domestic labor to keep the family going. Another aspect that might have been attractive to social conservatives is the way in which the film closely connects romance (or desire) with the goal of having children and giving birth, avoiding the messy reality of polymorphous human sexuality. In doing so, *March of the Penguins* follows a standard anthropomorphic script of television nature shows, in which animal mating and reproduction is consistently represented as a metaphor for human heteronormative romance and nuclear families (Mitman 1999; Wilson 1992).

What makes this adoption of penguins as promoters of a moral majority particularly ironic is the already iconic status of penguins as devoted gay couples and parents. The bonding of same-sex penguin pairs, it turns out, is not simply fairly common but was actually enjoying an unprecedented amount of publicity in the two years just before the film arrived. In fact, as several letter writers to the *New York Times* pointed out in their response to the article,[5] the disjuncture between these two popularized images of penguins shows how radically separated from each other are communities of gay people and communities of right-wing religious conservatives: if the Christian fundamentalists had looked up "gay penguins" or even "penguins" on the Internet, they would have encountered several gay penguin sites, including the story of Roy and Silo, the Central Park Zoo gay penguin couple about whom a children's book was written; the saga of the gay penguin community at a German zoo; and the campaign of Gay Penguin for President (whose slogan was "George W. Bush talks the talk, but Gay Penguin walks the walk"). If better prepared for the likelihood that the penguin could be employed as a symbolic saboteur of Christian conservatism, they would not have been so surprised and outraged by the liberal, tolerant moral of the 2006 children's film *Happy Feet*. In each of these cultural phenomena, discourses of the natural are flexibly used in the culture wars around sexuality.

Roy and Silo were two penguins that lived at the Central Park Zoo and were deeply bonded to one another. As is often the case, because penguin genitalia are not obviously sex-differentiated, the keepers did not know that the pair was same-sex until they noticed that an egg was never produced. Upon closer examination (necessitating, most likely, a DNA test to distinguish sex), the keepers discovered that Silo and Roy were both male. Though the couple went through all the usual courting displays, sexual activity, and nest-building behaviors, they were missing an essential element of their reproductive ambitions: an egg. The zookeepers decided to help them out by providing them with another penguin's egg (what arrangement was made with the surrogate mother is unclear). Roy and Silo successfully raised their egg into a healthy chick, named Tango. The couple and their baby were celebrities in the Central Park Zoo and became a tourist stop on many gay (and straight) people's visits to New York City. This charming penguin family romance was memorialized in the children's book *And Tango Makes Three* (Parnell and Richardson 2005). The book proposes the moral that all kinds of families, and all kinds of reproductive methods, are equally valuable as long as love, stability, and nurturing are involved. A back-cover blurb of *And Tango Makes Three* by well-known openly gay actor Harvey Fierstein says, "This wonderful story of devotion is heartwarming proof that Mother Nature knows best." The assertion that love and parenting naturally—indeed, biologically—come in both heterosex and same-sex forms was a moral lesson based on nature that enraged many right-wing religious homophobes. Right-wing religious activists in many U.S. communities sought to keep *And Tango Makes Three* out of libraries and schools.[6] Roy and Silo's story and the publication of the book were not merely innocent and diversionary stories but stand as cultural tokens of the political contest around gay marriage and gay parental and adoption rights. For human beings, the Central Park penguins were made into a living symbol of the naturalness and success of gay marriage and, depending on one's position in this contest, were celebrated or excoriated by humans as a result.

Of course, *And Tango Makes Three* did not cover the continuing saga of Roy and Silo's relationship. After raising Tango, they eventually broke up, and Silo became sexually involved with a female penguin named Scrappy. Some of New York's gay community took it hard that the apparently committed relationship of Silo and Roy was not as solid as they had hoped. Given the powerful legitimating force in the United States of the idea of nature underlying what is acceptable in human behavior, these cultural contests were about serious, material issues, particularly for gay, lesbian, bisexual, and transgendered people's lives. For queer activists involved in struggling against right-wing attacks on their communities and families, the relationship of the gay penguins served as welcome proof of the natural nature of same-sex love, romance, parenting, and domestic stability. In their lives, threatened by heteronormative institutions—which, far from protecting their relationships (and the property accumulation and parental obligations stemming from them), were openly hostile toward them—the symbol of the gay penguins was not a trivial thing. Presumably, they were therefore relieved when, in another twist of the story, Silo abandoned Scrappy and returned to Roy. Whether Silo was really gay or was instead bisexual might be a matter for human gossip columns (and possible fodder for the complicated debates around bisexual identity and definitions of gayness), but since as far as we can tell, penguin society has little interest in the nuances of sexual identity politics, we can presume that the other penguins were not particularly concerned with the goings-on in the love triangle of Roy, Silo, and Scrappy.

The saga of the German penguins shows similar human political and emotional investments in the durability and naturalness of same-sex penguin pairs. In February 2005, it was announced that of the five pairs of Humboldt penguins at the Bremerhaven Zoo in Bremen, three were same-sex pairs, all males (lesbian penguins, though they exist in nature and in captivity, seem invisible in these stories, perhaps because examining tuxedo-wearing birds who were female would raise questions of cross-dressing that would complicate the morality tales). As in the Central Park story, the Bremerhaven zookeepers noticed the same-sex pairings only because of their lack of reproductive success. Rather than attempt adoption of eggs to realize all zoos' mission of promoting reproduction among their animals, the Bremerhaven strategy was to bring in four female penguins from a Swedish zoo. The announcement of this program to introduce "foreign females" to seduce and break up the gay male penguin pairs outraged the German gay community, a community with a history of strong sensitivity to the implication of the extermination of gay people and the prevention of their reproductive capacities. Demonstrations outside the penguin cages against "the organised and forced harassment through female seductresses," to quote one of the German gay activists, produced a policy reversal on the part of the zoo, which flew the Swedish female penguins home unrequited. As Heike Kuek, the director of the zoo, said, in explaining the policy reversal, "Everyone can live here as they please."[7] Bremerhaven's gay penguins were thus protected from the incursions of heteronormative reproductive agendas, adding along the way a bit of nationalist pride to the underlying symbolism of the naturalness of homosexuality.

Ironically, though both the gay community and the religious right have been invested in the symbolic importance of penguin monogamy and long-term pair bonding, an assumption of the permanence of penguin bonds appears to be problematic in terms of actual penguin behavior. Penguin sexuality turns out to be quite variable, with breeding behaviors based on homosexual, heterosexual, trios, quartets, and single-parent relationships. Within all species of the genus, partners frequently break up and choose another mate after a season or two of reproductive pairing, though some, such as the Humboldt penguin, frequently form long-term, multiyear bonds. Penguin family values may include monogamy but usually only if it is serial—whether same-sex or heterosexual monogamy does not seem to matter too much to the penguins (Bagemihl 1999).

Arguments from the natural about sexuality, of whatever kind, especially when one uses penguins as one's touchstone, turn out to be pretty slippery (Alaimo n.d.; Haraway 1995). In general, the sexual practices of animals are so variable that little can be proved about human sexuality using animal examples, though it is a common narrative in popular culture. Furthermore, as Roger Lancaster points out, though there might appear to be short-term advantages to arguing that gayness is biological, inherent, and therefore natural and immutable, there are serious dangers in using these arguments. Arguments from nature about sexuality not only play into the logic of conservative versions of the family and biological determinism alike but also carry dangerous possibilities for many people:

> At best, then, the new innatist claims [that homosexuality is genetically determined] carve out a protected niche for homosexual exceptionalism. At worst, they reify the prevailing logic of heterosexual metaphysics and thus actively contribute to the reproduction of an exclusionary homophobic—and sexist—environment. For gays can only be gay "by nature" in a "nature" that already discloses men and women whose deepest instincts and desires are also different "by nature." In the resulting sexual imaginary, biologically engineered "real" men are always in hot pursuit of "real" women, who always play coy. In such a paradigm, every conventional gender norm, down to the last stereotype, is attributed to a fixed, immutable biology. Men do better at math and science because of that thing in the brain. Women are better at housework and childcare because of their hormones. Men are aggressive and women are nurturing because we are hunters and gatherers in our heart of hearts. And gay men are gay because they inherited a genetic defect, which caused something to go wrong in that thing in the brain. It's normal. It's natural. It's just the way men are and women are.
>
> Norms reified; men and women trapped in their "natures"; a radical division of gay people from straight people, of queer sex from normal sex, of our experiences from theirs. . . . One scarcely has to imagine

extreme scenarios to see that this is not good for gay people. Or for straight people, either. (Lancaster 2003, 280)

Finally (as I have stated before), in both pro-heterosexist and pro-gay cases, arguing for the naturalness and superiority of the U.S. nuclear family form ignores its implications in environmental problems. But this does not prevent penguin family values from playing a role in environmentalist popular culture.

Environmentalist Penguins Fight Back

Among the other Web sites that right-wing fundamentalist fans of *The March of the Penguins* might have found is Gay Penguin for President, which makes a point about the vacuity of George W. Bush's presidential promises. The success of this parody, of course, depends on the idea that the penguin is a fairly vacuous or at least ridiculous animal.[8] Predating *The March of the Penguins* (as well as the exposure of Bush-era Republicans such as Congressman Mark Foley, Senator Larry Craig, and Christian conservative leader Reverend Ted Haggard as gay), the site implies that Gay Penguin is gay because that makes him as far from a Bush supporter as possible. The creator of Gay Penguin for President has no interest in the naturalness of penguins but instead plays off the ludicrousness of penguins. This is the element that for many makes ridiculous the claims of right-wing fundamentalists that *The March of the Penguins* demonstrated the believability of the idea of an intelligent designer. Something about penguins—their waddling walk, their cute black and white uniforms, and, for the emperor penguins in the movie, the irrationality of their survival in one of the harshest environments on the planet—makes them laughable candidates for the outcomes of a divine intelligent designer. Many letter writers responding to Miller's *New York Times* article were quick to point out this irony.[9]

In fact, if one were worried not about what emperor penguins might symbolize for human sexual mores but about the penguins' reproductive health, one would focus not on their domestic, political, or sexual arrangements but on the important relationship between their biology and their environment, their adaptation to their particular environmental niche.[10] Emperor penguins are supremely and exactly suited to the particularities of their challenging Antarctic climate, and the method of protecting their eggs and raising their chicks that so thrills both the Christian right and the gay penguin supporters is the only way that they have managed to maintain their population and continue their reproductive cycles. Whether this adaptation demonstrates an intelligent design or not could no doubt be a point of debate, depending on whether one admires the amazing feat of the survival of the penguins in such a demanding climate or whether one would want to argue that a truly intelligent designer would have provided a more secure and sensible warm spot for the penguin's egg other than balancing it on two very hard and wobbly feet. Nevertheless, to see the emperor penguin as just a survivor is to miss a central part of its existence: that it is matched in specific and fairly inflexible ways to its environment. The emperor penguin is not a survivor but an integral element of its environment, existing nowhere else but the Antarctic. This element of integration with and dependence on environmental particularities is something we are comfortable with when thinking about animals but not when we are thinking about human societies, because our dominant frameworks see us as separate from and in control of nature.

What focusing narrowly on mating habits as political signifiers misses is the undeniable fact that the penguin's Antarctic environment is rapidly changing because of the warming trend called global climate change. The southern polar ice is melting at a rate faster than at any other time in the geological record. For the emperor penguin, this means walking farther and farther to find ice thick enough to support the huddled penguins for the length of time needed for the birth and raising of the penguin offspring. This imminent threat to the existence of the emperor penguins as a species is the unspoken backdrop to *The March of the Penguins*, as director Luc Jacquet admits. The director and the producers deliberately refrained from mentioning global warming in the movie, as they were worried about giving the movie a "political" message (Miller 2006). But they clearly did hope that the movie would raise people's consciousness about the beauty and value of the penguins, so that when discussion of their status as a newly endangered species becomes more well known, people would have sympathy for these special animals and be interested in saving them.

Indeed, the movie does seem to have produced a widespread attachment to the image of the penguin as a symbol of good and beauty, especially when portrayed as under environmental threat. For example, Al Gore's documentary on global warming, *An Inconvenient Truth* (2006), covers the crisis of the melting Antarctic ice at length. Interestingly, though his movie never refers to the emperor penguins (using the more common icon of the polar bear as an endangered animal), those marketing *An Inconvenient Truth* chose an image for an ad in the *New York Times* that could easily have been from *The March of the Penguins*. The ad shows a line of emperor penguins on their long march, making a clear connection to the other award-winning documentary and counting on the public's affection for the penguins to increase their concern about global warming. The caption for the ad says, "We're all on thin ice."[11] Another consciousness-raising documentary on global warming, Tom Brokaw's 2006 Discovery Channel documentary, *Global Warming: What You Need to Know*, likewise uses images of Antarctic penguins to drive home the danger of the melting polar ice. The good feelings produced by portraying penguins as the ultimate in natural family and moral behavior are manipulated into environmental concerns by stressing the endangered status of the penguins. This also leads to a rise of the use of penguins in advertising of the period. As pointed out in an article in the *New York Times* on the increasing use of penguins in various marketing venues: "'There's obviously something about these little guys that is leading advertisers to think it says something about us as consumers to associate ourselves with penguins,' said Michael Megalli, a partner at Group 1066, a corporate identity consulting company in New York. One theory Mr. Megalli offered is what he called 'the Al Gore thing'—that is, 'we want to reassure ourselves penguins will have a place in a world with global warming'" (Elliot 2007). Similarly, a 2008 Ad Council promotion for the organization Earth Share shows a family of emperor penguins (with a large parent watching over three smaller penguins) on a grassy expanse, under the caption "How can you help protect the prairie and the penguin?" as though penguins and prairies could ever be found in the same place. Once again, penguins are removed from their singular habitat and constructed as a humanlike family (emperor penguins have only one chick at a time) to appeal to a desire to protect "the prairies and the penguins and the planet."

This use of penguins as symbols of good family morals endangered by human-caused environmental problems appears again in the movie *Happy Feet*. Because of this plot, the movie could have been discussed in chapter 4, but I examine it here so that we can follow the trail of environmentalist penguins in popular culture. In this 2006 Academy Award–winning animated children's movie, an emperor penguin community is held together by their reverence for singing. Each penguin, in an individualistic twist improbable in a species that has almost no visible differentiation (including, as mentioned above, little obvious sexual difference), must find its own "heartsong." Their heartsong not only defines them as singular beings but also is essential to enabling them to find their one single true love and therefore to breed successfully, another popular cultural version of romanticized monogamous heterosexuality determined by nature. The hero of the film, the boy penguin Mumble, cannot sing, however—though he can dance, an ability that is treated with horror and shame by his parents, peers, and elders. Like homosexuality, his desire to dance not only is different but also threatens to restrict him to a life of infertile relationships with other different outcasts, because without a heartsong, he will not attract a mate. In this case, the outcasts that Mumble befriends are another species of penguin, a small band of male chinstrap penguins he meets. Interestingly enough, the five male chinstrap penguins are marked by their Latino accents, quite different from the dominant "white" accents of Mumble's family (though his father has a Southern accent that could be read as black, his name, Elvis, reassures us that Mumble does not come from an interracial family, since Mumble's mother, Norma Jean, is clearly meant to be white). References to homosexuality are frequent in the film but are flavored with the kind of liberal tolerance covering over ultimate rejection that is a thin veneer for heterosexist anxiety. In one of the movie's trailers, when the tribal chieftain of the chinstraps (voiced by Robin Williams) commands, "Turn to the penguin next to you, and give him a great big hug," two of the male penguins show a homophobic anxiety meant to be even more humorous because of the "Mexican" accents: "Wha-chu hugging me for?" "He tol' me to." "Get away!" "Nah, you liiike it!"

When Mumble's difference is blamed for the decreasing availability of fish that is causing a famine for the emperor penguin society, he is cast out by the high priests and vows to find the cause of the food scarcity, which turns out to be overharvesting by human fishing corporations. By the end of the movie, Mumble's penguin charm, along with his dancing ability, has mobilized human beings to stop overfishing. His love of his community, his success in bringing back the fish, and his over-the-top dancing also destroy the intolerance of his community to difference. Not incidentally, Mumble ultimately wins over the (female) love of his life and ends up in a happy, heterosexual, and successfully reproductive nuclear family. That the resolution of all of his problems seems to require the restoration of his "natural" status as the head of a heterosexual family undermines the message of inclusion around sexuality quite a bit, but this did not prevent Christian conservatives from being outraged at the barely disguised attack of the movie on their positive interpretation of *March of the Penguins* (Medved 2006). An example of this reaction from very close to home for me was an editorial in my local daily, the *Moscow-Pullman Daily News*. The writer, Ed Iverson, railed against *Happy Feet* as "one of the most blatant agenda pieces I have ever had to sit through . . . pure piffle, drivel and swill." He claims that the movie takes direct aim at Christian conservatism and pictures it as responsible for environmental evils as well as racism, sexism, and homophobia: "We know that the culprits [who cause the overfishing] are stand-ins for Western civilization because as hero and friends arrive at the scene of the destruction, the view that leaps onto the screen is a Christian church, cross and graveyard included." (Iverson 2006) Iverson is the librarian for a extremist Christian college called St. Andrews, whose leader is infamous for his stated belief that homosexuality is the cause of AIDS and that American slavery as a Christian system was benevolent for black people, so one should not be surprised at his elision here between "Western civilization" and far-right Christianity.

Beyond the extremism of conservative Christian positions such as Medved's and Iverson's, the influence of *The March of the Penguins* and *Happy Feet* have combined to promote penguins as popular symbols that conflate heterosexist family ideals and the need to resist environmental threats. Cashing in on the popularity and specific connection made between normality, healthy and happy families, and penguins, Roche Pharmaceuticals contracted with the copyright holders of *Happy Feet* to produce an ad campaign. A Roche ad depicting a mother penguin from *Happy Feet* protecting a baby penguin, uses the caption "It's flu season: protect your family like never before."

There is no question that real, as opposed to symbolic, penguins are endangered by human-caused environmental problems. Penguin reproduction, as individuals and as a species, is closely dependent on systems of planetary reproduction, including global climate systems. Presently, those systems are set on a course of rapid change by the carbon and methane emissions produced by human industrialization, air pollution, and factory farming practices, economic practices not unrelated to the high-consuming, decentralized formation of the U.S. nuclear family structure. Seeing the penguins as representative of natural human family forms, whether hetero- or homosexual, completely misses the actual nature of the penguin's reproductive system, which is interfused with the Antarctic environment. The lesson of the penguins is not a lesson in intelligent design or in patriarchal heroics or in the naturalness of gay marriage; rather, it should be a lesson in the ways in which human social reproduction is interrelated with environments both regional and planetary, and vice versa.

Deconstructing Polar Opposites: Endangered Peoples, Endangered Cultures, Endangered Natures

It is interesting that in the face of this popular cultural emphasis on the negative environmental effects of climate change on animal reproduction and hence survival, there is little mention of people's reproduction and survival; where this appears, it often only stresses problematic ideas about particular people's supposed over-reproduction. Missing from the popular culture arena, for the most part, is any attention to the immediate threat to numerous groups of people that are especially vulnerable to climate change because of geography, poverty, or political discrimination. The use of a group of people as a symbol of endangered species is uncomfortable for the authors of popular culture (as it should be), partly because it calls up questions of unequal responsibility and unequal consequences that are difficult to deal with in the arena of popular culture as entertainment. Both of the recent global warming documentaries mentioned above, Gore's and Brokaw's, use images of penguins and polar bears to dramatize the consequences of melting polar ice, but neither mentions the impact of climate change on Arctic indigenous peoples, one of the groups of people already most seriously impacted by climate change. I juxtapose this story with that of the emperor penguins with trepidation, because indigenous people are not penguins and endangered tribal cultures are not endangered species, that is, Indians are not animals. Seeing indigenous people as endangered species and thus equating them with animals is dangerous because such depictions can be racist.[12] Such a parallel reenacts the questionable trope of the "disappearing Indian," a dominant narrative that discounts and obscures the struggle of real Indians to exist and successfully transform their cultures strategically for survival, as discussed in chapter 2. Arctic indigenous tribes may be threatened by climate change, but they are resilient and experienced in resisting threats to their people. As Chickaloon grand chief Gary Harrison says in *Through Arctic Eyes* (2005), a movie documenting the effects of climate change on Arctic indigenous people, "We've adapted in the past, which is why we are still here."

Yet as a story about the environmental politics of reproduction, the ways in which cultural reproduction needs to be valued as much as biological reproduction, the relation of planetary reproduction to human reproduction, and the need to comprehend human beings as embedded in environmental systems on which they are dependent, the experience of the indigenous peoples of the Arctic region needs to be more widely known.[13] As many sources note, because of the rigors of survival in Arctic areas, Arctic native peoples are necessarily close to an environment that is particularly sensitive to the effects of climate change, a region tied to the global ecological system in so many intricate ways that changes in the Arctic have worldwide consequences.

Rather than seeing themselves as an endangered species, vulnerable and helpless, Arctic First Nations were politically active in publicizing the problem of global warming and suggesting solutions for many years before other people began to pay attention to the issue.[14] They have known that the threats they face to their culture and livelihoods are early warnings for the threats that people around the world will face. As Sam Johnson (from Teslin, Yukon Territory) says in *Through Arctic Eyes*, "The elders have talked about how everything is always going to change. Everything changes. But as long as you can learn to adjust with it, it will all pass again. All I want to say is good luck to everyone." Patricia Cochran (2007), former chairperson of the Inuit Circumpolar Council, points out the worldwide implications of what Arctic First Nations are experiencing now: "All of this will have a profound impact on the viability of indigenous cultures throughout the North, and further afield. Everything is connected in nature; what happens in Alaska will affect all other places of the world as a cascading effect, as scientists call it, will occur."

I learned something about what the indigenous Arctic peoples are facing during an event sponsored by the Smithsonian in Washington, D.C., in October 2005. As part of a celebration of all things Arctic, which spotlighted its excellent collection of Arctic art and animals and publicized its support of research on the Arctic, the Smithsonian Museum organized a panel primarily of Yu'pik people on the topic of global warming and its effect on their lives and their land. Between the morning and afternoon performances of Native Arctic dancers, who drummed and sang under the watchful eye of the preserved African elephant in the main lobby, an audience gathered in the auditorium to listen to the panel, whose title was based on an indigenous description of the crisis: "The Earth Is Moving Faster Now" (Krupnik and Jolly 2002).

The title refers to the fact that global warming has had a measurable impact on the lives of these indigenous people for many years. Over 8 percent of the sea ice has melted, with severe consequences for marine life, caribou herds (disrupting migration patterns), and coastal villages (because sea ice creates a buffer for coastal settlements against large waves). Increased thunderstorms and lightning cause more forest fires. Dangerous levels of UV radiation cause increased incidence of skin cancer and damage to eyesight. Ecological stress and disruption to traditional plant and animal food sources force a turn to a diet of storebought foods that cause diabetes (Krupnik and Jolly 2002; *Through Arctic Eyes* [2005]).

On the Smithsonian panel, Cristina Alava, a Yu'pik elder and teacher, spoke about the difficulty of bringing back edible meat from long-distance hunting trips if the weather continues to warm. As the permafrost melts earlier and freezes later, transporting meat over the softened tundra becomes very difficult, as does keeping the large carcasses cold enough so they do not rot before getting to the hunters' families. Orville Huntington, an Athabascan employee of the U.S. Fish and Wildlife Service, showed slides of the ice retreating and talked about the "silence of the moose" in the region, as their seasonal travels were disrupted by the changing climate. Huntington emphasized the depth and complexity of indigenous knowledge about the area and the possibility of losing this knowledge along with the animals and the ice. Harry Brower Jr., an indigenous whaler, scientist, and subsistence hunter, spoke about the ways in which subsistence living was part of cultural survival and an important method for keeping the world in balance. Other panelists echoed this theme, describing the Yu'pik understanding of the way in which the environment was part of a larger universe with moral and cultural aspects that have been maintained by the practices of indigenous peoples who have lived in the land for thousands of years.

One of the striking aspects of the discourse of the panelists was their insistence on speaking as knowledgeable experts based on their cultural expertise, their beliefs and experience as indigenous people, even when they mentioned that some of them had degrees in biology and wildlife management as well as careers in education and literacy work. It was crucially important for them to try to get across to the audience that their knowledge arose from their way of life, which similarly was embedded in the environment, and that this interdependence of cultural identity, expert knowledge, and land and animal existence was at the brink of extermination from global warming. In contrast, the white scientists who introduced and commented on the panel consistently referred to the indigenous panelists as community members and artisans rather than as scientists and researchers, undercutting their status as "experts." The point the indigenous panelists were making, however, was that the extensive knowledge they had about sustainable practices, whether it was supported by scientific expertise or traditional experience, was knowledge that arose from a particular way of life, one that needed to be respected and maintained. It was not knowledge gained from the mystical identity of being Ecological Indians (see chapter 2) but sophisticated information needed now by all those, indigenous or not, trying to understand and redress climate change. In contrast, the panelists implied, an industrialized and consumer economy's dependencies on nonrenewable fuels, emission-producing technologies, wide-ranging mobility, and manufactured goods were not merely nonsustainable but gave those who lived in these ways false understandings of the way in which material life-sustaining practices worked. Material practices of reproduction and production have epistemological implications, that is, they affect what we know and how we know it. We are all, like the penguins, suited or not suited to particular ecological contexts; living without respect for those contexts has consequences. Worse, from the perspective of the indigenous panelists, global capitalist-based industrialized ways of living and (not) knowing threaten the existing knowledge base needed to live in sustainable ways, not least because the cultural existence of indigenous people is threatened.

The worst example of white condescension and willful misapprehension of the point being made by these indigenous experts was the introduction to the event by a retired white Alaskan politician. While acknowledging the likelihood that indigenous Arctic cultures are being irreversibly changed by global warming, he referred admiringly to the idea that an ice sculpture is made more beautiful because it is transient and proudly pointed out that the State of Alaska had made computers available to tribal villages to allow native artisans to more effectively sell their crafts in a global economy. From his point of view, this was a sufficient way to preserve Native Alaskan culture in the face of what he clearly accepted as the inevitable transience of their existence and their way of life because of global climate change and the requirements of a global economy.

Randel Hansen (2005) calls this situation the "ethnocide via climate change of Arctic indigenous communities." How do we think about this as these processes accelerate so that, within a generation, these indigenous communities may not survive? Is this "natural"? What kind of environmental politics can encompass both the threat to emperor penguins and Alaskan Natives from global warming? The disjuncture between the politics of species preservation and the politics of environmental justice presents a barrier to thinking through the relation between these looming disasters. For instance, in Al Gore's film, *An Inconvenient Truth*, there is a lengthy discussion of the consequences of the melting of the northern and southern polar ice. There is no mention of the consequences of this drastic change on Arctic indigenous peoples. Instead, there is a wrenching depiction of an animated polar bear trying unsuccessfully to get onto a melting ice floe in a vast iceless sea. Yet the ecologies of the polar bear and of the Arctic indigenous peoples are interrelated, and surely, both are worth concern and intervention. They are also ecologies interrelated with industrialized ecologies. The reproduction of industrialized economic systems, particularly by the United States and Western countries, has consequences for planetary ecological workings on a global scale as well as on the scale of communities, families, and species, determining the ability of animals, families, and cultures to reproduce in healthy and sustainable ways.

In a point that is relevant to my earlier discussion of the penguins, we should understand family structure in these indigenous communities as arising from interrelationships among animals, land, and economic practices. Family does not float free in nuclear groupings of two adults (heterosexual or not) and two children, independent of the consequences of their material practices, whether they are industrialized or hunter-gatherers. The idea that families are either separate from or purely reflect a romanticized or anthropomorphized "nature" is an illusion—whether they are Western or indigenous or any other kind of family. So the point is not that we all have to or should replicate the family structures of Arctic indigenous peoples (which are various), but we might try, as environmentalists, feminists, and gay activists, to be cognizant of the material interrelationships produced by particular familial forms so that we can choose responsible ways of living, producing, consuming, and reproducing on our planet. Romanticizing indigenous people and ignoring the technological and ecological underpinnings of all ways of living are different forms of racism, both of which can make ecological ethnocide invisible.

Too Many People, Too Few Penguins

The silence around issues of environmental reproductive justice and the preference for an environmentalism that values "pure" nature is apparent throughout Gore's film, especially in its reliance on the moribund politics of overpopulation. Though Gore does point out that the industrialized Western economies, particularly the United States, are the biggest culprits in terms of harmful greenhouse gas emissions, his narrative proceeds for the most part as though all U.S. citizens are equally responsible as individuals for problematic ways of using fossil fuels. He does mention the support by Exxon Mobil for the disinformation campaign that has undermined scientific warnings about the dangers of global warming, but Gore's is a very mild version of an environmental justice analysis that would stress the ways in which corporate domination of politics and social inequalities, rather than separate individual consumer decisions (less about "choice" than people believe, as they operate within complex economic systems), are driving the creation and maintenance of environmental problems.

Instead, Gore's scariest and most visually arresting image of the cause of global warming is the steeply rising population curve, the one slide of his slideshow that requires him to mount a moving vertical platform to follow its rapid and inexorable growth. Slides depicting the disasters already caused by global warming show black people devastated by Hurricane Katrina and brown people fleeing flooding caused by monsoons. Thus, the reproduction of the planet is presented as most threatened by the reproduction of people, especially particular people of color, those that are "overpopulating" the planet. In most popular discussions of the causes of increasing global warming, those in the Global South (who have yet to industrialize as much as Global North countries) are the ones portrayed as likely to push us over the brink. China, in particular, is often held out as a threat to reining in global warming, as it is the largest Global South country to industrialize and is beginning to voraciously use the oil, gas, and coal technologies that produce most greenhouse emissions. The Gore film is careful not to demonize the Chinese but to show them as struggling with the implications of their growing dependence on nonrenewable fuels, which is indeed consequential for stopping global warming. For instance, he points out that the Chinese have better automobile emission standards than does the United States. But because of the context he offers, the Chinese are still presented as the symbol of the upcoming threat presented by the combination of overpopulation and increasing industrial emissions. Ironically, this overpopulation is presented as "natural," and no explanations are offered for it. As in the *Schoolhouse Rock* clip discussed in chapter 3, people are assumed to naturally need more and more "elbow room." No recognition is made of the possibility that the Chinese, and the people of other "developing" countries, may be able to construct different patterns of consumption, different family forms, and different ways of production that are environmentally sound and do not fit the pattern of a "natural" evolution toward an industrialized consumer economy presented as "progress."

Gore's film, with its relative sensitivity to the possibility of demonizing Global South peoples and its recognition of the responsibility of the United States and the role of corporate greed, is one of the better examples of mainstream environmentalism's approach to the topic of overpopulation. But its reliance on this trope as part of the explanation unfortunately legitimates other, less sensitive or outright racist versions of environmentalist arguments about overpopulation. As the Committee on Women, Population and the Environment notes, since the early 1990s, a disturbing political climate has developed in which older population-control rhetoric, undermined in its effectiveness by international women's and antiracist movements, has been revived under the rubric of "environment and security," a paradigm in which intra- and interstate conflict is explained by "overpopulation" producing "resource scarcity" and environmental degradation (Gosine 2005; Silliman and King 1999). This point is borne out by examples such as Gore's film, in which human reproduction (especially that of the poor, immigrant groups, and the Global South) is depicted as a major environmental problem, as in those environmentalist arguments that overpopulation is a serious threat to the Earth, such that some environmentalists argue against having children at all. In most popular culture versions of the "problem of overpopulation," the reproduction of the population of "Others" (that is, Global South peoples') is portrayed as the central issue: environmentally (especially in terms of energy use) and socially (because of the struggles in the Global South with AIDS, armed conflict, poverty, and famine). The reproduction of "our" ("developed" industrial societies) population, in contrast, despite the vastly greater amount of resources consumed, the reliance of the economy on the exploitation of Global South resources and labor, and the political domination of other countries by the Global North, is made invisible by this way of thinking about the problem of overpopulation, especially when coupled with the promotion of the suburban nuclear family in environmentalist popular culture.

For example, a former board member of the Sierra Club, John Tanton, has since the 1970s built a set of anti-immigration organizations (including founding the Federation for American Immigration Reform) that are virulently racist while he simultaneously supported organizations (such as Population-Environment Balance) that claim that immigrants and overpopulation are the source of environmental problems. In this environmentalist discourse blaming overpopulation for environmental problems, the reproductive capacities of poor brown women are portrayed both as natural (in the sense of uncontrollable and inevitable) and as unnatural (in the sense of damaging the health of the environment) (see www.populationconnection. org). In some versions of this discourse, through a perverse kind of putative feminism, one of the qualities that constitute these families' backwardness is the assumption that they are patriarchal structures that restrict women's rights and prevent women from engaging in family planning that would bring down their birth rates. Though patriarchal power within families may indeed prevent women from controlling their own reproductive capacities, this analysis ignores international family planning policies such as those imposed by the United States that insist on a priority on abstinence-only programs rather than birth control and do not provide the educational, health, political, and legal support to enable women to gain control over when they become pregnant.

Once again, we return to the question of just what kind of family forms, embedded in what kind of economic processes, are best for the interrelated survival of people, animals, and the planet. The discourse of overpopulation presents as problematic large extended families, primarily agricultural, often depicted as "premodern" and "patriarchal," without critically analyzing the global regimes that produce poverty, encourage large families, impose moralistic and impractical sexual attitudes such as abstinence, and prevent women from gaining political rights and independence. When these global regimes also are primarily responsible for climate change that results in drought, desertification, and crop failure, let alone the militarism and conflict that produces internal displacement and destroys ecologies, it is outrageous to portray overpopulation in the Global South as the main cause of environmental problems. Andil Gosine argues, after rehearsing the long history of a connection between environmentalist emphasis on overpopulation and racist attitudes toward nonwhite and Global South peoples,

> When environmentalists sound warnings about overpopulation, they are usually expressing fears over the reproduction of (poor) nonwhite people, not of white people, whose populations in all Western countries are in decline (but whose consumption habits generally are not). Calls for educational fixes to inform "populations" about why they should want to bear fewer children advance an imperialist cultural agenda that demands that nonwhite people adopt the cultural, social and economic practices and systems of organization dominant in Western countries (e.g., the prototypical nuclear family), while blaming the foolishness of Third World men and women (since the solution is Western education) for environmental degradation. (Gosine 2005, 80–81)

Environmental Justice Family Values

Given the issues I have raised with discourses about overpopulation, the use of penguins as symbolizing environmentalist and family values simultaneously, and narratives that make invisible the plight of native peoples, what kind of rhetoric should environmentalists use to bring people to their side? One thing they probably should not do is depict environmentalism as a heteronormative family romance. Such rhetoric obscures the need to put pressure on corporations to change their labor practices—including health care, child care, pay equity, and global labor practices (all, I would argue, important to real family values)—as part of an environmentalist agenda. In sidestepping these issues, the environmentalist family romance (common also in children's environmentalist films, as discussed in chapter 4) runs the risk of undermining people's willingness to recognize the ways in which families built on Global North consumerism may need to change their understandings of their relationship with the natural world and thus their practices of living and working, a critical stance that also requires challenging heterosexist norms. Examples of these family romance tropes abound, from both corporate and environmentalist sources. From the corporate angle, for instance, a 2007 television ad by Phillips (the lighting company) for its energy-saving light bulb Ecotone, shows a baby on a melting ice floe in the midst of giant threatening icebergs; as the camera zooms in on the baby's frightened eye, the eye becomes the light bulb and the baby is miraculously transported to the safety of mother's backpack and father's protection as the white nuclear family strolls through a park.

Another environmentalist example is a 2006 ad for the Sea World/ Busch Gardens Conservation Fund, an example that brings together many of the motifs discussed in this chapter. Starting with the sun rising on a wild world, followed by wildebeests and gazelles gamboling in herds, the ad first focuses on two lion cubs. "Sisters," the caption pronounces, as we sigh in appreciation of the cute and cuddly cubs. Then we are shown dolphins playing in the sea, leaping above the ocean. "Cousins," says the ad. A frilled lizard, its distinctive bonnetlike membrane spread widely, rushes toward the camera with comical aggression. "Little Brother," says the ad (assuming that we know that all little brothers are adorable brats). Next we see two bighorn rams, colliding in fierce challenge. "In-Laws," says the caption, naturalizing the clichéd sitcom plot of fighting in-laws. A chinstrap penguin appears, a baby bird protected on its feet. "Father," says the ad, proving that once again, as *The March of the Penguins* shows, those penguins are really great dads. Then the camera pans rapidly outward from the Antarctic continent, like reversing GoogleEarth, pulling far enough out to show Earth as seen from space.[15] "Mother Earth," says the caption, making a common and problematic move that results in the feminization of the planet. "We all belong to the same family," says the penultimate frame of the ad, and while the caption is replaced by the mission of the Conservation Fund ("Research, Protection, Rehabilitation, Education"), the Earth floats beautifully in space, magically free of all the conflict, power, inequality, and policy failure that actually undermine effective environmentalism. The ad closes on a picture of a mountain lake, with the Sea World/Busch Gardens Conservation Fund logo superimposed on it and the caption "Conservation: It's in our nature."

Do we really all "belong to the same family"? Is conservation "in our nature"? What does this mean for understanding our environmental problems? What kind of family is environmentally sustainable, and how can we encourage such considerations? If corporations such as Roche and Phillips and environmentalists such as the Conservation Fund use the same narrative frames and images of nature that legitimate heterosexist white middle-class nuclear families, how will we develop a useful critique of that family form's complicity in environmental problems? If the family we think of as natural and normal is white, Western, heterosexual, and middle class, how will we raise consciousness and concern about indigenous and Global South families, many of which suffer more severely from environmental problems today? The rhetoric of penguin family values limits us to the same ideas of what is natural that are promoted by those institutions and corporations that cause environmental destruction. To value nature and to correct social inequalities, we might want to shake off these normative ideas about nature, to see it as more dynamic, more interrelated with human practices, more agentive, and more complicated than we can if we rely solely on these dominant stories about nature. Donna Haraway's term *naturecultures* is designed for just this kind of conceptual understanding of the relation between nature and culture, nature and human, human and animal, and human and machine (Alaimo n.d.; Haraway 2004).

The importance of seeing reproduction in a planetary environmental justice context involves conceptualizing reproduction as an environmental issue that crucially rests on realities of human nature in ways not usually entertained. For example, one essential aspect of human nature that we need to recognize and seriously consider is our ability to change our biology, to construct terrestrial environments, and to collectively choose (hopefully not coercively impose) what kind of social arrangements are most productive, sustainable, and pleasurable. To me, the most important characteristic of human nature is this ability to change and control one's environment, precisely to *not* be determined by one's biology or one's genes (or one's god, but that is perhaps another matter). Recognizing this natural human capacity, I argue, is the only perspective that is the responsible one, for it requires us to be accountable for the societies we support, the lives we live, the resources we use. If we recognize this characteristic as the essential aspect of being a biological human, it does not follow that humans are therefore in control of every aspect of the world, however (Bird 1987; Cuomo 1998; Merchant 2004; Warren 2000). As discussed in chapter 3, we are not outside the Earth looking down upon it. Instead, we are inside of complex relationships with other biological entities; we impact and are impacted by the interrelationships of those entities. Responsibility to those networks and dynamics can be brought into view only if we understand ourselves as animals among other animals, with varied sexualities, complicated family relationships, and multiple desires—perhaps peculiar animals with astounding abilities but still part of an interconnected world and thus answerable to it.

PART III

Naturalizing Globalization

6

Planetary Security, Militarism, and the Nature of Violence

I examine many issues in the preceding chapters, but mostly I follow two themes of naturalization in popular culture: the naturalization of violence and conquest and the naturalization of the white, suburban, nuclear family. In each case, I argue that these patterns of naturalization have both negative environmental consequences and negative impacts on social equality.

In this chapter, I draw these two themes together and extend them by using the tools of a critique of naturalization and a critique of dualism to generate an understanding of the environmental and social consequences of U.S. militarism and the global political economy.[1] What do myths of conquest and myths of gendered, sexed families have to do with each other? How do the naturalization of war and the naturalization of heteronormative, gendered reproduction come together as an obscuring web to prevent us from imagining and acting on alternative visions of social relations and environmental practices? Militarism (not merely the support of militaries but the promotion of military values throughout the culture, such as using camouflage patterns in fashion and Humvees as status symbols [Enloe 2004]) and the glaring inequality seemingly inevitably built into our global economy are huge obstacles toward building ways of living that are more equal and more sustainable, and most environmentalist analyses are daunted by attempting to address them (Some exceptions are Hollander 2003; Hossay 2006; Wall 2005). Despite my criticism of Michael Jackson's *Earth Song* (1995) video in the first chapter, I recognize the importance of including the devastation of war in an environmentalist analysis, as the video does by including the Bosnian war scene in its purview. My attempt at trying to understand these interconnections arises from several insights:

first, processes of naturalization in dominant culture prevent us from even making the attempt to think of a peaceful, economically just future; second, war and unequal economic structures are incredibly damaging to the environment; and third, there are intricate relationships between the exploitation of nature, the devaluation of "women's work," global economic inequality, and militarism.

What can a global feminist environmental justice analysis offer us in understanding the causes of war and terrorism today or, seen from another angle, as a guide to reach the elusive goals of planetary peace and security? The development of such a perspective arose through the process of direct theorizing (Sturgeon 1995) involved in a particular set of social movement histories. The challenge facing this kind of analysis is to provide a useful understanding of the present post–cold war situation—the U.S. invasions of Iraq and Afghanistan, terrorist attacks around the world, and several intractable violent flash points (including the ongoing Israeli occupation of Palestine and ethnocide in the Darfur region of the Sudan). A global feminist environmental justice analysis yields four useful analytical approaches: arguments against the inevitability of war, arguments for the effectiveness of nonviolent approaches to conflicts, arguments for the importance of an environmental perspective for achieving peace, and an analysis of the relation between the globalization of capital, the exploitation of women and the environment, and the persistence of violence and militarism.

Undermining the Nature of War

The first thing a global feminist environmental justice perspective can offer us is some small hope, because such a perspective rejects the popular assumption that war, organized violence, and exploitation are inevitable consequences of human (especially male) nature. As I have shown throughout this book, arguments from nature are highly suspect, though they have been used strategically for liberatory purposes. In particular, the use of arguments from nature to support social inequality has a long history. For example, slavery was supported by arguments about natural racial inferiority; the exploitation of women sexually and as domestic laborers was (and is) legitimated by arguments about women's natural capacities to cook, clean, and reproduce; and imperialist endeavors by Europeans and by the United States have been justified by beliefs in the White Man's Burden and Manifest Destiny that proposed white people as naturally superior to darker-skinned, supposedly "uncivilized" Others and supported a frontier myth that portrayed conquest as evolutionary progress.

Given this legacy, arguments assuming that organized violence and war are natural parts of human instinctual makeup should be treated critically. The way in which violence in many cultures, particularly in popular culture, has been problematically but positively associated with strength, power, and masculinity while nonviolence is associated with passivity, ineffectiveness, and femininity should lead us to reject (or at least question very deeply) easy assumptions that war is an inevitable part of human nature (whether it is organized military violence, intragroup violence motivated by ideologies of racism, sexism, or imperialism, or individual-on-individual violence). A determination of whether people are biologically capable of violence, individually or in groups, should not make us accept that war and militarism, organized and institutionalized as part of nation-states, are inevitable and unassailable.

There is a long history of feminist antimilitarism and women's peace movements across the globe. Some of the arguments used in these movements promoted the idea that women were biologically attuned to peace, while war was naturally a man's business (Alonso 1993). But in the context of contemporary global antiwar movements, such as those manifested throughout the world in the widespread opposition to the U.S. war on Iraq, such arguments from nature about men's and women's relative propensities for war and peace are now more often seen by antimilitarist feminists as inaccurate and ethnocentric, based as they are on ahistorical frameworks and unfounded cultural universalisms (Featherstone 2004).[2] For while some men in some cultures and some men in some classes are encouraged and rewarded for their propensity for violence, others are not; and while some women may be celebrated as nurturers, others are not (Mageo 2004). Rejecting the idea that men (and women) are biologically prone to violence, particularly when violence is used as a justification for organized militarism, is a hopeful position, since it allows for the possibility of achieving nonviolent societies. Nonviolent societies would not necessarily be societies in which there is no physical, individual violence, but they would be ones in which militarism, social inequality, and environmental exploitation have been rejected in favor of frameworks of substantive peace.

Such a feminist antimilitarist perspective is foreign to many of us; indeed, it may seem laughably idealistic, partly because popular culture is filled with easy assumptions about the naturalness, effectiveness, and social value of violence. This has been especially true in contemporary popularizations of discoveries in genetic science. In the past twenty years, many writers, bloggers, television commentators, and movie scriptwriters have uncritically portrayed human nature as determined by genetic forces beyond our control, a kind of discourse that often results in rationalizing behaviors claimed to be underlying unfair economic competition, masculinist violence, social inequality, heterosexist dominance, and military conflicts (despite their sexist, heterosexist, and racist implications). Too frequently, portraying genetics as a determining aspect of people's lives becomes an unthinking way of justifying unequal social arrangements as natural and inevitable.

For example, popular genetic scientific discourse is frequently resorted to in a superficial way to claim that competition and violence are the driving forces behind reproductive success (a position located in what is sometimes called "sociobiology").[3] The human male's so-called drive to spread his genes, to dominate a given territory, and to successfully reproduce (above all other goals) is depicted as a natural imperative; thus, that men would be more adulterous, less willing to take on domestic chores (sometimes articulated as a resistance to commitment), or comfortable with sexually exploitative attitudes toward women is made to appear normal and inevitable. Sexual desire in this discourse (see chapter 5) thereby becomes significantly reduced from its social, complex, and polymorphous variation to some kind of genetically determined force focused on having babies.

Furthermore, links between these supposed evolutionary reproductive instincts and the reoccurrence of complicated social phenomena such as wars, economic colonialism, and male supremacy are assumed in the popular culture sphere to be obvious and thus phenomena that are impossible to eradicate. In actual scientific discourse, the existence of causal relationships between individual social behaviors and genetic makeup (let alone causal relationships between complex forms of collective action and genetic factors) is intensely debated and deeply contested; any such claims by responsible scientists tend to be narrowly applied. Yet this scientific caution does not stop various agents of popular culture from presenting stories of genetic determinism as scientific truths. Roger Lancaster (2003, 96–97) points out,

> What is intellectual folly in sociobiology is the leap from general pronouncements about "biological potentiality" to categorical statements about a "hardwired biological program." What is logically unwarranted is the selective, self-serving, or commonsensical derivation of this particular form or that particular practice—monogamy, nuclear families with breadwinner dads and stay-at-home moms, polygyny, polyandry, male aggression, compulsory heterosexuality, Puritanical morality, playboy exploits, imperialism, capitalist business practices, collectivism, to name but a few contradictory instances—from made-

to-fit stories about evolution served up as scientific bromides. What ought to be suspicious, prima facie, is the characterization of nature in terms of a male "wildness" so plainly cultivated in Western culture.

This popular narrative about so-called genetic determinants of complex human behavior is particularly consequential when we are trying to ascertain whether living in societies that reject violence and war as a means of resolving problems is possible. War, in particular, is portrayed in our popular imagination as a natural environment for male achievement and success. Far from being "natural," however, the deliberate socializing of men and women to accept and desire masculinist violence or militarism requires quite a bit of cultural energy. In popular culture products such as video games, television shows, and traditional U.S. war movies, war (and the violence that characterizes it) is presented as the ultimate prerogative of men, the place where, despite suffering pain, loss of their war buddies, and trauma, they can revel in physical expression, anger, homosocial camaraderie, and right moral action. Movies produced about the Gulf War and the Iraq War are no different. The movie *Jarhead* (2005) is quite clear about this process, though its ironic self-critique has not been apparent to every reviewer or viewer. In *Jarhead*, the young men brought to the Kuwaiti desert in Desert Storm long for their first kill and create highly sexually charged homosocial relationships out of hazing and bullying rituals. When this pattern of male violence and competition is confirmed in the popular imagination because it is connected by popular science discourse in an unbroken line to the anger, aggression, and territorial imperatives of male primates (such as our closest ancestors, the chimpanzees) or men in "primitive" societies, then there seems to be no point in questioning the apparent inevitability of war or its pride of place in achieving male identity, power, character, and citizenship. After the feminist movement became influential, popular culture through movies such as *Courage under Fire* (1996) and *G.I. Jane* (1997) began to allow women to participate in the drama of war as fighters, but they achieve the status of true citizen only if they become like male fighters and welcome violence, competition, and pride in their status as killers. Otherwise, women are relegated to the "home front," providing the rationale for men's violence in war as protectors of the "weaker sex" but not naturally able to participate in war themselves (Feinman 2000).

What is interesting is that this broad popular culture consensus on a depiction of war, violence, and killing as the ultimate proving ground for American masculinity is materially consequential only for certain men, those in less privileged positions, who are recruited to become the troops, rather than for the strategists, defense intellectuals, diplomats, and politicians who initiate and manage wars. Popular culture celebrations of bloodbaths welcomed by men glorying in heroic military violence (such as in the movie 300 [2007], a thinly veiled analogy justifying the Iraq War)—let alone movies too numerous to mention that celebrate nonmilitary violence as the ultimate in male achievement—are expected to be a real experience only for men who are likely to seek out military combat, not men whose ambitions are for corporate or political leadership. Different forms of masculinity are naturalized for different classes of men; those who are poor and lack access to education and whose power as men is likely to be restricted to violence against those they live with are special targets of the naturalization of violence. Men of all classes can identify with and take pleasure in masculinist violence in popular culture, but it is mostly the poor who are expected to actually practice it on the streets or on the battlefield. Meanwhile, the violence they suffer from is justified by its glorification in popular culture.

For example, though there are many video games that glamorize violence, there are also games created for specific, instrumental efforts to recruit for the U.S. military through selling games to young, especially working-class men. In a video game expressly designed for recruiting soldiers, *America's Army* (2007), players can experience "a virtual test-drive of the Army, with a focus on operations in the Global War on Terrorism." Players are presented with examples of "Real [American] Heroes," such as Sergeant First Class Gerald Wolford, whose "dad drove logging trucks" while his "mother worked as a waitress." SFC Wolford's exploits in the first days of the invasion of Iraq, as he put himself at risk to lead his men to attack Iraqi soldiers, earned him a Silver Star. The conflation of a game with actual fighting and the presentation of war heroes as exemplary, defined in *America's Army* (under the heading "Overview: Real Heroes") as "a person of distinguished courage or ability, admired for *his* brave deeds and noble qualities" (emphasis mine), combine to make the war experience one of desirable masculinist expression.

Other games, such as *KUMA/WAR* (2007), are constructed to put players into actual war situations gleaned from the recent news and events, allowing them to "experience some of the fiercest engagements in the most hostile territories in the world"; this game includes blogs in which soldiers presently deployed in or recently returned from Iraq can post their comments and thoughts on their experiences. The several games put out under the *SOCOMM* label likewise advertise the attraction of the reality of war games, using the Sony slogan "Live in Your World, Play in Ours" and featuring moving, heroic martial music on the company's Web site. A television spot for SOCOMM: Navy SEALs shows young men, each in his own home, playing together. Suddenly, one of the young men begins shooting the virtual soldiers on his team accidentally, because he is distracted by watching two blonde women in bathing suits apply suntan lotion to each other, emphasizing that the all-male nature of "your world" is the same in "ours," both dependent on women remaining outside as sexual objects. SOCOMM includes a link to the U.S. Navy SEALs on its Web site, so those interested in becoming one can find out how. The tagline for the game is "Courage. Command. Country," nicely encapsulating the natural equivalencies made between masculinist violence, militarism, and patriotism.

The U.S. military is not alone in creating these popular culture avenues to recruit young men into military action. Similar war games are created by those fighting against the U.S. military and its allies. According to Game-Pro magazine (2005, 39), the trade magazine for video games, "UnderAsh was developed by a Syrian company [and] reflects its missions from the Palestinian point of view. . . . In 2003, [the] Lebanese radical Shiite group Hezbollah also released a game, Special Force, which lets players take aim at Israeli forces—proving that wars of ideology can be fought virtually." It is interesting that GamePro seems to feel that America's Army, KUMA/WAR, and SOCOMM are not fighting "wars of ideology" but that games from the point of view of those occupied by Israeli and U.S. militaries are. If these games were not connected to justifying actual wars on the ground, perhaps it would be an improvement to allow wars to be fought virtually and decide who won based on the outcomes of video games rather than on the slaughter of human beings and the destruction of environments.[4]

In analyzing the masculinist nature of these popular culture sites and their connection to militarism, I want to be clear on one point: I am not arguing that men *are* violent. Rather, I am trying to decouple violence from maleness by questioning the naturalization of this association. Nor am I arguing that this popular cultural association between violence and masculinity is the cause of war; I am suggesting instead that seeing that association as biologically determined prevents us from considering and promoting nonviolent solutions to conflict. Today, feminist intellectual frameworks are shaped by two overarching precepts: the idea that gender roles and gender difference (ideas of proper masculinity and femininity) are socially constructed, historically specific, and culturally variable; and the idea that gender is a category of analysis that can be usefully applied to almost every aspect of life. In fact, it is better to talk, from a contemporary feminist perspective, about masculinities and femininities in the plural, to allow one to distinguish the way in which gender roles are inflected by class, cultural, racial, or sexual social locations. Adopting a feminist perspective does not require one to deny biological difference; what is required is that the social meanings attached to those apparent biological differences be deeply questioned and that so-called natural differences be understood as fluid and variable. The particular form of masculinity offered by the movies and video games I discuss here is only one kind of possible masculinity, one that must be addressed critically if it is to be rejected. A form of violent masculinity that requires men to see themselves as strong because they can destroy others at will, including causing extreme destruction of environments without consequences, assumes a separation between huMANs[5] and Others that prevents us from seeing ourselves as part of and responsible to complex planetary and local living systems. If, as I suggest in chapter 5, we were instead to emphasize our "natural" ability to change, control, and choose gendered and sexualized social arrangements, then we would be in a position to create and reward versions of nonviolent masculinity rather than continue to present violence and war as inevitable and, in many cases, desirable.

Thus, while a global feminist environmental justice perspective would discard the notion that men are naturally violent and women are naturally nonviolent, we could still recognize patterns of gender difference through critical examination of the social institutions that create them in discrete cultural and historical locations. For example, this would allow us to account for what has been called, at least in the United States, "the gender gap" in men's and women's support for war—that, given a few fluctuations, men are more likely to support war than are women. This can be explained by the social (not natural) relegation of domestic labor and caretaking mostly to women, which splits the values of caring and nurture from narrow ideas of strength and command. Thus, military institutions can be seen as "masculinist"—that is, legitimated by ideologies of patriotism involving strength through violence, equating all three with a form of extreme masculinity that is misogynistic and homophobic—regardless of whether men or women are the ones being trained as soldiers (Feinman 2000). Gender divisions of labor that assign most caretaking work to women and underrate that work may produce different value systems in men and women (but not necessarily ones uninflected by race, class, and cultural differences) that can explain the gender gap. Making arrangements of domestic labor more equal may therefore be necessary (but not sufficient) to eradicate violence and militarism.

Feminist Nonviolent Solutions to Conflict

Consonant with a position that rejects essentialist assumptions about a natural huMAN propensity to war, a global feminist environmental justice position would argue for nonviolent solutions to conflict, holding to an understanding of peace as a substantive concept, involving planetary security rather than national security. This is the second useful perspective that a global feminist environmental justice analysis can offer.

Peace, in this view, is not merely the absence of war, nor is it the achievement of security for a few. Often, the dominant ideal of "security" assumes that threats to health and safety are beyond solution and that the most that can be done is to make only some people secure from such threats. A global feminist environmental justice position understands that the threats we face today—to the global environment, to food security, to political equality, to human rights—are threats not to any one group of people but to us all and to the health of the planet. Militaristic and nationalist arguments for "security" usually arise from positions of privilege; witness the reaction of the hegemonic U.S. cultural/political interpreters to the terrorist attacks of 9/11 in New York. The dominant perception that these were the first such attacks on U.S. territory (aside from Pearl Harbor) and that the American people had been "safe" before this moment comes out of a privileged perspective that not only ignores previous incidents of genocidal violence (such as massacres of Native peoples) and other politically motivated mass violence (such as the bombing of the Federal Building in Oklahoma City) in the United States and redefines "terrorism" to exclude U.S.-supported violence in other countries (such as the United States' past support for Osama bin Laden, for example) but also overlooks the extreme conditions of fear, insecurity, and violence that many poor people in the United States live in every day (Bunch 2002). This perspective enables ready acceptance of the Bush administration's characterization of 9/11 as an act of war between nations rather than a criminal attack, best dealt with through law enforcement practices rather than military action. A global feminist environmental justice definition of peace (like the idea of global environmental reproductive justice introduced in the previous chapter) would include (besides substantive rights to food, health, political equality, environmental quality, and control of one's own body) freedom from fear of violence, whether that violence is state sponsored or generated by militant opposition to states or consists of widespread gender-specific forms of personal violence such as rape or battering of women (the latter are social practices that have been identified as a form of terrorism aimed at control of women; International Peace Research Institute 2001). Achieving this state of security for all would include supporting sustainable practices attentive to biosystems health and dynamism; all in all, this would mean planetary security.

The practice and philosophy of nonviolence most suited to a global feminist environmental justice perspective is not a traditional Gandhian perspective but a version influenced particularly by activists such as Ella Baker and Barbara Deming, as well as groups including the Women's International League for Peace and Freedom and Women in Black. It would involve a nonviolent practice that is not self-sacrificing, dependent only on achieving a change of mind in individuals, or located in a specific religious tradition but confrontative, diverse, strategic, persistent, humorous, and aimed at hegemonic structures of inequality and institutionalized violence. It would allow the possibility of people refusing to support war without being identified automatically as nonpatriotic. It is a theory of nonviolence that depends on a political theory of participatory consent rather than passive consent and on citizen obligation to act against state-sponsored violence directly rather than to accept coercive practices of the state, social institutions, or cultural practices (Sturgeon 1995).

Part of the preference for this form of nonviolent practice as a feminist tool for change and substantive peace, embedded in participatory democratic forms, comes from the knowledge that war, even war fought for what seems like moral purposes or some sort of national or ethnic self-defense, deeply affects women in long-term ways. Women are likely to experience excruciating suffering as a result of war (UNIFEM 2007). This is not to say that war does not have an impact on men—most of the direct casualties in a war are male, and men are subject to torture and imprisonment at greater rates than women are. But the prevailing belief that war is mostly men's business, one which naturalizes violence as a man's prerogative and requires a willingness to commit violence as the definition of normal, appropriate manliness, is built on masculinist versions of honor and revenge and expects (and therefore tolerates) male casualties as part of the cost of war. The effects of war on women need to be more deliberately revealed, because these are often hidden by our popular cultural depiction of war as a male arena.

The 2002 report commissioned by UNIFEM, *Women, War and Peace* (Rehn and Sirleaf 2002), details the horrendous impact that war has on women. As the UNIFEM report shows, women are killed in wars as combatants and, along with children and older men, as "collateral damage." In our wars today, as opposed to the past, a majority of the casualties can be noncombatants, so the toll on women's lives has been growing. Women are also more subject to gender-specific forms of violence. The UNIFEM report observes,

> Violence against women during conflict has reached epidemic proportions. . . . [Women's] bodies become a battleground over which opposing forces struggle. Women are raped as a way to humiliate the men they are related to, who are often forced to watch the assault. In societies where ethnicity is inherited through the male line, "enemy" women are raped and forced to bear children. Women who are already pregnant are forced to miscarry through violent attacks. Women are kidnapped and used as sexual slaves to service troops, as well as to cook for them and carry their loads from camp to camp. They are purposely infected with HIV/AIDS, a slow, painful murder. (Rehn and Sirleaf 2002, 12)

The most conservative estimations are that over 250,000 women were raped in the Rwandan genocide (Rehn and Sirleaf 2002, 11) and over 30,000 women were raped in the Bosnian conflict (Enloe 2000, 140). In the Darfur conflict in Sudan, evidence of rape is widespread and appears to be systematic, involving thousands of women (Amnesty International 2004; Doctors without Borders 2005). The rape of designated "enemy" women does not occur only in active armed conflict but has been a part of official government policy in various militarized security states, such as Chile, Argentina, and the Philippines in the 1970s and, more recently, Guatemala, Iraq, Israel, India (in Kashmir), Haiti, Indonesia, Bhutan, Zaire, China, and Turkey (Enloe 2000, 123). In addition, there has been documentation of the prevalence of rape in the U.S. Air Force Academy, at U.S. military bases in the Philippines and Okinawa, and between U.S. men and women soldiers during the latest deployment in Iraq in 2003. Rape as a weapon of war further naturalizes male violence as it attaches itself to notions of sexuality that are assumed to be biologically determined.

War and its corollary, militarism, also cause the displacement of people on a massive scale. UNIFEM estimated in 2002 that 40 million people were displaced because of armed conflict and human rights violations, and 80 percent of these are women and children (Rehn and Sirleaf 2002, 21). At present, these numbers are likely to be even higher; estimates of the number of refugees from the conflict in the Darfur region in Sudan alone are over 1.2 million (Amnesty International 2004). Refugees need to find food, shelter, and health care, and women bear the brunt of this work because of their traditional responsibilities of child care, cooking, and caring for the ill. Women who are displaced and desperate to care for their families are frequently forced to choose sex work, or they are enticed and sold into sexual slavery.

After conflicts are supposedly over, women have to contend with a heavily militarized society, in which many men have guns and intramale and domestic violence is rampant. One of the most disturbing aspects of their study for the UNIFEM researchers was the finding that UN peacekeepers and workers in international charity organizations were also involved in sexually exploiting and violating vulnerable and displaced women in refugee camps (Lyall 2006; Rehn and Sirleaf 2002). Thus, the very presence of those meant to protect and help the refugees instead continued the exploitation of and violence toward women.

In addition, the cost of a militarized economy, as it sucks away money for social services, falls heavily on women. In the United States, women are the majority of those benefiting from public assistance, because they are more often the ones taking care of children. State and federal budget crises spurred by huge deficits from (among other things) military spending affect health care, public education, and other programs desperately needed by the poor, thus further exacerbating the situation of poor women and children. The naturalization of gendered labor roles and masculinist violence works simultaneously to obscure the real, long-term consequences of militarism for social health and prosperity.

These connections between feminism and antimilitarism could be summarized, using older U.S. feminist antimilitarist slogans, as the "guns versus butter" argument and the "take the toys away from the boys" argument against war. The guns versus butter argument is that women suffer from war because the gender division of labor means they have the most responsibility for the social, health, and educational aspects of a society that are underfunded by a militarist economy. The "take the toys away from the boys" argument is that militarism—the idea that violence is effective, necessary, and honorable—is built on a form of masculinism that promotes and depends on violence against women.

These two feminist antimilitarist arguments have been made for a long time, but in the 1980s a worldwide movement developed, using both of these arguments together, beginning by protesting against nuclear power and expanding into the creation of strong connections between feminism, environmentalism, and antimilitarism. However, this analysis did not come about without intensive internal struggle over various political issues, including what kind of culturally specific "masculinism" was the problem for feminist antimilitarists and what attention needed to be paid to the structures and dynamics of global capitalism. Global South feminists, U.S. feminists of color, and working-class and poor feminists all should be credited with changing the terms of the analysis being promoted by feminists in more-privileged social locations, a debate that took place in feminist antimilitarist demonstrations, U.N. women's conferences and meetings, and feminist policy institutions in many countries (Enloe 2001; Sturgeon 1997). The development through this political struggle of a more complex feminist antimilitarist analysis has become influential for the global peace and justice movement (Reed 2005).

War against the Environment

So far, I have been delineating a particular feminist antimilitarist perspective, but I have said very little about the connections between this perspective and an environmentalist analysis. This is the third aspect that a global feminist environmental justice position can offer us.

Looking for a moment at the recent U.S. wars against Iraq and Afghanistan, we can see the huge negative consequences that war has for the environment. Those consequences can be thought of as occurring in three ways.

The first is direct damage to the environment from war (bombing, oil fires, oil spills in the gulf, depleted uranium shells, land mines, disruption of sanitary and water distribution systems, draining of wetlands, destruction of animal habitat, emissions from burning, toxins that affect the health of Afghanis, Iraqis, and U.S. military personnel, and so forth) (Austin and Bruch 2000). Besides direct damage to the environment from active military engagements, the growth of the military means pollution and contamination of the environments used for testing, storage, and development of weapons (see chapter 3) and the exorbitant use of oil and petroleum by the military (Martinot 2007). Joni Seager estimates that the military is one of three of the most environmentally destructive institutions (along with governments and corporations), and it is often the most devastating because of the cloak of secrecy and the assumption of necessity that militaries enjoy (Seager 1993).

The second kind of environmental consequence is the strong official turn by the Bush administration away from alternative energy policies, a rejection of energy conservation, and the legitimation of a renewed emphasis on nonrenewable and environmentally destructive sources of energy: oil and nuclear power. As our sources for oil in the Middle East become increasingly seen as problematically out of U.S. control, the political will to search for more nonrenewable energy sources on U.S. lands increases. The result (unless we turn decisively toward the use of nonrenewable fuels, which may be happening now as a reaction) will be oil drilling in presently protected areas, oil spills, increased global warming, and the continued pollution of indigenous people's lands with nuclear wastes (Klare 2004; LaDuke 1999).

The third environmental consequence of war is what might be called broad indirect costs to a wider environmental agenda that desires a more globally integrated set of policies: the contempt shown by the United States for international law, the U.S. refusal to cooperate with international treaties to deal with global warming and other environmental problems, and the public relations cover that the war has provided the Bush administration's outright attack on environmental efforts in this country. From declaring environmental protesters "ecoterrorists" to gutting the Clean Air Act, diluting the organic label, easing restrictions on toxic waste siting, and shrinking budgets for Superfund cleanup, the Bush administration has been involved in a very serious rollback of hard-fought environmental achievements.

Showing the importance of engaging in popular culture as a strategy to change policy, Al Gore's film, *An Inconvenient Truth* (2006), has managed to support the work of environmentalists concerned with global climate change to resist some of this antienvironmentalist agenda and to turn the tide somewhat. But efforts to do so have been slow, given the intransigence of the U.S. administration as it is imbedded in a nationalistic framework in which the United States must protect its overuse of natural resources and an overconsumptive lifestyle, especially that of its elites, above all other concerns.

How do environmentalists deal with this attack in the context of a war polity and a war economy? What is needed is a clear alternative, a pragmatic political vision, integrating environmental issues with other social justice issues that can connect the dots for the general public, demonstrating the interrelationships between this attack on the environment and the Bush administration's simultaneous attack on working poor people, on women, on people of color, and on Global South peoples. In other words, a global feminist environmental justice approach should emphasize questions of environmental justice, an environmentalist perspective that makes connections between social inequalities and the production and continuation of environmental problems. In order to avoid a world in which only the privileged have a green future, a redefinition of national security to mean planetary security should include the need to keep our air, water, and food clean and healthy as well as ensure that environmental costs are not unequally distributed, a perspective that would require focus on global interconnections rather than nationalistic competition. Penguins and Arctic indigenous peoples would both receive concern and protection, and the results would benefit us all.

As Vandana Shiva (1997) and many others in the now-worldwide environmental justice movement point out, the negative consequences of environmental pollution, overexploitation of natural resources, and commodification of water, seeds, and foodstuffs is overwhelmingly borne by those in the world who are less powerful; conversely, environmental catastrophe is overwhelmingly caused by dependence on an economic system built on inequality and oppression. Environmentalists have a particular role to play in connecting the human and natural costs of war and in researching and promoting alternative decentralized energy and agricultural technologies. This is why we see environmentalist activism embedded in the broader alternative vision of the contemporary antiwar mobilization. In the United States, this is a development not new to the Seattle antiglobalization protests in 1999, as some seemed to think when expressing surprise at the visible coalition in those demonstrations between environmentalists, anti–corporate globalization activists, and labor organizers. Rather, these were connections forged through the 1980s nonviolent direct action movement against nuclear power, nuclear weapons, and U.S. intervention in El Salvador and Nicaragua (a movement that was global, environmentalist, feminist, and antimilitarist), as that movement made common cause with Global South anti–corporate globalization activists (Epstein 1991; Sturgeon 1991).

The Political Economy of Women's Work, Nature, and War

The cross-national interactions between these sites of activism produced analytic links between the politics of environmentalism, feminism, and antimilitarism. But what we see today in the present antiwar mobilization is a more self-consciously global movement, set firmly in the context of a critique of global corporate capitalism (Reed 2005). This kind of political economic analysis is the fourth aspect that a global feminist environmental justice perspective can develop, one arising out of political struggles between Global North and Global South feminists in the context of forging international feminist coalitions.

In an economy in which many large corporations have bigger budgets than entire countries (LaDuke 1999; Scott 2005), extreme, unprecedented inequalities of wealth are both feeding and resulting from militarism. Early in the post–cold war period that produced this economic situation, some Global South feminist and antimilitarist organizations demanded not simply that budget priorities change but that the military budgets of the industrialized countries be given over to women as reparations for their unpaid domestic work. Though this demand may seem unrealistic when first encountered, it was meant to bring out the connection between the creation of gross, unequal maldistribution of wealth and the resulting necessity to have a national security state supported by exorbitant military spending. These increasing inequalities of wealth are on a global scale, not a national scale, thus resulting in potential worldwide unrest that, to some, seems to require the United States' position as a massive military superpower, willing to use its military strength either preemptively (in the Bush administration's view) or at the behest of small collection of powerful nations on the U.N. Security Council (the more internationalist view of the U.S. Democratic Party and centrist Republicans) to maintain the structures that foster this inequality.

Of course, the many checks and balances, complications, and nuances involved in global political economic structures blur this picture considerably, on deeper analysis. What is undeniable is that extreme inequalities of wealth are driving global conflicts and that the resulting militarization deprives poorer countries and international institutions of the resources, access, and cooperation that would allow solutions to worldwide crises of health, education, human rights, and environment.

As I have said, this guns versus butter argument is an important feminist antimilitarist analysis. But many Global South feminists, socialist feminists, and U.S. feminists of color pushed this argument further—their argument was that the caring work that was done in most societies predominantly by women was *productive* work, work that produced value, work that as unpaid work was crucial to creating the surplus value that was the foundation of the growing global inequalities of wealth (Salleh 2004; Waring 1999). This creation of wealth enabled the capital accumulation that fueled neocolonialist endeavors and required militarism, whether large-scale state militarism or the support of death squads and private militias, to put down resistance to neoconservatism and neocolonialism, as well as violent responses by guerrillas, gangs, and warlordism designed to create protection for some groups of people. Thus, analyzing women's role as caregivers was not only about creating preferences for butter over guns but was also about understanding that this exploitation of women's labor, both underpaid and unpaid, was part and parcel of the structures of global capitalist accumulation that foments and requires militarism. Thus, "pay women, not the military," the 1983 slogan put forth by the London-based antimilitarist feminist-of-color organization Wages for Housework, was a slogan meant to challenge the basic structures of global capitalism and to denaturalize the unfair burden of women's work. However, paying women for their work is not enough to correct the problem. What matters is how much and under what conditions women (or men) are paid for this essential work.

The delegitimation of what many think of as women's natural work assignments is an important analytical focus. The caring work that had been socially assigned to women in many cultures becomes an externality in the capitalist economy, just as nature is an externality. Just as air, water, biodiversity, and ecosystem health are reified as externalities to the economy (such that the exploitation, pollution, commodification, and overuse of them as natural resources do not have to be paid for or accounted for), so too has the work assigned to women—the work of daily human maintenance, of feeding, of cleaning, of changing diapers, of elder care, of cooking, of loving, of celebrating, of teaching the young—been treated as an externality, with much of it separated off from the economy as though it were not part of sustaining life, to be exploited without recognition or proper recompense, because it is seen as women's natural skill and duty. Nature is expected to be all bountiful and usable, as women are expected to be all nurture and availability. If women are devalued, femininity feared, then women's work, and often nature itself, is also devalued. When their devaluation is naturalized, remedying the situation becomes difficult. A global feminist environmental justice analysis allows us to see these connections between the way in which women's labor and natural resources are treated.

Global South feminists and U.S. feminists of color argued further that economically privileged women, despite their supposed socialization to be more-caring individuals, were complicit in these exploitative economic structures. As pointed out in a letter to U.S. feminists written by Global Women's Strike (2003, 2), an organization that grew out of Wages for Housework, "Feminists in industrial countries (in the 1980s) . . . ditched welfare mothers fighting for survival, and this also meant ditching women of color with the least. They plumped instead for careers for a few and for integrating into the ruling class and the management class. The result is that women's wages, deprived of the floor that welfare provided, collapsed. (And men's [wages] followed, as they always do. This lowering of men's wages is what closed the gap between the sexes, giving the appearance of leveling [that is, bringing men's and women's pay rates closer together].)"

I would add to this analysis that the growth of the service sector during this neoconservative period was a way of commodifying women's work at low wages with poor or no benefits. One of the ironic results of this trend of falling wages is that working-class women in the United States began during this period to seek entry into the U.S. military, partly as a means to overcome the devaluing of their "service" work and to move themselves out of the ranks of the working poor (Feinman 2000).

The dismantling of welfare and other social services (or refusal to create them), coupled with the fall of real wages and the need for all family members to work at least one job and sometimes two, was one of the hallmarks of neoconservatism, accelerated in what was called the Reagan/Thatcherite era immediately following the cold war. The success of this neoconservatist reworking of the Keynesian welfare state was buttressed by the success of neocolonialism, justified by the tactics of fearmongering pursued by the Reagan administration, which spoke of the need to fight an "evil empire," which required an enormous military buildup (an ideological move repeated and intensified by the Bush administration in its cynical use of 9/11 to create enough fear and insecurity for Americans to support war and a huge military budget). What followed was a round of debt crisis for the Global South, inviting the imposition of structural adjustment programs, which set up stringent requirements for poor countries to receive international loans and aid, requirements that gutted social supports, depressed the price of basic agricultural products, increased environmental devastation for poor rural peoples in particular, and produced rising unemployment, hunger, and desperation (Hossay 2006; Stiglitz 2002).

These economic patterns, of which this is an incredibly brief summary, were and are thoroughly gendered. Through these processes, particularly in the Global South and poor areas of the Global North, men often became unemployed and unable to help to provide adequate food for their families, while poor (often young) women became the means for their families' survival as low-waged workers in maquiladoras and sweatshops for multinational corporations; as prostitutes, dancers, and entertainers in tourist industries (Enloe 2001); and as domestics and nannies for Global North women (Beneria 2003; Ehrenreich and Hochschild 2002).

As wages fell in the industrialized countries, the "family wage," that is, the ability of some men in middle- and upper-class jobs to bring home enough money to support a family on one income, became more and more rare. Almost all middle- and upper-class women entered the wage economy (a change often attributed only to "feminism" rather than economic necessity), although this was manifested differently at different class levels. The caring work that had been done by upper- and middle-class women became understaffed as they moved into the workplace, because generally men did not take on these jobs within the home, and no social services were funded to replace them, especially in the United States. With this change, almost all women came to face the tough situation that poor and working-class women had faced for centuries—they had a double shift on the job and at home and their overall workload increased. The service economy picked up some of the slack, providing fast and take-out food, laundry services, day care, and health care using poorly paid, mostly female workers. This breakdown of the post–World War II "contract" between organized labor and corporations that supported the "family wage," caused by the forces of increasing economic globalization, was one major source of the sense in U.S. culture of the time that "the family" was under attack, providing the logic behind the popular culture narratives examined in previous chapters in which saving nature is equated with saving the family.

This situation created what has been called a "care deficit" in Global North countries and a corresponding "care drain" in Global South countries (Ehrenreich and Hochschild 2002). Poor Global South women have become one of the largest exports from their countries, as domestics, elder-care workers, and nannies for elite Global North women. The remittances these Global South women send back to their countries are sometimes the largest source of foreign currency for indebted and cash-strapped Global South governments, and as they leave to take care of other families, their own families lose their caring work (Parreñas 2002). Barbara Ehrenreich and Arlie Russell Hochschild (2002, 8–9) point out, "It would be a mistake to attribute the globalization of women's work to a simple synergy of needs among women. . . . [T]his formulation fails to account for the marked failure of Global North governments to meet the needs created by the entry of its women into the workplace . . . [and] omits the role of men [who refuse to do "women's work"]. . . . So, strictly speaking, the presence of immigrant nannies does not enable affluent women to enter the workforce; it enables affluent men to continue avoiding the second shift."

Yet affluent men feel threatened by the entry of elite women into formerly male domains. They feel the "care deficit" as well—the shift in control over women in their class. I speculate here, with others, that this is part of the underlying reason for the rise in sex tourism, sex trafficking, and mail-order brides, the third stream of the expanding flow of women forced to work in other countries (Ehrenreich and Hochschild 2002, 9). Some of these women may be working by choice in these jobs, if sex work is a better situation than other kinds of available work, but many of them are working in conditions of extreme coercion and sometimes outright slavery (Ebbe and Das 2008; Kempadoo and Doezema 1998). Their clients are overwhelmingly rich men from industrialized countries, and I would theorize that many are resistant to changing gender roles in their own societies in which women in their class are no longer under their complete control.

A global feminist environmental justice perspective pays attention to these connections, to the way in which the World Bank's and the International Monetary Fund's control over the economic choices of indebted countries destabilizes cultures and creates the conditions for conflict, encourages the rapid export of natural resources from poor countries and the accompanying environmental devastation, and leads ultimately to the export of a country's women and the accompanying exploitation and suffering (Kempadoo and Doezema 1998). We need to look at the connection of these trends to the growing militarization within these countries and within our own, as well as the growth of cults of violent masculinity. Arguments from nature that support aggression and violence as natural tendencies, especially for men (in the belief that violence is part of a set of genetically programmed needs to attain reproductive success), naturalize war as honorable, necessary, and a matter of pride, fueled by masculinist tropes such as "Bring it on" and reflected in the war movies and video games mentioned earlier in this chapter. Sut Jhally argues in his movie *Tough Guise* (1999) that, contrary to being a natural and transhistorical phenomenon, the appearance and promotion of a particular form of American masculinity in the 1980s—the image of the superbeefy, extraviolent Rambo male— was partly a backlash against feminism and the rapid changes in gender relations and partly a response to increasing unemployment for working class and poor men. Furthermore, this "tough guise" drives U.S. support for violence at home and throughout the globe (Mageo 2004).

Various versions of this form of extreme, violent masculinism are socially constructed, not natural, accessed differently by people in different gender, class, race, religious, and national formations. What kind of different connections between violence and particular masculinities are leveraged in different situations? For instance, how are ideas about male pride and prowess hitched to ideas about national pride, religious purity, and ethnic affiliation in many cultural contexts? What are the connections between the unemployment of men in Global South countries and the rise of Islamic militant fundamentalism? How, along with economic insecurity and resistance to U.S. dominance and support for Israel's occupation of Palestine, are the possibility of changing roles for Muslim women connected to the appeal for many young Muslim men of suicide bombing, guerrilla jihad, and the kidnapping and murder of hostages? How are similar forces (economic stress, racism at home, and changing gender roles) connected to the appeal for many young American men of participating in militarist adventures abroad?

These are questions I cannot answer, but I hope to suggest through asking them the value of moving decisively away from a position that militarist violence is something men do because they are men, so that we can analyze the structural and economic character of various forms of masculinist attachment to violence and connect them to other gendered trends currently driving military conflicts (and other forms of violence) around the globe. The increasing numbers of immigrant domestics and nannies are related to the rise of sex trafficking and mail-order brides, as well as to the existence of predominantly female sweatshop labor, and all of these are part of a specifically gendered set of global changes that underlie the World Bank/IMF structural policies, in which male unemployment and the lack of basic food, health, and reproductive services produce the global circulation and exploitation of Global South women by Global North city dwellers on the one hand and increasing desperation, fundamentalism, and militarization for Global South and poor Global North men on the other. Although masculinist violence can be appropriated by women to gain the civic, ethnic, and nationalistic power it may represent, what we primarily see at present is a war between several forms of masculinist fundamentalism— the Bush administration's Christian version, a extremist Zionist version, and an Islamic militant version—all of which are deeply patriarchal, fueled by different versions of masculinity in crisis. Unless these gendered, raced, classed, and naturalized aspects of the situation we face are recognized, real solutions to the problems of war cannot be found. Instead, as is happening in Afghanistan and is likely to happen in Iraq, women who suffered under one form of violent, patriarchal regime will continue to suffer under another version of violent patriarchy.[6]

Seeking a Just and Full Peace from a Global Feminist Environmental Justice Perspective

What are some answers to the problems we face? Should we be paying women for all the work they do, put a price, an hourly wage on that work? That, in fact, has been happening, albeit in an economy in which women and women's work are the least valued (this often goes by the phrase "the growth of the service economy") (Beneria 2003). Similarly, the externalities of natural resources have been increasingly subjected to commodification if only companies can control and market them. This is what Bechtel tried to do with the water in Bolivia, until the corporation was stopped by indigenous activists in the Cochabamba region (Brecher, Costello, and Smith 2000).

If the commodification of what was previously thought of as free externalities is going to happen, then that caring work and those natural resources have to be valued much more and much differently than they are now. They have to be valued as the most important work and the most precious resources we have. And if we start to pay fairly for "women's work" (not necessarily work done only by women) and for natural resources, then we also need a simultaneous cap on profits and overvalued kinds of work to ensure that we value caring work and natural resources adequately. As I suggest in more detail in the concluding chapter, those of us who are consumers in the Global North economies could play a role in insisting on a more sustainable economic process that mitigates global inequalities and environmental degradation.

The other aspect that needs to be stressed is insisting on women's participation in peace making and nation building. A few years ago, the United Nations passed Resolution 1325, which required that women be part of these processes in significant rather than token ways (Abdela 2004). Here in the United States (as of this writing in 2008), only 16 percent of our elected representatives in the U.S. Congress are women, yet we present ourselves as having achieved political equality for women.[7] Because of the gender gap, in countries where that ratio is much higher, there are better social services and less economic inequality (Seager 2003). Particularly in areas that are presently or were recently suffering from military conflict, there is a need to involve women, who have so much at stake in attaining peace rather than waging war and therefore should be deeply involved, in political resolutions of conflicts. Focusing on the situation of the world's women—on their access to health care, to education, to civil rights, and to the control of their own bodies—is a means to raise the level of education for all, to ensure adequate health care, more environmental protections, and widespread well-being. Using the status of women as a benchmark changes priorities in radical and meaningful ways, bringing us closer to peace, a just and full peace, than we have ever been before. Hopefully, full of hope, a global feminist environmental justice perspective can provide part of the means to see these connections and inspire the political will to make these changes.

Purity and Privilege or Justice and Sustainability?

Natural Consumers in the Global Economy

In thinking about my obsession with the myriad ways that the idea of "natural" is used in U.S. culture and politics, I realized that there was an origin story for this interest, based in my childhood. For, I confess, I grew up in Woodstock, New York, in the 1960s and 1970s, one of two major hotbeds of the hippie movement—the other being the San Francisco Bay Area. Woodstock and San Francisco have similar cultural histories, too, despite one being a tiny town in the rural Catskills and the other a big urban center by the Pacific Ocean. They were both homes to eccentric utopian artist colonies (such as Peter Whitehead's in Woodstock) and to the Beat poets. They were havens for writers, musicians, and painters (such as my parents); oddballs, rebels, and freethinkers (okay, my parents again), way before "hippies" were discovered and labeled by the burgeoning mass media of the cold war period. And of course, as children of Thoreau, these artistic and political movers and shakers were fascinated with the natural, with the idea of a pure, wild, open, and unfettered nature as opposed to the bland, mechanistic, repressive, Organization Man promoting of technology, progress, industrialization, and modernization. The hippies were primarily white, and in positive but ultimately racist ways, they associated black people with a primitive connection to sex, music, and the body and Native Americans with pagan spirituality, peyote, and wild nature (though there were black and Indian hippies, too). But many were also civil rights and antiwar activists. They were in rebellion against the conformism and consumerism of the suburbanization that had taken over much of the countryside in the late 1950s and early 1960s, so this widespread movement was called "the counterculture." It resisted the confining framework of the nuclear family and as such was part of the groundwork that produced the feminist and gay liberation movements.

Hippies were also anticapitalists, trying out cooperative forms of living and working, and promoting an ethics of sharing food and housing. Though most of the people who were hippies in the 1960s and 1970s eventually found their cooperative practices unsustainable in the face of economic realities, these efforts formed the basis for much of the cooperative movement, organic food production, alternative energy businesses, and fair trade efforts that we see forming the heart of "green business" today. Yet these alternative economic creations were originally intended as oppositional to the exploitation and inequality of the dominant economic system. Today, the green business that we see developing in leaps and bounds presents itself as part and parcel of our usual business practices, a natural outgrowth of capitalism. This is a controversial outcome for those who believed that countercultural economic initiatives were more than simple reform of business as usual. Is the new wave of green business a sign of success of this older agenda for change, or is it a dangerous co-optation of widespread desire for radical change in business-as-usual? How would we decide? Divorced in popular culture from this history of resistance, the idea of "hippies" has now become commodified as a form of retro fashion or reductive farce. When my kid's generation goes trick-or-treating during Halloween dressed in "hippie" costumes, it comes as a bit of a shock.

"Back to nature" was a major trope for the hippies in the sixties. "Free love" was a celebration of the "natural" body and the "natural" impulse to make sexual connections to everyone (and a handy way to justify the sexual exploitation of young women and girls). "Free love" was also part of an antiwar stance against the Vietnam War: "Make love not war" and "Girls say yes to men who say no" (to the military draft). It was the time of "natural" foods (such as the diet promoted by Adele Davis, someone we would call now a "whole foods" cookbook author), "nature" spirituality (often ripping off Native American religious traditions, as noted in chapter 2), and "natural" medicine (including the beginning of major alternative health trends that are now well accepted, some trading on stereotypes of Eastern medicine, such as Transcendental Meditation, acupuncture, yoga, massage, and homeopathic drugs). In the 1970s, a "back-to-the-land" movement involving the establishment of communes and organic farms was a major project for many of those involved in the counterculture, including many radical lesbian activists (Sandilands 2002, 2004).

How I came to suspect the political implications of this adoration of nature has to do with my experience in the 1980s in the antinuclear, antimilitarist direct action movement and other movements that were multi-issue, that wanted to make connections between political work against racism, sexism, heterosexism, colonialism, militarism, and environmental degradation. With a political theoretical education steeped in Marxist ideas of social construction, ideological critique, and materialism, as well as the feminist precept of intersectionality—that all these oppressions were connected and that no one social location existed without being impacted by different aspects of inequality—I came to the contemporary environmental movement with a deep distrust of purist concepts of nature. The analysis I have offered in this book was born of that process of engagement, dispute, listening, and changing my mind and practices. In making it, I am indebted to many other thinkers and activists (some also descended from the sixties movements) similarly struggling with how best to understand, resist, and change the damage caused by unequal and antienvironmental social and economic systems.

By way of a conclusion, then, I offer some suggestions about how such a critical analysis might work to guide us in our everyday economic practices to create positive social change. If we are to avoid the dystopian version of our future (as outlined earlier), in which green ways of living are embraced by the rich while the poor live in unsafe, violent, and toxic environments, then we have to think carefully about how to take advantage of the greening of global capitalism. This will involve thinking about social inequalities as much as we think about environmental problems even while we attempt to understand the interrelations of the two.

From the introduction of organic food sections in mainstream retailers such as Wal-Mart and Safeway and the rise of organic and natural food chains such as Whole Foods and Living Foods, to the popularity of "natural" product catalogs such as that of Gaiam, to the introduction of successful hybrid vehicles such as Toyota's Prius, to the rejection of bottled water by major restaurants and cities, to the success of farmer's markets and the increase in Community Sustainable Agriculture (CSA) programs, to the interest in eco-conscious investment funds, to the efforts to produce green building practices, to the greening of urban centers such as New York City (and many other examples too numerous to list), to the promotion of fair trade practices (that is, promoting nonexploitative economic relationships with Global South workers and craftspeople) we are suddenly seeing an unprecedented greening of capitalism.

Using some of the tools I have discussed in this book as a means of distinguishing which of these economic phenomena contribute to real change, we can look carefully at the ways in which the marketing of this corporate environmentalism is taking place. Are these green products being sold to advance the privilege of elites, or are they aimed at reducing inequalities in a global framework? For example, is organic food made to seem desirable because it increases the safety and health of rich white people, who are buying it because they think they will be protected from toxins or illness (Szasz 2007)? Or are consumers also concerned about protecting workers who produce the food from exposure to harmful pesticides and herbicides and about creating more long-term productivity in healthy soils? Are "natural" beauty products trafficking in notions of purity that reinforce racial stereotypes, or are consumers becoming interested in products that do not harm animals for testing and are safer for the people who put the products together and for soils and water when they are thrown away? Are consumers of green products focused on attaching themselves to symbols of a protected, uncontaminated wilderness, or are they demanding that their economic choices encourage fair trade practices, ensuring that Global South workers and their environment are not exploited and polluted by transnational companies? Is environmentalist consumerism only about preserving a privileged lifestyle, or can it be used to insist on the major changes in family structure, labor practices (including domestic labor practices), corporate policies, government regulation, and international politics that will be necessary for both a more just and a more environmentally sound way of life in a global context?

In some cases, the decision to "green" one's business practices can be read cynically as a corporation's attempt to deflect concern away from labor or pollution issues through hitching itself to the positive connotations of environmentalism. In this category there are many examples; one is the series of ads by British Petroleum (BP) showing a variety of individuals being asked if they were concerned about their carbon footprints, while continuing to promote the use of nonrenewable petroleum products. Another example is Wal-Mart. In the early 2000s, Wal-Mart's image and profits began to be affected by an effective coalition between environmentalists and labor activists determined to disclose its generation of enormous profit made on the backs of low-wage workers, working-class consumers, and a profligate use of resources (including the practice of building bigger stores near older Wal-Marts and leaving the first ones empty) (Lichtenstein 2006). In October 2005, in response to this relentless criticism, Wal-Mart attempted to split the anti-Wal-Mart environmentalist/labor coalition by making a decision to go green, forming an association with the National Wildlife Federation, selling organic food in its stores, committing itself to energy efficiency for its fleet of trucks, and promising to use green construction in its future stores (Gogoi 2006; Kastel 2006; Scott 2005). Such a political move, if it is successful in breaking up the oppositional green/labor coalition, clearly shows the dangers of separating environmental concerns from social justice concerns. In fact, Wal-Mart's support of organic food is likely to be a mixed bag, since the economies of scale involved mean that on the one hand, organic farming receives a huge boost through Wal-Mart's demand and can be sold at significantly lower prices (Warner 2006), while on the other hand, the pressure from Wal-Mart to meet its needs, in terms of both quantity and price, means that organic agriculture must shift its production practices into larger, monoculture-based, low-wage–labor-intensive farms as well as increasing reliance on imports from China, where oversight protecting the integrity of organic certification is almost nonexistent (Gogoi 2006). All of these practices ironically may have negative environmental consequences despite the end result of large-scale conversion to organic production.

Indeed, Wal-Mart's effort is only one aspect of a broader shift; since the USDA's creation of organic certification in 2002, the growth in consumer interest in organic food products has spurred the rapid acquisition of numerous independent organic brands by large multinational distributors, investment firms, and huge food processors (Howard 2008). This trend has affected the organic food industry's original commitment to humane treatment of animals, economic justice for family-scale farming, and quality and integrity in organic food production (Kastel 2006). Michael Pollan nicely brings out the contradictions of Wal-Mart's organic conversion: on the one hand, organic food loses its elitist connotation, becoming available to poor and working-class people because of lower prices, and millions of acres of land worldwide will be farmed without pesticides, inorganic fertilizers, and herbicides; on the other hand, how will Wal-Mart achieve that lower price?

> To do so would virtually guarantee that Wal-Mart's version of cheap organic food is not sustainable, at least not in any meaningful sense of that word. To index the price of organic to the price of conventional is to give up, right from the start, on the idea, once enshrined in the organic movement, that food should be priced not high or low but responsibly. As the organic movement has long maintained, cheap industrial food is cheap only because the real costs of producing it are not reflected in the price at the checkout. Rather, those costs are

charged to the environment, in the form of soil depletion and pollution (industrial agriculture is now our biggest polluter); to the public purse, in the form of subsidies to conventional commodity farmers; to the public health, in the form of an epidemic of diabetes and obesity that is expected to cost the economy more than $100 billion per year; and to the welfare of the farm- and food-factory workers, not to mention the well-being of the animals we eat. (Pollan 2006, 2)

Note the complexity of figuring out where social justice and environmental values lie and how to meet them both. What is more important: the need for cheaper food for poorer people; the desire to treat animals well; the working conditions and wages of agricultural and processing workers? The list could go on, but assuming that these values are inevitably in conflict would be a mistake. Only seeing those "natural" and social indices as interrelated and interdependent on each other will lead toward practices and policies that can achieve both environmental and social health and equity. The activist response to the Wal-Mart green initiative has prominently displayed the necessity to see issues of labor, global justice, and environmental sustainability as going hand in hand. A critique of Wal-Mart's sustainability initiative was written by twenty-two organizations concerned with fair wages, health care, environmental protection, economic justice, community health and sustainability, global corporate power, racism, the exploitation of women workers, and global climate change; it vividly demonstrates the connections between these issues (Anderson 2007). Granted, in efforts focused on critique, downplaying possible disagreements (especially on details of strategy and policy) is easier than working them out to produce pragmatic policy, but still this kind of integrated attention to environmental and social justice issues is encouraging.

The complexity involved in figuring out the practical details about how to have an economy that is both environmentally sound and socially just requires more knowledge and research than I can offer here. But a way to decide what approach is most useful is to look at whether what is being suggested makes connections between environmentalism and social justice. Though there is a rich literature on ecological economics (see Hawken et al. 2000) much of it does not necessarily deal with social justice issues. However, many thinkers and scholars are working on the integration of these issues. Derek Wall (2005) offers an excellent overview of many efforts to analyze the relationship between global capitalism, the environment, and the production of inequality. The work of Hazel Henderson (2006) and Mary Mellor (1992) is particularly interesting in their articulation (though in different ways) of the relationship between women's unpaid domestic and underpaid service work and environmentally exploitative practices (see chapter 6).

Despite the need to think differently about these questions, it should not be surprising that the trend of corporate environmentalism does not display this kind of integrated approach but deploys the kind of dominant U.S. and Western ideas about nature I present throughout this book, ideas that support and reflect social hierarchies and exploitative economic processes, often intertwined with mainstream environmentalism. An examination of green business marketing reveals many of the same patterns of naturalization that I identify in this book: images of the whole Earth as environmentalist icon, the constant portrayal of green products as a cement to hold together a white, middle-class nuclear family, and racialized images that identify people of color or Global South people as closer to nature, more "primitive," and occupying a doomed cultural location on the evolutionary economic scale.

One can see this narrative in many arenas of popular culture, such as the 2008 Franklin Templeton Investments television ad that starts by showing an Asian woman holding a child making her way through a street market that is dirty and crowded, with glimpses of sellers washing chicken carcasses in a bucket. "You see a traditional market," says the narrator. The next scene shows the same woman pushing her child in a shopping cart through a blindingly white and bright supermarket, in which every item of food is enclosed in separate, see-through plastic containers. "We see an opportunity for growth," says the narrator. In this ad, danger, impurity, and exposure to disease are placed firmly in the context of a local economic practice that is operated by poor, darker, and "traditional" peoples, while the excessively packaged, energy-intensive supermarket is presented as safe, white, and healthy, despite the environmentally questionable practices pictured. That Franklin Templeton is under pressure from organizations such as Save Darfur to disinvest from PetroChina (the oil company many see as responsible for funding the genocide in the region) fits into this picture of the deceptive promotion of "growth" without taking responsibility for environmentally problematic and socially devastating economic institutions (see the YouTube video *Franklin Templeton Is Making a Killing* [2008]).

The appearance of these tropes in close alliance with environmentalism is part of a post–cold war political and global economic regime in which the United States promotes itself as the single global superpower (as I have argued in previous chapters). In particular, a reification of purity that acts as a foundation for individualistic and consumerist notions of health and safety often results in upholding existing economic privileges and, thus, problematic economic and cultural practices that exploit both people and the environment. Andrew Szasz (2007) talks about this phenomenon using the interesting concept of "inverted quarantine," in which consumers are encouraged to see environmental problems not in terms of society-wide issues suitable to collective action but in terms of the protection of individuals and their families from contamination and illness, creating an inversion of the strategy of quarantining dangerous elements away from people, so that privileged people, particularly white suburban families, are enclosed inside "safe" and "pure" zones away from dangerous (darker) peoples and cultures. This can produce consumer phenomena such as a demand for "pure" water in individual bottles, which has deeply antienvironmental consequences in terms of plastic waste and lack of political action against causes of the pollution of public water sources. The inverted quarantine framework is fundamental to the development of suburbanization, with all of the environmental and social consequences noted earlier: the overdependence on cars, the promotion of overconsumption, the enclosure of agricultural or wild land, class and race segregation, the increased domestic exploitation of women, the alienation of its occupants from comprehending the global inequality that sustains it (Szasz 2007).

In particular, I have noticed two common racialized tropes in much of green marketing, in both corporate environmentalist marketing and green fair trade marketing, which have complex implications for whether these increasingly profitable market sectors have actual positive results for the poor workers and craftspeople invoked. One is the common equation made between generically Asian products as markers of less-developed, more-natural cultures (whether identified as such through aesthetic associations, claims of origin, or references to various Asian health traditions) and human health and environmental quality. The other is the depiction of poor brown Global South women as deserving recipients of help directed by affluent, white Global North people. To illustrate these tropes and other problematic patterns, we can look at the catalogs produced by Gaiam, a "conscious living" company that sells high-end green lifestyle products (bedding, furniture, clothing, cleaning products, and exercise and health-related appliances) with a commendable attention to questions of economic justice (Gaiam 2007).

Gaiam commits itself to offer "products created responsibly," that is, manufactured with environmental criteria in mind as well as whether producers of its products are paid fairly and work under safe, healthful conditions (in other words, the company promotes fair trade practices).

Gaiam also pays attention to the environmental consequences of its own production, shipping its products in recycled boxes and printing its catalog on recycled paper. Additionally, it encourages its consumers to become active on environmental and social justice issues and prominently displays its relationship with Co-Op America (whose slogan is "economic justice for a green planet" and which joins together a huge range of activist organizations as well as economic efforts making headway on these issues), the Conservation Fund, the Nature Conservancy, Doctors without Borders, Heifer International, Action against Hunger, and other environmentalist and fair trade organizations. On every fourth page or so of its catalog, inset next to pictures of its products, Gaiam features a short description of a fair trade effort. Clearly Gaiam, like *Captain Planet* in chapter 4, is an exceptionally commendable example of a green business that promotes fair trade and on-the-ground engagement in social change, trying to move its customers toward action above and beyond buying its products.

But looking at its self-presentation through the framework of the analysis presented in this book, one sees several problematic patterns. The recipients of Gaiam's fair trade efforts are almost all from Global South, traditional (that is, "peasant") Asian cultures (Thailand, India, Afghanistan, China, and Vietnam are prominently featured), painting those cultures as at once "primitive" and closer to nature—automatically environmentalists as in the Ecological Indian stereotype—and therefore a prime source of green products. The consumers, in contrast, are all pictured as affluent, white, Global North women, taking part in the construction of women as primary consumers in a suburban economy, as discussed earlier (in the catalogs I receive several times a year, only one light-skinned African American model has been used). This may make a great deal of sense, as poor Global South workers are desperately in need of fair trade and healthy working conditions—but so are workers in all countries of the world, including the United States. Gaiam's wealthy (and feminized) customer base, people who are expected to be able to afford $219 for a set of organic cotton sheets or $126 for a mission solar light, are appealed to on the basis of their paramount need for individual protection from dangerous impurities, personal luxury, and control over their own narrow space, in a clear use of the inverted quarantine narrative identified by Szasz (2007). Much of this appeal is couched in terms of stunning disregard for how others with access to much fewer resources might be unable to protect themselves as well, including the deployment of a colonialist discourse that justifies the idea that what is of paramount importance is the safety and comfort of the rich and the imperialist. A "Deluxe Mini Personal Air Supply" unit delivers a "steady stream of pure, clean air to your breathing space . . . ideal for cars and airplanes where pollutants become concentrated" (Gaiam 2007, 34). A "PlasmaWave Air Purifier" is introduced by a customer testimonial that reads, "Recently I moved to Cairo, where the air is infamously bad. The air got even worse when the farmers began burning the rice fields at night. I had been waking up sick from sinus problems. I ordered your PlasmaWave and now I can breathe again! I am so grateful" (Gaiam 2007, 35). The idea that it is fine to have one individual, someone who regularly uses polluting cars and airplanes and who can afford to travel to Cairo, be protected from air pollution while farmers, urban residents, and others not able to buy their own "personal air supply" will continue to suffer from respiratory illnesses and cancer should be deeply disturbing. Just the concept of owning a "personal air supply" speaks to an amazing ideological construction of air—one of the most globally integrated, necessary, and heretofore non-commodified natural resource—as able to be owned, sold, and controlled for individual benefit.

The relationship between the affluent, female, white American Gaiam consumer and the poor, Asian, "primitive," brown female Global South producer is frequently constructed as one of colonialist appropriation and paternalistic charity. "Organic Cotton Bangalore Sheets" are sold as the opportunity to "Experience your own passage to India" (Gaiam 2007, 63), a reference to the 1924 novel *A Passage to India* by E. M. Forster, which is, ironically, highly critical of British colonialism in India. Ultimately, obscured by its environmentalist and social justice veneer, Gaiam constructs a female world of wealthy white women exploiting poor brown women for their own individual advantage. The name of the company, created through "a fusion of Gaia—an ancient word for Mother Earth—and 'I am', symbolizing the connection between the Earth and all living things" (Gaiam 2007, 41), nicely encapsulates this individualistic, feminized naturalization of inequality.

The racialized trope in Gaiam of the image of brown or black women from Asia (but also Africa and Latin and South America) as wholesome recipients of the charity of U.S. middle-class white people is common in fair trade advertising, so much so that FINCA International, soliciting donations for its microcredit loaning program for poor Global South women, places a dark-skinned woman with a basket of apples on her head on the front page of one of its brochures under the heading "This woman doesn't need your charity . . . all she needs is a chance." The anxiety about political consequences of straightforwardly advocating the redistribution of wealth from the affluent to the poor is clearly on display. Much of this kind of environmentalist and social justice–oriented marketing deploys several underlying themes familiar to us by now: the United States as a privileged site of purity and health under threat from impure Others; the United States as innocent and beneficent promoter of modernization and progress in the world (American exceptionalism); and (what may seem to be in contradiction, in a repetition of the Ecological Indian motif) the United States as a nation in need of redemption.

There are valid debates about fair trade and microcredit programs (in which banks lend small amounts of money to very poor people who usually would not be able to get credit, the majority of them women, to assist their efforts to become small-scale entrepreneurs and try to lift them out of poverty).[1] Microcredit programs in which high rates of interest can be charged—between 20 and 50 percent (Dugger 2004)—may still be enriching the lenders at the expense of the poor. In addition, the context of women's lives needs to be taken into account in assessing the success of microcredit programs; for example, access to microcredit may provide women who have abusive male partners resources to escape the abuse, but it may also exacerbate male violence when women are perceived as empowered by the loans to stop conforming to gendered expectations of them (Schuler, Hashemi, and Badal 1998). Whether microcredit and fair trade programs can significantly reduce poverty when the main thrust of their attempts is to turn poor Global South women into small entre-preneurs in a global economy in which they will remain at a significant disadvantage depends on whether these efforts can ultimately address the unequal and environmentally damaging structures of that economy. If the outcome of creating some small benefits for individuals while accepting that the appeal of their products depends on their remaining within a ste-reotype of more "primitive" (closer to nature and entirely responsible for their families) while encouraging affluent Global North customers to con-tinue their high-volume consumption, it would seem to be a questionable kind of "green" economic structure. Taking Gaiam as an example, we can clearly see that what its customers are purchasing, besides green products, is the pleasure of feeling that they are contributing to the welfare of an abstracted Mother Earth as well as a poor brown woman (perhaps seen as one and the same) who will be grateful for the purchase of her "traditional" handmade goods. In this way, the stereotype is consumed along with the product, and the women who are the actual people behind the stereotype are locked into meeting its expectations or risking economic failure. They must remain poor, traditional artisans in narrow ways to satisfy this need of their affluent customers. Seeing Global South women as complex, agentive members of their communities is difficult to maintain if they are fixed as images of worthwhile but reductive objects of beneficence by those who are more powerful (Padmanabhan 2001; Spivak 2004).

Despite this critique, there are plenty of worthwhile environmental justice and fair trade efforts being developed, and I do not want to sound hopelessly cynical—because I am not. These efforts are crucial tools to get to what we want: a socially just and environmentally sustainable economy. But I do not want to repeat the mistakes of the counterculture that nurtured the beginnings of the environmentalist movement, ensuring in its romanticization of the "primitive" that it would not appeal to working-class people, people of color, or people from the Global South. The new environmentalist consumer wave has the potential to move far beyond the utopian hopes of the "back to nature" desires of the sixties or the purist biocentrism of much of the mainstream environmentalist movement, because it is more sophisticated, more technologically adept, more realistic, and more situated in global contexts. But it must move beyond individual modifications of ways of living to address the systematic, institutionalized structures that maintain inequality and promote environmental devastation. As Patrick Hossay says,

> We are not going to find salvation in lifestyle changes. Riding a bike to work, recycling, carrying a reusable shopping bag, or planting a tree will not make the current global system either morally or physically sustainable. The focus on these sorts of lifestyle solutions reveals what I see as a grave weakness in the dominant environmental agenda. We've become passive, accepting, and far too timid. We're trying to fix a machine that is fundamentally broken by tinkering lightly on the edges. Most disturbing of all, we seem to have accepted, in a matter-of-fact sort of way, the legitimacy of the individualistic, profit-centered thinking that underpins the system we're trying to change. As a result, we imagine environmental solutions as consumer-based, and friendly to the consumption-centered world-view that inflicts the global crisis. (2006, 221)

Similarly identifying some of the problems with the green marketing practices examined here, Hossay writes, "Our dissent is commodified and sold back to us" (2006, 223).

A focus on individualistic environmentalist solutions makes sense only if one ignores questions of social justice in a global context. When evaluating products, strategies, policies, or our political representatives, we should look to how and whether connections between social justice and environmentalism are being made, and if they are, whether they are being made without the kinds of problematic narratives identified here. Judging whether those connections are being made with integrity can provide us with much better guides to actually solving the environmental crises we face, and we can choose to join only those community groups, activist efforts, and larger movements that address environmental issues from social justice perspectives or vice versa. An educated, critical approach born out of forging coalitions between movements that were separated and in conflict in the sixties can offer us the understanding that environmental and social justice goals must be connected at every turn, that we must insist that the greening of the economy also involve reducing inequities of wealth and exploitative labor conditions around the world (Pellow and Brulle 2005).

Furthermore, though individualistic solutions to environmental problems will not produce the significant changes in material practices that are required to make real change, it would be folly to completely reject the potential power of consumer pressure to change business practices—but only if those efforts are also connected to questions of social equity. As long as the twin foundations of our economy are environmental unsustainability and inequality (the exploitation of the poorer and less powerful), we will not meaningfully produce change. The developing green business context is widespread and dynamic, involving many different kinds of products and business practices, as well as decentralized efforts by municipal, local, and state governments and activist organizations. This has the potential of giving consumers, voters, workers, managers, investors, and leaders multiple avenues to press for real change. Green business will not magically or automatically produce more equality or even environmental sustainability if left to its own devices, and it will not do so simply through consumer demands for different products; it must be constantly shaped, prodded, critiqued, resisted, imagined, regulated, engaged, and modified by an activist public through collective strength. Doing things differently has to be the responsibility of corporations and political institutions as well, not only consumers and activists. But these things are interconnected; corporations are consumers, too, and people make up, resist, control, and shape political institutions. Luckily, there are plenty of examples of collective efforts to make such real change, efforts that we can support and join (Danaher, Biggs, and Marks 2007). Education in the ways in which environmental and social justice issues are connected is crucial to ensure that this unprecedented opportunity to make real change is not wasted. Given the magnitude of the threats we face to the environment and to equitable ways of living, the consequences—for people and nature alike—of *not* taking action are catastrophic (Hossay 2006).

In the late 1960s and early 1970s, in the United States as well as numerous other places around the world, the combined agitation of the counterculture, the antiwar movement, the New Left, the civil rights movement, the Black, Brown, and Red Power movements, the women's movement, the lesbian and gay movement, and the environmental movement produced real change in a whole host of areas of life, culture, and economics. It is hard to convey to those who were born after this period and have only reductive popular culture versions to represent it the exciting sense of huge possibility as well as deep fear generated by this widespread agitation for social change, for a better world. Versions of what that better world would look like varied widely, of course. But the sense that change was possible was very real. And that the change was deep is undeniable—particularly in areas of gender and racial equality and in the successes of the early environmental movement and the anti–Vietnam War movement. But the fear and realities of change also generated a huge backlash that ushered in the Moral Majority and the Reagan Revolution. In addition, attempts to form strong coalitions between these movements fell apart in the face of internal racism, sexism, classism, and U.S. ethnocentrism, including a tendency among some radicals to valorize violence and purist left sectarianism that alienated many people who otherwise deeply desired a different society.

Though this book is focused on popular culture and environmentalism, analyzing the narratives of naturalization of social inequality and problematic versions of nature that prevent an understanding of the need to connect environmentalism with social justice to produce real, positive social change, I also hope that some of the critical perspectives I suggest might be useful in evaluating the claims of all movement activists, political campaigns, and economic reforms. Is violence—especially violence connected to masculinist ideas of power, effectiveness, revenge, and honor— valorized as a necessary means to an end? Are questions of care, education, the nitty-gritty work of daily sustenance ignored because they are seen as feminized externalities? Is there only one narrow notion of what kind of community or family should benefit from change? Are achievement and discovery presented as a means of attaining a new frontier in ways that are aimed at increasing nationalistic power and access to natural resources at the expense of poorer countries? Are differences between people naturalized and fixed in ways that allow them to be exploited or excluded from being equal partners in processes of social change? Are groups of people and ways of living romanticized as closer to nature in ways that relegate them to inferior roles in working on the problems we face?

Couched as it is in the pages of a book, my effort to advocate for seeing the connections between environmentalism and social justice tends to produce an analysis heavy on criticism and light on solutions. Even so, I hope engaging in such a critical endeavor is still useful. I am fully aware that such an analytic practice may not always lead us to a clear path to follow in our daily lives or our collective actions. But if we cultivate a way of thinking that requires us to understand the practical impacts of our conceptual apparatus, then we may be inspired to better material and political practices. Such an analysis can show us why and how certain ways of thinking about the natural and nature are not conducive to collaborative and effective solutions to our problems. In particular, such a focus could guide us to better form coalitions between privileged and excluded groups, a requirement, I argue, for effective political action. The images we choose, the language we use, and the particular strategies we promote have consequences. If popular culture is one powerful way to reach others—to persuade, to educate, and to consciousness-raise—then we need to choose ways of creating that culture that reflect our desire to be inclusive and effective, not to shore up practices of exclusion, inequality, and privilege. Attending to the ways in which we conceive of nature and the natural can be one important tool to use in this effort, to help us understand which changes and which goals we should support, and to create a global feminist environmental justice movement that has broad appeal. Greening without justice, without equity, will not sustain the Earth or our future.

Notes

The book epigraph is from Haraway 1995, 70–71.

Introduction

1. The terms *Global North* and *Global South* have generally replaced older terms used to indicate structures of global economic inequality, such as *First World* and *Third World* or *Western* (meaning Euro-American) and *non-Western*, or *developed* and *underdeveloped*. The newer terms have the advantage of moving away from a no-longer-applicable cold war framework (which divided along communist and noncommunist lines with "First World" and "Second World" being the superpowers and "Third World" being the nonaligned or less powerful) or a description of the more powerful nations that left out non-Western powers such as Japan or a framework that assumes "development" as an uncritically positive term. Another advantage of *Global North* and *Global South* is the way in which the terms can accommodate the fact that there are poor and disempowered groups within the more powerful nations, affected negatively by histories of exclusion and discrimination and the globalizing economy, such as indigenous people in the United States. I do use *Western* when I am looking at a specifically Euro-American ideological construction, such as the frontier myth or in my discussion of naturalization.

2. In using the term *radical environmentalisms* for only three approaches, I depart from the more conventional use of the term, used for environmentalisms that are aimed at systemic change, usually including biocentric environmentalism. In terms of my argument in this book, however, environmentalisms that separate nature from culture, as biocentric positions do, are not aimed at fundamental change. From this point of view, biocentric environmentalisms such as bioregionalism, Earth First! and deep ecology are closer to mainstream positions than radical positions. As I mention below, I have left out animal liberation movements, which deserve a fuller treatment.

3. Sometimes this field is called cultural environmental studies rather than

environmental cultural studies, but I prefer the latter because I see it as an approach built on scholarship often incorporated into contemporary "cultural studies" as a field. I would characterize the following academic approaches as contributing to environmental cultural studies (in a list not meant to be exhaustive): newer versions of *ecocriticism* (Buell 2005), primarily literary critical efforts to understand the role of nature and environment in literature, which include the fields of ecojustice ecocriticism (Reed 2002) and ecofeminist ecocriticism (Gaard and Murphy 1998); *ecocritique* (Luke 1997), a broad term for a variety of social scientific and cultural studies efforts to analyze the relation between environmental practices and forms of social inequality; newer versions of *environmental history*, historical endeavors that account for histories of nature as well as people; *the production of nature* (Smith 1984), a materialist approach to understanding nature as a dynamic and social entity; *environmental cultural geography* (Seager 1993), for instance, as addressed in the journal *Gender, Place and Culture*; and *feminist science studies* (Haraway 1989), which has for a long time criticized the ideological uses of concepts of nature to justify social inequalities and has recently included examinations of environmental issues such as the use of animals in scientific research. In all cases, I would include the work in these areas, which attends to the intertwining of power, race, class, gender, sexuality, and the environment, in environmental cultural studies, an intertwining that has been at the heart of the activist and theoretical efforts that I gather under the label "radical environmentalisms" for this book. T. V. Reed has used the term *environmental justice cultural studies* to define similarly interconnected academic efforts (see http://www.wsu.edu/~amerstu/ce/ce.html). An important area of relevant scholarship that I have left out of this list—and, unfortunately, this book—is work that addresses the exploitation of animals. My excuse for not sufficiently incorporating such work, which I respect and recognize as often relevant to the questions I address here (Adams 1999; Gaard 1993), is unsatisfactory to me and certainly will be to those working on these issues, but including questions of animals in the theoretical framework I develop here involved complexities that I felt unable to tackle in the time and space I had to do this work.

An incomplete list of scholars whom I see as especially influential in creating an environmental cultural studies approach includes Joni Adamson, Stacey Alaimo, William Cronon, Chris Cuomo, Giovanna Di Chiro, Greta Gaard, Andil Gosine, David Harvey, N. Katherine Hayles, Annette Kolodny, Winona LaDuke, Timothy Luke, Carolyn Merchant, David Pellow, Devon Peña, Jennifer Price, Laura Pulido, Andrew Ross, Catriona Sandilands, Joni Seager, Vandana Shiva, Neil Smith, Zoë Sofoulis, Rebecca Solnit, Rachel Stein, Julie Sze, Anna Tsing, Richard White, and Alexander Wilson. The figure who represents the most complete example of environmental cultural studies as I define it here, and who has taught me the most about the necessity of interwining these fields, is Donna Haraway, though I have no idea whether she would accept this label. See the reference list for works by many of these authors.

Chapter 1. Natural Patterns in U.S. History and Popular Culture

1. For many years, I have taught an upper-level undergraduate class called "Gender, Race and Nature in American Culture" at Washington State University. I have also taught this material in Santa Cruz, California, as well as in Perth, Australia; Berlin, Germany; Taipei, Taiwan; and Kunming, China.

2. Described on her Web site, http://www.judybaca.com/art/worldwall/WW_Philos.html.

3. The *Earth Song* video can be seen on YouTube at http://www.youtube.com/watch?v=Rch7ey-v7ks. The song is on the popular Jackson album *HIStory—Past, Present and Future—Book One* (1995).

Chapter 2. Frontiers of Nature

1. Shepard Krech coined the term *Ecological Indian* in his book of the same name, though he argues that it appeared well before the post–cold war period that I identify here. My chronology does not constitute a disagreement with Krech, because I agree with him that the environmental movement of the 1970s made the figure of the Ecological Indian much more prominent (Krech 1999). I am looking at the appearance of the figure primarily in movies, in which there is an evolution from the Noble Savage to the critical Noble Savage (with ecological overtones) to the Ecological Indian, particularly in Westerns, from the 1950s to the 1970s to the 1980s–present period. Annette Kolodny (2007) argues that the Ecological Indian figure was used strategically by Indian activists well before the 1970s environmental movement made it an important political device. My thanks to David Warner, whose interest in the Ecological Indian figure in U.S. movies spurred me to think more deeply about the phenomenon.

2. The myth is not limited to American culture. Jean-Jacques Rousseau famously deployed the figure of the Native American to stand for his Natural Man, which he used to develop a political theory of human nature and to criticize the corruption of his contemporary French society. As European colonialism developed, different forms of racism appeared, in which black African people were always dehumanized even while the "redskins," discovered as part of the conquest of the New World, were often depicted as Noble Savages (perhaps partly because Indians were not widely enslaved in North America and thus served no commercial use as long as they could be driven off their land).

3. Jeffrey Walker (1998) examines the differences between the 1986 film and the original Cooper novel.

4. See Cooper [1826] 1958, 333–38.

5. In the credits of *The Last of the Mohicans*, AIM (American Indian Movement) is thanked for the presence of Dennis Banks in the movie. For more about the relation between American Indian activism and movies, especially the role of what James Stripes calls "actorvists" such as Banks, Means, and John Trudell, see T. V. Reed (2005) and Stripes (1999).

6. Iron Eyes Cody was born Espero De Corti, the son of Sicilian immigrants. He became well known acting in roles as an Indian in numerous films, and he claimed to be Cherokee and Cree, denying his Sicilian heritage. See http://en.wikipedia.org/wiki/Iron_Eyes_Cody.

7. Shepard Krech III begins his important book *The Ecological Indian* (1999) (to which I am clearly indebted in this chapter) with a discussion of the major influence on U.S. culture of the "crying Indian" ad featuring Iron Eyes Cody, including an illustration of the original print poster. The 1971 television spot can be found on the Internet in several places, along with references to various parodies inspired by the ad. These parodies include a 2006 version by Plan4.blogspot.com, which shows the crying Indian in a spacesuit floating past the blue planet and shedding his tear upon sighting an orbiting garbage truck with the NASA logo on it. This image is relevant to themes in chapter 3. In 1998, Keep America Beautiful made another crying Indian television spot, entitled "Back by Popular Neglect," which shows people littering at a bus stop and the face of Iron Eyes Cody on the bus shelter's wall, crying a fresh tear.

8. The controversy over the origins of two supposed Chief Seattle utterances, one a speech and the other a letter, is well documented (esp. see Kaiser 1987). The speech, represented as a transcription of Chief Seattle's address to the governor of Washington in 1855, was more likely written by a Dr. Henry A. Smith (Clark 1985). The letter (or message; see Jeffers 1991) was apparently written by a scriptwriter named Ted Perry for a documentary in 1971. For the original Ted Perry version of Chief Seattle's letter, see http://www_formal.stanford.edu/jmc/progress/fake2.html.

9. Jeffers lists herself as the illustrator rather than the author, retaining the fiction that the statement's author is Chief Seattle (Jeffers 1991).

10. Many children's films also use the Ecological Indian narrative structure, in which white boys (and sometimes girls) encounter the combined force of indigeneity, nature, and animals as a redemptive mechanism: *Once upon a Forest* (1993), the *Free Willy* movies (1993, 1995, 1997), *Ferngully: The Last Rainforest* (1992), *Pocahontas* (1995), *Jungle 2 Jungle* (1997), and *Brother Bear* (2003), among others (see chapter 4). An interesting example of the Ecological Indian—in a movie that shifts the theme by focusing on white people's integration into nature rather than white people's integration into indigenous society but still follows a similar structure (except for its contemporary setting) as in the frontier movies I've been discussing—is the *Free Willy* trilogy. In these movies, about a young white boy, Jesse, who befriends an orca and enables it to be set free, it is a Native American character, Randolph (played by the great indigenous actor Augustus Schellenberg), who facilitates Jesse's acceptance into the whale society (reversing the process of the Ecological Indian motif) and, in the sequel *Free Willy 2* (1995), through providing "traditional" medicine, heals the whale when it falls sick through encountering pollution. While the Randolph character and his indigenous friends are contemporary, modern figures with scientific educa-

tions, their close relation to the whales and to the environmental issues involved in the plot are assumed as part of their culture. The complexity of the environmental issues faced by contemporary Northwest Coast indigenous peoples and their complicated cultural and material relation to the whales barely surface in the story. One of the main differences in plot structure in these children's films as opposed to most of the films discussed in this chapter is that redemption comes in the form of reconstituting a home for lost, abandoned, and orphaned children within a nuclear family structure. I discuss this aspect of the environmentalist narrative in children's environmentalist films in chapter 4.

11. For the tagline from *Dances with Wolves*, see http://www.imdb.com/title/tt0099348/. Another example of this narrative of ecological indigenous redemption of guilty white men through the medium of an animal, and the recovery of a violent masculinity on righteous grounds, can be found in the children's movie *White Fang 2: The Myth of the White Wolf* (1994). The movie, set in the Pacific Northwest in the late 1880s, concerns a young white man who, along with his wolf sidekick, befriends a Northwest Coast tribe. The tribe is threatened by the greedy, violent, and ecologically destructive actions of white miners. After the miners are defeated by an explosion set up by the young man, his wolf, and his Indian helpers, he is taken into the tribe, through marrying an Indian maiden, who, coincidentally, also has a wolf sidekick. Once again, with some attempt at cultural authenticity, the main character is a white male who becomes Indian through the auspices of his connection with an animal and, in doing so, is able to right ecological wrongs. The ecological issue, as well as the "authenticity" of the Indians, is set firmly in an unreachable past. (See chapter 4.)

12. The claim of authenticity for the story of Hidalgo—made by its scriptwriter, Joe Fusco, and seemingly supported by Viggo Mortensen—was met with anger by many people, particularly the members of the Long Riders Guild, a group of people who engage in lengthy endurance rides on horseback in rugged country around the world. In particular, critics of the movie objected to the wholesale creation of the "Ocean of Fire" horse race in Arabia, which is the heart of the movie (and which Fusco admits "embellishing"). The Long Riders depiction of the "Hidalgo Hoax" can be found at http://www.thelongriders guild.com/hopkins.htm. Fusco, who is also an activist for the preservation of the mustang, made a lengthy statement about the controversy, which can be found at http://www.frankhopkins.com/articles28.html.

13. *Hidalgo* and *The Last Samurai* use almost the same plot structure to extend the critical Noble Savage narrative into a global frame. *The Last Samurai*, starring Tom Cruise, does not use an ecological motif, but like *Hidalgo*, it concerns a guilty U.S. Seventh Calvary officer involved in the 1890 Wounded Knee massacre who becomes involved in trying to save a "vanishing tribe": in this case the Japanese samurai, who are (like the Bedouins in *Hidalgo*) identified by the movie in numerous ways (especially their status as premodern warriors) as akin to American indigenous peoples.

Chapter 3. "Forever New Frontiers"

1. Though I did not accept all of her excellent suggestions, I am deeply indebted to Phaedra Pezzullo for her close reading of an earlier version of this chapter.

2. The link between colonialist rhetorics and images of space exploration is not merely a U.S. phenomenon but also occurs in the culturally different context of space programs in China, Japan, France, and the Soviet Union. Generally, these links are a staple of the cold war. See Mazin and Tourkina 1998.

3. The "Forever New Frontiers" ad campaign was designed by the advertising company Foote, Cone and Belding. All ads also contain the tagline "What will tomorrow bring?" and have sometimes been referenced by that phrase. Six 60-second "Forever New Frontiers" television commercials were released, one each year from 2000 to 2005. All of them were still occasionally in circulation on television in 2006. The keywords or concepts emphasized in the ads consist of "Farmers" (2000), "Monk" (2001), "Horizons" (2002), "Knowledge" (2003), "Privilege" (2004), and "Freedom" (2005) (these are my labels for them). They could be seen at http://www.boeing.com/companyoffices/aboutus/advertising until around March 2007 but have since been taken down. Foote, Cone and Belding did not archive them either. Goldman, Papson, and Kersey include two of the commercials ("Farmers" and "Monk") in their searchable database at http://149.175.1.56/global/fmpro.

4. See http://www.lclark.edu/~goldman/global.

5. See http://www.space_frontier.org.

6. See http://www.highfrontier.org.

7. In 1993, three new segments were made, and in 1999, ABC showed *Schoolhouse Rock* again as part of its Saturday morning children's line-up for a time. Several existing parodies of other segments of *Schoolhouse Rock* also speak to its lasting cultural resonance. One is in a Simpson's episode, a bit called "I'm an Amendment to Be," which is a parody of the popular "I'm Just a Bill" (*The Simpsons*, March 17, 1996, an episode entitled "The Day the Violence Died"). Another parody of *Schoolhouse Rock* is *Pirates and Emperors: Or, Size Does Matter* (2004) by Eric Henry, which criticizes U.S. imperialism. The creators of *Schoolhouse Rock* were Lynn Ahrens, Bob Dorough, David McCall, George Newall, Radford Stone, and Tom Yohe. It was originally greenlighted by Michael Eisner. See http://www.school-house-rock.com.

8. The Web site for *Schoolhouse Rock* describes "Elbow Room" as about "the pioneers opening the West" and explaining "the concept of Manifest Destiny." See http://www.school-house-rock.com.

9. In reality, the moon and all other celestial bodies are specifically excluded from national territorial claims, in accordance with the Outer Space Treaty of 1967. See http://www.fas.org/nuke/control/ost/intro.htm.

10. See http://www.apolloalliance.org/about_why.php.

11. See http://www.fas.org/nuke/control/ost/intro.htm.

Chapter 4. "The Power Is Yours, Planeteers!"

1. Some of the listeners to presentations of the essay that was the precursor to this chapter have asked me whether I would include in this criticism nature-based spiritual and cultural practices, such as those found in many indigenous cultures, which use animals and natural entities as significant characters in educational stories and spiritual practices. But I think there is a fundamental difference between stories from cultures that do not display a Western culture/nature dualism and the way in which animals are used as characters in moral stories for young children in Eurocentric cultures.

2. I am confident in my conclusions here but have not done a comprehensive study of all environmental culture for kids. A useful anthology engaging in ecocritical attention to the subject is Dobrin and Kidd 2004. There is little research, as far as I am aware, into the frequency of environmentalist themes in children's education and culture worldwide and cross-culturally. There was some work done in the United States, mostly prompted by conservative concerns that kids were being "brainwashed" by environmentalists in the public schools, but this scholarship is seen as biased and unreliable (Sanera and Shaw 1999; Williams 2000). Moreover, this research does not cover popular culture. I am therefore forced to make tentative statements here, backed up by my attention to this phenomenon in the United States and Europe over a period of seventeen years of personal observation and, it should be said, with the assistance of my son, who parried my constant questions and critical observations with his own and brought to me numerous examples of this material as he came to understand my interest in it. So I thank Hart Sturgeon-Reed for his research assistance. I would also like to thank the Center for Cultural Studies at UCSC, Patsy Hallen and Peter Newman of the Institute for the Study of Technology and Policy at Murdoch University, and the many audiences whose comments contributed to this final version. In addition, I am indebted to Rachel Stein and anonymous reviewers for their excellent suggestions concerning a previous version of this essay published in Stein 2004. This chapter is dedicated to Zoë Sofoulis, who over the years has taught me a lot about the problems with Planeteer tendencies, especially my own.

3. A worthwhile research endeavor would be to explore the reception of these children's products in different cultural contexts, in which I would expect to find them the subject of surprising and different narrative reconstructions and oppositional practices. This should be true not only in non-U.S. contexts but also in subjugated cultural contexts internal to the United States. In particular, it would be interesting to examine the films of Hayao Miyazaki, especially *Monoke-hime* (in English, *Princess Monoke*; 1997). Miyazaki's films have strong environmentalist themes, strong young girls as heroines, anticorporate messages, and fascinating depictions of social difference.

4. In the post-9/11 context, we seem to be seeing a revival of the binary, black-versus-white framework familiar from the cold war era. The *Spy Kids* mov-

ies, the *Star Wars* prequel trilogy, and the *Lord of the Rings* trilogy are just some examples of children's movies moving away from an environmentalist framework to a Manichean vision like that of the second Bush administration (though in Episode Six of the *Star Wars* movies, *Revenge of the Sith*, a critique of the Bush vision finally appears—a bit late, I would say, despite Lucas's good intentions).

5. A student of mine makes the excellent point that the third hyena, Ed, is a disabled character, presented as mentally challenged and almost unable to talk (Schatz 2007). This makes the Nazi imagery even more faulty, as disabled people were among their targets, not acceptable as loyal followers.

6. Audiences to early versions of this chapter as a talk have disputed my characterization of *The Lion King* as homophobic by pointing out that *The Lion King*, whose famous musical team included the openly gay Sir Elton John, also portrays a happy and helpful gay male couple in the loving and committed relationship of Timon the meerkat and Pumbaa the warthog. Though I think this is an accurate reading of a relationship that should have been far scarier to the Jerry Falwells of the world than the proclivities of the purple Teletubby, Tinky-Wink, or Spongebob Squarepants (and despite the further celebration of this loving relationship between two male animals found in the television spin-off of *The Lion King*, *Timon and Pumbaa*), the central resolution of the plot in *The Lion King* requires the restoration of Simba to the throne and to a heterosexual, nuclear family form quite unlike that of real lions.

7. Another student of mine has pointed out that the family in *Over the Hedge* (2006) is an example of a positive depiction of a non-nuclear family in that the animals gathered under the guidance of the turtle, Vern, are from different species and play multiple familial roles. She also points out that the family is still a patriarchal one, however (Day 2007).

8. Though I strongly believe in this positive reading of *Babe*, the movie is alarmingly sexist in its portrayal of the farmwife. For other analyses of the non-naturalizing effect of *Babe*, as well as other interesting insights into the message of the movie, see Plumwood 2002, esp. 600–606.

9. I have written elsewhere about the dangers of assuming that racial balance in numbers is the solution to creating effective antiracist coalition politics (Sturgeon 1997).

10. "Mission to Save Planet Earth" section of *Captain Planet* Web site, http://www.turner.com/planet/static/index.html.

11. The idea for *Captain Planet* came from Ted Turner in 1989. *Captain Planet*'s first season aired in 1990, and a second, called *The New Adventures of Captain Planet*, aired in 1993, both on Turner Broadcasting System ("Mission to Save Earth," http://www.turner.com/planet/static/index.html). Altogether, there were six seasons and 114 episodes ("Episode Listing," http://www.turner.com/planet/static/index.html).

12. For "Planeteer Alert" tips, see http://www.turner.com/planet/static/alerts.html.

13. See http://captainplanetfoundation.org, retrieved July 29, 2007. The information on the Atlanta Braves event was retrieved from an earlier version of the Web site on April 14, 1998.

14. From "Mission to Save Planet Earth," http://www.turner.com/planet/static/alerts.html. The last sentence I quote here was on the Web site in 1998 but had been removed by 2002.

15. See "Ecovillains," http://www.turner.com/planet/static/heros.html.

16. See "Captain Planet's Top Ten Ecotips," http://www.turner.com/planet/static/index.html; "How You Can Help," http://captainplanetfoundation.org/default.aspx?pid=32&tab=environment.

Chapter 5. Penguin Family Values

1. In considering these questions, I have greatly benefited from the help of others. An earlier version of this chapter was accepted for publication in Sandilands and Erickson's edited collection of essays, with a working title of *Queer Ecologies: Sex, Nature, Biopolitics and Desire*. Thanks to all of the participants in the Queer Ecologies workshop for their excellent feedback (fairy penguins unite!), with special thanks to Cate Sandilands and Bruce Erickson for their support. Thanks also to Nishant Shahani for his insightful suggestions and to Hart Sturgeon-Reed for his technical assistance with retrieving and capturing photos, films, and ads and for his T-shirt's motto, "One by one, the penguins steal my sanity."

2. For example, one of the most powerful contemporary popular discourses that naturalize inequality is genetic determinism (see chapter 6).

3. For discussions of toxins in the environment that are affecting human fertility, see Di Chiro n.d. and Colborn, Dumanoski, and Myers 1997. The science on this issue is still preliminary, but indications are that chemicals commonly found in plastics may mimic or disrupt endocrine systems, producing results such as falling sperm counts in men, reproductive system diseases in women (including cancer), and learning disabilities in children (Cone 2007). If these data prove convincing in the long run, the impact of these toxins on human reproduction may (ironically) produce a crisis of underpopulation, rather than the overpopulation that many mainstream environmentalists worry about now. The movie *Children of Men* (2006), with its dystopian vision of a world without new babies, may well seem prescient.

4. For an example of how fundamentalist Christians describe the proper relationship between husband and wife, see Christian Answers 2006.

5. See letters by Michael Shober, Gitta Zomorodi, and Rick White in "About That March" in the Science Times letters section of *New York Times*, September 20, 2005, p. D4.

6. Attempts to either remove *And Tango Makes Three* from libraries or to move it from children's fiction to areas of the libraries less likely for children to go to on their own were made in Illinois, Missouri, Georgia, Tennessee, North Carolina, Iowa, and Wisconsin (Huh 2006).

7. See http://www.ananova.com/news/story/sm_1275591.html and http://www.ananova.com/news/story/sm_1284769.html.

8. The origin of Gay Penguin for President was a little more complex than this. According to the creator of the site, Scout Thompson (who may also be the video artist Eryk Salvaggio), the idea for the site came from a "guy on a NYC subway who my friend asked if he would vote for Giuliani again, a few years back. 'Fuck Giuliani.' He said. 'I'd vote for a hamburger. I would vote for a gay guy in a spacesuit.'" Thompson, in response, started a campaign for "Gay Guy In A Spacesuit for President." Later he decided that "a Gay Penguin might be more sophisticated. . . . [A] Gay Penguin wouldn't have got us into war, wouldn't have given us this deficit, wouldn't lose this many jobs, and would, in fact, allow Gays the right to marry. I would actually vote for a Gay Penguin over George Bush because, literally, a gay penguin would do a better job running the country than our current President." See http://www.one38.org/a177/2004_02_08_archive.html.

9. See letters by John Karl, Louis Kalikow, and Sharon Raymond in "About That March" in the Science Times letters section of New York Times, September 20, 2005, p. D4.

10. In an article by Hillary Mayell, several scientists point out the ways in which anthropomorphizing penguin mating and sexual behavior as "love" produces misleading understandings of penguin behavior. But as marine biologist Gerald Kooyman says in this article, "Simplifying some aspects of the penguins' life story makes it more accessible to the general public" (Mayell 2005). What I would point out is that this form of heteronormative romanticizing is not merely simplifying but conveys a normative ideology.

11. New York Times, June 17, 2006, p. A23.

12. For an important discussion of the racist and heterosexist implications of the use of the concept of species, see McWhorter n.d.

13. The main groups of Alaskan Natives are Athabascans, Aleuts, Alutiiqs, Tlingit/Haidas, Inupiaqs, and Yup'iks. Athabascans live in the central-eastern part of Alaska. The Aleuts (not their name but the Russian label for the people) and the Alutiiqs live along the Aleutian Archipelago to the southwest. The closely related Haida and Tlingit groups live in southeastern Alaska, the southwest of Yukon Territory, and northwestern British Columbia. The Inupiaqs live in the northern Alaskan interior and on the Seward Peninsula. The Yu'piks, or Yupiits, live in western Alaska, along the Bering Sea coast and inland, and on St. Lawrence Island, which is forty miles from the Siberian coast, home to the Siberian Yu'piks in what is now Russia. Other Arctic First Peoples include the Samis, indigenous to what is now Scandinavia and Greenland (who have an immigrant presence in the Alaskan area, along with their reindeer), the Canadian Inuits, the Inuvialits of western Canada, and the Kalaaiits, or Greenlanders. With a reliance on fishing and hunting (particularly of caribou, elk, moose, whales, and seals), the Arctic indigenous history of living off the land

extends at least as far back as 400 BC. Extensive knowledge of animal behavior and weather patterns were essential to their survival for this long period of time (Chaussonet 1995).

14. Because of the transnational context of these peoples' homelands, Arctic indigenous political activism spans several national locations and has been intervening in the international arena for some time; see the work of the Inuit Circumpolar Conference (www.inuitcircumpolar.com) and the Circumpolar Conservation Union (www.circumpolar.org). In December 2005, the Inuit Circumpolar Conference submitted a petition to the Inter-American Human Rights Commission saying that the United States was denying the Arctic indigenous peoples their human rights by refusing to halt greenhouse gas emissions (Crowley and Fenge 2005). The petition was denied.

15. I discuss the problems with the environmentalist use of the Earth-seen-from-space image in chapter 3. Also see Garb 1990.

Chapter 6. Planetary Security, Militarism, and the Nature of Violence

1. This chapter has had several previous lives and thus has incurred multiple obligations. An early version was first given as a speech at the Public Environmental Law Conference at the University of Oregon on the eve of the 2003 invasion of Iraq. I thank Chaone Mallory for her invitation and intelligent responses to my argument. A more developed written version was presented to the faculty in the International Christian University (Japan)/Washington State University (U.S.A.) Partnership for Peace, Security and Kyosei, and I thank all of the participants, but especially Professors Chin Shiba and Noriko Kawamura, for their insightful comments. Once again, I must thank Hart Sturgeon-Reed for his research assistance, particularly his help with finding various video games focused on war.

2. Somewhere between 5 million and 30 million people marched in coordinated protests around the world the week of February 8–15, 2003. Despite disagreement on the numbers, sources agree that these were the largest coordinated antiwar demonstrations ever seen (Frenkel 2003; Koch 2003; Leupp 2003; McFadden 2003; Reed 2005).

3. Much literature exists on the arguments pro and con about whether genes determine human behavior. For critical arguments against genetic determinism, see Duster 2003; Geller et al. 2004; Hubbard and Wald 1997; Lewontin, Rose, and Kamin 1984; and Nelkin and Linee 2004.

4. This is the position my son takes when I express my concern over violence in video games. He contends that he can distinguish between real violence and game play, and he argues that it would be better to play out international conflicts through video-game contests rather than real wars, like a cyborg version of the original idea behind the Olympic Games. The idea of video-game players (mostly male but increasingly female)—stereotypically

post-adolescent, geeky, brainy, and far from the tough, brutal masculinist ideal promoted by violent products in popular culture—deciding world-changing questions about territories, political dominance, and economic control is somewhat stunning but intriguing. (A version of this idea animates the science fiction novel *Ender's Game*, by Orson Scott Card [1991/1997]), resulting in less positive outcomes than my son's vision.) Violence in popular culture may not directly translate into violence in real life, yet the sexism and racism of many of these video game products still create a "dreamworld" (*Dreamworlds II* [1997]) for young males that undoubtedly affects their apprehension of their identities and their life choices, legitimating violence as effective and pleasurable. Hence, unless video games and video game players changed considerably, I would be wary of giving them the decision-making power in this way (despite my confidence in my son's decisions).

5. As in chapter 3, I use this formatting of the term, *huMANs*, to point to the feminist critique of the use of the concept of "humanity" as a universalism that obscures male privilege and advantage and normatively places men in the position of representing all humans. Here, I am using the term to stress that in the narrative of natural determinism that I am critiquing, while war is seen as an inevitable outcome of "human" nature, what is really meant is that men are naturally prone to kill each other.

6. See Revolutionary Association of the Women of Afghanistan Web site, http://rawa.fancymarketing.net/index.html.

7. See Center for American Women in Politics Web site, http://www.cawp.rutgers.edu/Facts.html.

Chapter 7. Purity and Privilege or Justice and Sustainability?

1. See, for some examples of the debate around microcredit, the exchange between Susan Davis, the president of Grameen Bank (the initiator of microcredit programs), and Vandana Shiva, the Indian ecofeminist scientist and activist (*Democracy Now!* [2006]) and the exchange between Bowman and Stone (2007) and Leonard and Leonard (2007). When Mohammed Yunus, the founder of Grameen Bank, won the Nobel Peace Prize on December 9, 2006, this debate was reenergized, and one can find countless references to the issues in the mainstream and alternative press in late 2006 and early 2007.

References

Books and Articles

Abdela, Leslie. 2004. "No place for a woman." In *The W effect: Bush's war on women*, ed. L. Flanders, 258–62. Old Westbury, NY: Feminist Press.

Adams, Carol. 1999. *The sexual politics of meat: A feminist-vegetarian critical theory*. 10th anniversary edition. New York: Continuum Press.

Adamson, Joni, Mei Mei Evans, and Rachel Stein, eds. 2002. *The environmental justice reader: Politics, poetics and pedagogy*. Tucson: University of Arizona Press.

Alaimo, Stacey. n.d. "Posthuman desire: Queer animals, science studies, and environmental theory." In *Queer ecologies: Sex, nature, biopolitics, desire*, ed. Catriona Sandilands and Bruce Erickson. Publication pending.

Alonso, Harriet. 1993. *Peace as a women's issue*. Syracuse, NY: Syracuse University Press.

Amnesty International. 2004. *Darfur: Rape as a weapon of war: Sexual violence and its consequences*. July 19. http://web.amnesty.org/library/index/engafr 540762004.

Anderson, Sarah, ed. 2007. "Wal-Mart's sustainability initiative: A civil society critique." Report coordinated by Trina Tocco. Big Box Collective. September 6. http://www.bbc.wikispaces.net/space/showimage/ CounterSustainability.

Applegate, K. A. 1997. *The change*. Animorph series, vol. 13. New York: Scholastic.

Austin, Jay, and Carl E. Bruch, eds. 2000. *The environmental consequences of war: Legal, economic and scientific perspectives*. Boston, MA: Cambridge University Press.

Bacchetta, Paola, Tina Campt, Inderpal Grewal, Caren Kaplan, Minoo

Moallem, and Jennifer Terry. 2001. "Transnational feminist practices against war." Circulated on the Internet Sept./Oct. 2001; reprinted in *The W effect: Bush's war on women*, ed. L. Flanders, 263–67. Old Westbury, NY: Feminist Press.

Bagemihl, Bruce. 1999. *Biological exuberance: Animal homosexuality and natural diversity*. New York: St. Martin's Press.

Barthes, Roland. [1956] 1972. *Mythologies*. Trans. Annette Lavers. New York: Hill and Wang.

Beale, Frances. 1970. "Double jeopardy: To be black and female." In *The Black woman*, ed. Toni Cade Bambara, 90–100. York, ON: Mentor Books.

Beneria, Lourdes. 2003. *Gender, development and globalization: Economics as if people mattered*. New York: Routledge.

Berger, John. 1972. *Ways of Seeing*. New York: Penguin.

Berlant, Lauren. 1997. *The queen of America goes to Washington City*. Durham, NC: Duke University Press.

———, and Michael Warner. 1998. "Sex in public." *Critical Inquiry* 24 (winter): 547–566.

Bird, Elizabeth. 1987. "The social construction of nature: Theoretical approaches to the history of environmental problems." *Environmental Review* 11, no. 4: 255–64.

Boeing. 2000. "Boeing advertising campaign rolls out." Press release, May 1. http://www.boeing.com/news/releases/2000/news_release_000501c.html.

Bowman, Betsy, and Bob Stone. 2007. "Can Grameen Bank–style microcredit eliminate poverty?" Center for Global Justice/Centro para la Justicia Global. http://www.globaljusticecenter.org/articles/report_microcredit.htm.

Brecher, Jeremy, Tim Costello, and Brendan Smith. 2000. *Globalization from below*. Boston: South End Press.

Brown, Wilmette. 1983. *Black women and the peace movement*. London: Falling Wall Press.

Brulle, Robert J., and David Naguib Pellow. 2005. "The future of environmental justice movements." In *Power, justice, and the environment*, ed. David Naguib Pellow and Robert J. Brulle, 293–300. Boston: MIT Press.

Buell, Lawrence. 2005. *The future of environmental criticism*. Malden, MA: Blackwell Publishing.

Bullard, Robert, ed. 1994. *Unequal protection: Environmental justice and communities of color*. San Francisco: Sierra Club Books.

———. 2005. *The quest for environmental justice: Human rights and the politics of pollution*. San Francisco: Sierra Club Books.

Bunch, Charlotte. 2002. "Whose security?" *Nation*, Oct. 23.

Burbick, Joan. 2006. *Gun show nation*. New York: New Press.

Bush, George W. 2004. "A renewed spirit of discovery: President Bush announces a new vision for space exploration program," Address delivered January 14, 2004, at NASA Headquarters, Washington, DC. http://www.whitehouse.gov/news/releases/2004/01/20040114-3.html.

Campbell, Joseph, with Bill Moyers. 1988. *The power of myth*. New York: Doubleday.

Card, Orson Scott. [1991] 1997. *Ender's Game*. 3rd ed. New York: Tom Doherty Associates.

Carson, Rachel. 1962. *Silent spring*. Boston: Houghton Mifflin.

Center for American Women in Politics. 2007. "Facts and Findings." http://www.cawp.rutgers.edu/Facts.html.

Chaussonet, Valerie. 1995. *Crossroads Alaska*. Washington, DC: Arctic Studies Center/Smithsonian.

Chea, Terence. 2004. "Immigration debate fuels battle over Sierra Club's fate." *Boston Globe*, Feb. 18. http://www.boston.com/news/nation/articles/2004/02/18/immigration_debate_fuels_battle_over_sierra_clubs_fate/.

Chivers, C. J. 2007. "Eyeing future wealth, Russians plant the flag on the Arctic seabed, below the polar cap," *New York Times*, Aug. 3, 2007, p. A8.

Christian Answers. 2006. "Should Christians support women's liberation movements?" http://www.christiananswers.net/q-eden/edn-f003.html.

Clark, Jerry L. 1985. "Thus spoke Chief Seattle: The story of an undocumented speech." *Prologue* 18, no. 10 (spring). National Archives. http://www.archives.gov/publications/prologue/1985/spring/chief-seattle.html.

Cochran, Patricia. 2007. "Arctic Natives left out in the cold." *BBC News*, Jan. 4. http://news.bbc.co.uk/2/hi/science/nature/6230731.stm.

Colborn, Theo, Dianne Dumanoski, and John Peterson Myers. 1997. *Our stolen future: Are we threatening our fertility, intelligence and survival?* New York: Plume/Penguin.

Cone, Marla. 2007. "Scientists: Plastics Pose Risk." *Los Angeles Times*, Aug. 3. http://www.latimes.com/news/science/la-na-plastic3aug03,1,7038922.story?coll=la-news-science&ctrack=1&cset=true.

Coontz, Stephanie. 1992. *The way we never were: American families and the nostalgia trap*. New York: Basic Books.

Cooper, James Fenimore. [1826] 1958. *The last of the Mohicans*. Ed. William Charvat. Boston: Houghton Mifflin.

Cronkite, E. P., R. A. Conrad, and V. P. Bond. 1997. "Historical events associated with fallout from BRAVO Shot/Operation Castle and 25 years of medical findings." *Health Physics: The Radiation Protection Journal* 73, no. 1: 176–87.

Cronon, William, ed. 1996. *Uncommon ground: Toward reinventing nature.* New York: W. W. Norton.

Crowley, Paul, and Terry Fenge. 2005. "Inuit petition Inter-American Commission on Human Rights to oppose climate change caused by the United States of America." Inuit Circumpolar Council. http://www .inuitcircumpolar.com/index.php?ID=316&Lang=En.

Cuomo, Christine. 1998. *Feminism and ecological communities: An ethic of flourishing.* New York: Routledge.

Danaher, Kevin, Shannon Biggs, and Jason Marks. 2007. *Building the green economy: Success stories from the grassroots.* A Global Exchange Book. Sausalito, CA: Polipoint Press.

Darnovsky, Marcy. 1991. "Stories less told: Histories of U.S. environmentalism." *Socialist Review* 22 (1991): 11–54.

———, Barbara Epstein, and Richard Flacks, eds. 1995. *Cultural politics and social movements.* Philadelphia: Temple University Press.

Dauer, Susan Jaye. 2004. "Cartoons and contamination: How the multinational kids of Captain Planet save Gaia." In *Wild things: Children's culture and ecocriticism,* ed. Sidney J. Dobrin and Kenneth B. Kidd, 254–66. Detroit, MI: Wayne State University Press.

Davis, Susan. 1996. "Touch the magic." In *Uncommon ground,* ed. William Cronon, 204–17. New York: W. W. Norton.

Day, Robin. 2007. "Female and family roles as they relate to environmentalism in the film *Over the Hedge.*" Unpublished ms.

Di Chiro, Giovanna. 1992. "Defining environmental justice: Women's voices and grassroots politics." *Socialist Review* 22, no. 4: 599–617.

———. 2008. "Living environmentalisms: Coalition politics, social reproduction, and environmental justice." *Environmental Politics* 17, no. 2 (2008): 276–98.

———. n.d. "Polluted politics? In(toxic)ating alliances for environmental justice." In *Queer ecologies: Sex, nature, biopolitics, desire,* ed. Catriona Sandilands and Bruce Erickson. Publication pending.

Dobrin, Sidney, and Kenneth Kidd, eds. 2004. *Wild things: Children's culture and ecocriticism.* Detroit, MI: Wayne State University.

Doctors without Borders. 2005. "The crushing burden of rape: Sexual violence in Darfur." March 8. http://www.doctorswithoutborders.org/ publications/reports/2005/sudan03.pdf.

Dugger, Celia. 2004. "Debate stirs over tiny loans for world's poorest." *New York Times*, April 29. http://query.nytimes.com/gst/fullpage.html?res =9D07E4D8163DF93AA15757C0A9629C8B63&scp=1&sq=Dugger %2C++April+29%2C+2004&st=nyt.

Duster, Troy. 2003. *Backdoor to eugenics*. New York: Routledge.

Eaton, Heater, ed. 2003. *Ecofeminism and globalization*. Lanham, MD: Rowman and Littlefield.

Ebbe, Obi N. I., and Dilip K. Das. 2008. *Global trafficking in women and children*. Boca Raton, FL: CRC Press (Taylor and Francis).

Edelman, Lee. 2004. *No future: Queer theory and the death drive*. Durham, NC: Duke University Press.

Ehrenreich, Barbara, and Arlie Russell Hochschild, eds. 2002. *Global woman: Nannies, maids, and sex workers in the new economy*. New York: Metropolitan Books.

Elliot, Stuart. 2007. "A procession of penguins arrives on Madison Avenue," *New York Times*, Jan. 10. http://www.nytimes.com/2007/01/10/business/ media/10adco.html?ex=1184043600&en=efcbe26c4bea35f0&ei=5087& mkt=bizphoto.

Enloe, Cynthia. 2000. *Maneuvers: The international politics of militarizing women's lives*. Berkeley: University of California Press.

———. 2001. *Bananas, beaches and bases: Making feminist sense of international politics*. Rev. ed. Berkeley: University of California Press.

———. 2004. *The curious feminist: Searching for women in a new age of empire*. Berkeley: University of California Press.

Epstein, Barbara. 1991. *Political protest and cultural revolution: Nonviolent direct action in the 1970s and 1980s*. Berkeley: University of California Press.

Featherstone, Liza. 2004. "Mighty in Pink." In *The W effect: Bush's war on women*, ed. L. Flanders, 244–49. Old Westbury, NY: Feminist Press.

Feinman, Ilene. 2000. *Citizenship rites: Feminist soldiers and feminist antimilitarists*. New York: NYU Press.

FINCA. n.d. "This woman doesn't need your charity." Brochure. Washington, DC: FINCA International.

Fisher, Elizabeth. 1975. *Women's creation: Sexual evolution and the shaping of society*. New York: McGraw-Hill.

Fiske, John. 1989. *Understanding popular culture*. New York: Routledge.

Flanders, Laura, ed. 2004. *The W effect: Bush's war on women*. Old Westbury, NY: Feminist Press.

Forster, E. M. [1924] 1989. *A passage to India*. Orlando, FL: Harcourt Brace.

Foucault, Michel. 1980. *Power/Knowledge: Selected interviews and other writings, 1972–1977*. Ed. and trans. Colin Gordon. New York: Pantheon Press.

Frank, Thomas. 2004. *What's the matter with Kansas?* New York: Henry Holt.

Frenkel, Glenn. 2003. "Millions worldwide protest Iraq War." *Washington Post*, Feb. 16, p. A.01.

Gaard, Greta. 1993. *Women, animals and nature.* Philadelphia: Temple University Press.

————, and Patrick Murphy, eds. 1998. *Ecofeminist literary criticism: Theory, interpretation, pedagogy.* Champaign: University of Illinois Press.

Gaiam. 2007. *Gaiam-Living: Harmony.* Spring catalog.

Gaiam: A Lifestyle Company. 2008. http://gaiam.com.

GamePro, The. 2005. "Next-generation war." July, no. 202: 28–46.

Garb, Yaakov. 1990. "Perspective or escape? Ecofeminist musings on contemporary earth imagery." In *Reweaving the world*, ed. Irene Diamond and Gloria Orenstein, 264–78. San Francisco: Sierra Club.

Geller, Lisa, Joseph S. Alper, Catherine Ard, Adrienne Asch, and Jon Beckwith, eds. 2004. *The double-edged helix: Social implications of genetics in a diverse society.* Baltimore, MD: Johns Hopkins University Press.

Global Women's Strike. 2003. "Letter to feminists in the US." February 3. http://www.globalwomenstrike.net/English/a_letter_to_us_feminists .htm.

Gogoi, Pallavi. 2006. "Wal-Mart's organic offensive." *Business Week*, March 29. http://www.businessweek.com/bwdaily/dnflash/mar2006/nf2006 0329_6971.htm.

Gosine, Andil. 1994. "Roots of flight: Environmental refugees in Latin America." *Refuge* 15, no. 2: 27–32.

————. 2005. "Dying planet, deadly people: 'Race'-sex anxieties and alternative globalizations." *Social Justice* 32, no. 4: 69–86.

Gottlieb, Robert. 1993. *Forcing the spring: The transformation of the American environmental movement.* Washington, DC: Island Press.

Grahame, Kenneth. [1908] 1983. *The wind in the willows.* 75th anniversary edition. Boston: Atheneum.

Gramsci, Antonio. 1971. *Selections from "The Prison Notebooks."* Ed. and trans. Quentin Hoare and Geoffrey Nowell Smith. New York: International Publishers.

Griffin, Susan. 1978. *Woman and nature.* New York: Harper and Row.

Grossman, Zoltan. 1995. "Linking the Native movement for sovereignty and the environmental movement." *Z Magazine* 8, no. 18 (Nov.): 42–50.

Guha, Ramachandra. 1989. "Radical American environmentalism and wilderness preservation: A third world critique." *Environmental Ethics* 11, no. 1:71–83.

————, and Joan [Juan] Martínez-Alier. 1997. *Varieties of environmentalism: Essays North and South*. London: Earthscan Publications.

Gunn, Ian. 2007. "Canada to reclaim Arctic waters." *BBC News Online*, July 10. http://news.bbc.co.uk/go/pr/fr/-/2/hi/americas/6287436.stm.

Hall, Sarah. 2004. "Jackson can't heal the world." *E! Online*, March 24. http://www.eonline.com/News/Items/0,1,13776,00.html?newsrellink.

Hansen, Randel. 2005. "The future is now: Arcs of globalization, indigenous communities, and climate change." Presentation at the American Studies Association Annual Meeting, Washington, DC, November.

Haraway, Donna. 1989. *Primate visions: Gender, race, and nature in the world of modern science*. London: Routledge.

————. 1991. *Simians, cyborgs, and women: The reinvention of nature*. New York: Routledge.

————. 1992. "The promises of monsters: A regenerated politics for inappropriate/d others." In *Cultural Studies*, ed. Lawrence Grossberg, Cary Nelson, and Paula Triechler, 295–337. New York: Routledge.

————. 1995. "Otherworldly conversations, terran topics, local terms." In *Biopolitics: A feminist and ecological reader on biotechnology*, ed. Vandana Shiva and Ingunn Moser, 62–92. London: Zed Books.

————. 2004. "Cyborgs to companion species: Reconfiguring kinship in technoscience." In *The Haraway Reader*, 298–320. New York: Routledge.

Hartsock, Nancy. 1983. *Money, sex and power*. New York: Longman.

Hausdoerffer, John. 2004. "George Catlin and the politics of nature." Ph.D. diss., American Studies Program, Washington State University.

Hawken, Paul, Amory Lovins, and L. Hunter Lovins. 2000. *Natural capitalism: Creating the next industrial revolution*. Boston: Back Bay Books.

Henderson, Hazel, with Simran Sethi. 2006. *Ethical markets: Growing the green economy*. White River Junction, VT: Chelsea Green Publishing.

Hollander, Jack M. 2003. *The real environmental crisis: Why poverty, not affluence, is the environment's number one enemy*. Berkeley: University of California Press.

Hossay, Patrick. 2006. *Unsustainable: A primer for global environmental and social justice*. New York: Zed Press.

Howard, Philip H. 2008. "Graphics showing organic industry structure." http://www.msu.edu/%7Ehowardp/organicindustry.html.

Hubbard, Ruth, and Elijah Wald. 1997. *Exploding the gene myth*. Boston: Beacon Press.

Huh, Nam Y. 2006. "Schools chief bans book on penguins." *Boston Globe*, Dec. 20. http://www.boston.com/news/nation/articles/2006/12/20/schools_chief_bans_book_on_penguins/.

Hull, Gloria, Patricia Bell Scott, and Barbara Smith, eds. [1982] 2003. *(All the women are white, all the men are black) But some of us are brave: Black women's studies.* Old Westbury, NY: Feminist Press.

Ingram, David. 2000. *Green screen: Environmentalism and Hollywood cinema.* Exeter, UK: University of Exeter Press.

International Peace Research Institute (PRIO). 2001. *Gender, peace and conflict.* London: Sage Publications.

Iverson, Ed. 2006. Opinion. *Moscow-Pullman Daily News*, weekend edition, Dec. 2–3, p. 7D.

Jeffers, Susan. 1991. *Brother eagle, sister sky: A message from Chief Seattle.* New York: Scholastic.

Kaiser, Rudolph. 1987. "Chief Seattle's speech(es): American origins and European reception." In *Recovering the word: Essays on Native American literature*, ed. Brian Swann and Arnold Krupat, 497–536. Berkeley: University of California Press.

Kasdan, Margo, and Susan Tavernetti. 1998. *Critical eye: An introduction to looking at movies.* Dubuque, IA: Kendall/Hunt.

Kastel, Mark. 2006. "Wal-Mart: The nation's largest grocer rolls out organic products: Market expansion or market delusion?" White paper, Cornucopia Institute, Sept. 27. http://www.cornucopia.org/WalMart/WalMart_White_Paper.pdf.

Kempadoo, Kamala, and Jo Doezema. 1998. *Global sex workers: Rights, resistance and redefinition.* New York: Routledge.

Kennedy, John F. 1961. "Special message to the Congress on urgent national needs." May 25. http://www.jfklibrary.org/j052561.htm.

———. 1962. "Address at Rice University on the nation's space effort." Sept. 12. http://www.jfklibrary.org/Historical+Resources/Archives/Reference+Desk/Speeches/JFK/003POF03SpaceEffort09121962.htm.

Kilpatrick, Jacquelyn. 1999. *Celluloid Indians.* Lincoln: University of Nebraska Press.

Klare, Michael. 2004. *Blood and oil: The dangers and consequences of America's growing petroleum dependency.* New York: Metropolitan Books.

Knobloch, Frieda. 1996. *The culture of wilderness: Agriculture as colonization in the American West.* Chapel Hill: University of North Carolina Press.

Koch, Connie, ed. 2003. *2/15.* New York: HELLO and AK Press.

Kolodny, Annette. 1975. *The lay of the land: Metaphor as experience and history in American life and letters.* Chapel Hill: University of North Carolina Press.

———. 1984. *The land before her: Fantasy and experience of the American frontiers, 1630–1860.* Chapel Hill: University of North Carolina Press.

————. 2007. "Rethinking the 'Ecological Indian': A Penobscot Precursor." *ISLE: Interdisciplinary Studies in Literature and Environment* 14, no. 1 (winter): 1–23.

Krech, Shepard, III. 1999. *The ecological Indian*. New York: W. W. Norton.

Krupnik, Igor, and Dyanna Jolly, eds. 2002. *The earth is faster now: Indigenous observations of Arctic environmental change*. Fairbanks, AK: ARCUS (Arctic Research Consortium of the United States).

Kuletz, Valerie. 1998. *The tainted desert: Environmental and social ruin in the American West*. London: Routledge.

LaDuke, Winona. 1999. *All our relations: Native struggles for land and life*. Boston: South End Press.

Lancaster, Roger N. 2003. *The trouble with nature: Sex in science and popular culture*. Berkeley: University of California Press.

LeGuin, Ursula K. 1989. "The carrier bag theory of fiction." In LeGuin, *Dancing at the edge of the world: Thoughts on words, women and places*, 165–70. New York: Grove Press.

Leonard, Bob, and Sue Leonard. 2007. "Microcredit and microfinance issues: Response to Betsy Bowman and Bob Stone's article on microcredit." Center for Global Justice/Centro para la Justicia Global. http://www.globaljusticecenter.org/articles/report_microcredit_REPLY1.htm.

Leupp, Gary. 2003. *Counterpunch*. Feb. 25. http://www.counterpunch.org/leupp02252003.html.

Lewontin, Richard, Steven Rose, and Leon J. Kamin. 1984. *Not in our genes: Biology, ideology, and human nature*. New York: Pantheon.

Lichtenstein, Nelson, ed. 2006. *Wal-Mart: The face of twenty-first-century capitalism*. New York: New Press.

Litfin, Karen. 1997. "The gendered eye in the sky: A feminist perspective on earth observation satellites." *Frontiers: A Journal of Women's Studies* 18, no. 2:26–47.

Lowe, Lisa. 1996. *Immigrant acts: On Asian American cultural politics*. Durham, NC: Duke University Press.

Luke, Timothy. 1997. *Ecocritique: Contesting the politics of nature, economy, and culture*. Minneapolis: University of Minnesota Press.

Lyall, Sarah. 2006. "Aid workers are said to abuse girls." *New York Times*, May 9, p. A8.

Mageo, Jeannette. 2004. "Migratory femininity in cultural fantasies, male gender instability, and war." Paper presented at the Gendering Research across the Campuses Conference, Washington State University.

Martínez-Alier, Joan [Juan]. 2002. *The environmentalism of the poor*. Cheltenham, UK: Elgar.

Martinot, Steve. 2007. "Militarism and Global Warming." *Synthesis/Regeneration* 42 (winter). http://www.greens.org/s-r/42/42–06.html.

Marx, Leo. 1964. *The machine in the garden: Technology and the pastoral ideal in America*. New York: Oxford University Press.

May, Elaine Tyler. 1999. *Homeward bound: American families in the cold war era*. New York: Basic Books.

Mayell, Hillary. 2005. "March of the penguins: Too lovey-dovey to be true?" *National Geographic News*, Aug. 19. http://news.nationalgeographic.com/news/2005/08/0819_050819_march_penguins.html.

Mazin, Victor, and Clessia Tourkina. 1998. "The golem of consciousness: Mythogeny's lift-off." Trans. Thomas Campbell. *Cultural Studies* 12, no. 2: 210–33.

MacDonald, Peter. 1980. "Navajo natural resources." In *American Indian environments: Ecological issues in Native American history*, ed. Christopher Vecsey and Robert W. Venables, 162–70. Syracuse: University of Syracuse Press.

McFadden, Robert D. 2003. "From New York to Melbourne, cries for peace." *New York Times*, Feb. 16, p. A1.

McWhorter, Ladelle. n.d. "Enemies of the species." In *Queer ecologies: Sex, nature, biopolitics, desire*, ed. Catriona Sandilands and Bruce Erickson. Publication pending.

Medved, Michael. 2006. "Don't be misled by crappy feet!" Nov. 17. http://michaelmedved.townhall.com/blog/g/5094f586–fed7-4cf4–872c-d20b94c78024.

Mellor, Mary. 1992. *Breaking the boundaries: Towards a feminist green socialism*. London: Virago Press.

Merchant, Carolyn. 1980. *The death of nature: Women, ecology and the scientific revolution*. New York: HarperOne.

———. 1992. *Radical ecology*. New York: Routledge.

———. 1996. *Earthcare: Women and the environment*. New York: Routledge.

———. 2004. *Reinventing Eden: The fate of nature in Western culture*. New York: Routledge.

Miller, Jonathan. 2006. "March of the conservatives: Penguin film as political fodder." *New York Times*, Sept. 13, p. D2.

Mies, Maria, and Vandana Shiva. 1993. *Ecofeminism*. London: Zed Press.

Mitman, Gregg. 1999. *Reel nature: America's romance with wildlife on film*. Cambridge, MA: Harvard University Press.

Morgan, Edmund S. 1975. *American slavery, American freedom: The ordeal of colonial Virginia*. New York: W. W. Norton.

Nash, Roderick Frazier. 2001. *Wilderness and the American mind*. 4th ed. New Haven, CT: Yale University Press.

Nelkin, Dorothy, and M. Susan Linee. 2004. *The DNA mystique: The gene as cultural icon*. Ann Arbor: University of Michigan Press.

Noble, Holcomb B. 1985. "Pondering man in 'The Emerald Forest.'" *New York Times*, June 30. http://movies2.nytimes.com/mem/movies/review.html?_r=2&title1=EMERALD%20FOREST%2c%20THE%20%28MOVIE%29&title2=&reviewer=Holcomb%20B%2e%20Noble&pdate=&v_id=15687&oref.

Omi, Michael, and Howard Winant. 1986. *Racial formation in the United States*. New York: Routledge and Kegan Paul.

O'Neill, Gerard K. 1976. *The high frontier: Human colonies in space*. New York: Morrow.

Ortner, Sherry. 1974. "Is female to male as nature is to culture?" In *Woman, culture and society*, ed. Louise Lamphere and Michelle Rosaldo, 7–88. Palo Alto, CA: Stanford University Press.

Padmanabhan, K. P. 2001. "Poverty, microcredit and Mahatma Gandhi: Lessons for donors." *International Social Science Journal*, 53, no. 169 (Sept.): 489–99.

Parnell, Peter, and Justin Richardson. 2005. *And Tango makes three*. New York: Simon and Schuster Children's Publishing.

Parreñas, Rachel Salazar. 2002. "The care crisis in the Philippines: children and transnational families in the new global economy." In *Global woman: Nannies, maids, and sex workers in the new economy*, ed. Barbara Ehrenreich and Arlie Russell Hochschild, 39–54. New York: Metropolitan Books.

Peet, Bill. 1970. *The wump world*. Boston: Houghton Mifflin.

Pellow, David Naguib, and Robert J. Brulle, eds. 2005. *Power, justice, and the environment: A critical appraisal of the environmental justice movement*. Boston: MIT Press.

Perry, Ted. 1971. "Ted Perry version [of the] Chief Seattle Speech." http://www.formal.stanford.edu/jmc/progress/fake2.html.

Plumwood, Val. 1994. *Feminism and the mastery of nature*. New York: Routledge.

———. 2002. *Environmental culture: The ecological crisis of reason*. London: Routledge.

Pollan, Michael. 2006. "Mass natural." Magazine section, *New York Times*, June 4, pp. 2, 15–18.

Prats, Armando José. 2002. *Invisible Natives: Myth and identity in the American Western*. Ithaca, NY: Cornell University Press.

Radway, Janice. 1986. "Identifying ideological seams: Mass culture, analytical method, and political practice." *Communications* 9: 93–123.

Reed, T. V. 2002. "Toward an environmental justice ecocriticism." In *The Environmental Justice Reader*, ed. Joni Adamson, Mei Mei Evans, and Rachel Stein, 145–62. Tucson: University of Arizona Press.

———. 2005. *The art of protest: Culture and activism from the civil rights movement to the streets of Seattle.* Minneapolis: University of Minnesota.

———. 2007. Environmental Justice Cultural Studies Web site. http://www.wsu.edu/~amerstu/ce/ce.html.

Reginald, James. n.d. "Ralph's teepee." *W Magazine*, with photographs by Michael Mundy.

Rehn, Elisabeth, and Ellen Johnson Sirleaf. 2002. *Women, war and peace: Progress of the world's women,* 2002. Vol. 1. New York: UNIFEM.

Ross, Andrew. 1996. "The future is a risky business." In *FutureNatural: Nature/science/culture,* ed. George Robertson et al., 7–21. New York: Routledge.

Salleh, Ariel. 2004. "Nature, women, capital: Living the deepest contradiction." In *Is capitalism sustainable? Political economy and the politics of ecology,* ed. Martin O'Connor, 106–24. New York: Guilford Press.

Sandilands, Catriona. 1999. *The good-natured feminist: Ecofeminism and the quest for democracy.* Minneapolis: University of Minnesota Press.

———. 2002. "Lesbian separatists and environmental experience: Notes toward a queer ecology." *Organization and Environment* 15, no. 2 (June): 131–63.

———. 2004. "Sexual politics and environmental justice: Lesbian separatists in rural Oregon." In *New perspectives on environmental justice: gender, sexuality and activism,* ed. Rachel Stein, 109–26. New Brunswick, NJ: Rutgers University Press.

———, and Bruce Erickson, eds. n.d. *Queer ecologies: Sex, nature, biopolitics, desire.* Publication pending.

Sandler, Ronald, and Phaedra Pezzullo, eds. 2007. *Environmental justice and environmentalism: The social justice challenge to the environmental movements.* Cambridge, MA: MIT Press.

Sanera, Michael, and Jane Shaw. 1999. *Facts, not fear: Teaching children about the environment.* Washington, DC: Regnery.

Schatz, Nicole. 2007. "Entertainment vs. ideology: An analysis of social ideologies present in Disney's *The Lion King* and their impact on viewers." Unpublished ms.

Schiebinger, Londa. 1993. *Nature's body: Gender in the making of modern science.* Boston: Beacon Press.

Schuler, S. R., S. M. Hashemi, and S. H. Badal. 1998. "Men's violence against women in rural Bangladesh: Undermined or exacerbated by microcredit programmes?" *Development in Practice* 8, no. 2 (May 1): 148–57.

Scott, Lee. 2005. "Twenty-first century leadership." CEO of Wal-Mart annual speech, Oct. 24. http://www.walmartstores.com/Files/21st%20 Century%20Leadership.pdf.

Seager, Joni. 1993. *Earth follies: Coming to feminist terms with the global environmental crisis.* New York: Routledge.

———. 2003. "Rachel Carson died of breast cancer: The coming of age of feminist environmentalism." *Signs: Journal of Women in Culture and Society* 28, no. 3: 943–72.

Seale, Doris. n.d. "Books to avoid." http://www.oyate.org/books-to-avoid/bro_eagle.html.

Seuss, Dr. [Theodore Geisel]. 1971. *The Lorax.* New York: Random House.

Shiva, Vandana. 1997. *Biopiracy: The plunder of nature and knowledge.* Boston: South End Press.

———. 2005. *Earth democracy: Justice, democracy, and sustainability.* Boston: South End Press.

Silliman, Jael, Marlene Garber Fried, Loretta Ross, and Elena Gutiérrez. 2004. *Undivided rights: Women of color organize for reproductive justice.* Boston: South End Press.

———, and Ynestra King, eds. 1999. *Dangerous intersections: Feminist perspectives on population, environment, and development.* Boston: South End Press.

Silverstein, Shel. 1964. *The giving tree.* New York: HarperCollins.

Slotkin, Richard. 1973. *Regeneration through violence: The mythology of the American frontier, 1600–1860.* Middletown, CT: Wesleyan University Press.

———. 1985. *The fatal environment: The myth of the frontier in the age of industrialization, 1800–1890.* New York: Macmillan.

———. 1992. *Gunfighter nation: The myth of the frontier in twentieth century America.* Boston: Atheneum.

Smith, Andrea. 1991. "For all those who were Indian in a former life." *Ms. Magazine,* Nov.–Dec., pp. 44–45.

———. 2005. *Conquest: Sexual violence and American Indian genocide.* Boston: South End Press.

Smith, Henry Nash. 1950. *Virgin land: The American West as symbol and myth.* Cambridge, MA: Harvard University Press.

Smith, Neil. 1984. *Uneven development: Nature, capital and the production of space.* Chicago: University of Chicago Press.

Sofia, Zoë. 1984. "Exterminating fetuses: Abortion, disarmament, and the sexo-semiotics of extraterrestrialism." *Diacritics* 14: 47–59.

Southern Poverty Law Center. 2002. "The puppeteer." *Intelligence Report* (summer). http://www.splcenter.org/intel/intelreport/article.jsp?pid=180.

Spivak, Gayatri Chakravorty. 2004. "Righting Wrongs." *South Atlantic Quarterly* 103, no. 2/3: 523–81.

Spotts, Peter N. 2003. "Lots in space." *Christian Science Monitor*, Oct. 9. http://www.csmonitor.com/2003/1009/p11s02-stss.html.

Starhawk. 1982. *Dreaming the dark*. Boston: Beacon Press.

Stein, Rachel. 2004. *New perspectives on environmental justice: Gender, sexuality, and activism*. New Brunswick, NJ: Rutgers University Press.

Stern, Megan. 1993. "Making the old myth new: The frontier in 'The Last of the Mohicans' and 'Dances with Wolves.'" *Wasafiri* 17 (spring): 49–53.

Stiglitz, Joseph. 2002. *Globalization and its discontents*. New York: W. W. Norton.

Stripes, James. 1999. "Strategy of resistance: The 'actorvism' of Russell Means." *Wicazo Sa Review* 14, no. 1: 87–101.

Sturgeon, Noël. 1991. "Direct theory and political action: The U.S. non-violent direct action movement, 1976–1987." Ph.D. diss., History of Consciousness Board, University of California, Santa Cruz.

———. 1995. "Theorizing movements: Direct action and direct theory." In *Cultural Politics and Social Movements*, ed. Marcy Darnovsky, Barbara Epstein and Richard Flacks, 35–51. Philadelphia: Temple University Press.

———. 1997. *Ecofeminist natures: Race, gender, feminist theory and political action*. New York: Routledge.

Sturken, Marita, and Lisa Cartwright. 2001. *Practices of looking: An introduction to visual culture*. Oxford: Oxford University Press.

Szasz, Andrew. 1994. *Ecopopulism: Toxic waste and the movement for environmental justice*. Minneapolis: University of Minnesota Press.

———. 2007. *Shopping our way to safety: How we changed from protecting the environment to protecting ourselves*. Minneapolis: University of Minnesota Press.

Sze, Julie. 2007. *Noxious New York: The racial politics of urban health and environmental justice*. Cambridge: MIT Press.

Taylor, Dorceta. 1997. "American environmentalism: The role of race, class and gender in shaping activism, 1820–1995." *Race, Gender and Class* 5: 16–62.

Taylor, Peter, and Frederick Buttell. 1992. "How do we know we have global environmental problems?" *Geoforum* 23, no. 3: 405–16.

Thompson, Scout. 2004. "Gay Penguin for president, and then . . ." Feb. 8. http://www.one38.org/a177/2004_02_08_archive.html.

Tompkins, Jane. 1992. *West of everything: The inner life of Westerns.* New York: Oxford University Press.

Tsing, Anna. 1997. "Environmentalisms: Transitions as translations." In *Transitions, translations, environmentalisms: International feminism in contemporary politics*, ed. Joan Scott, Cora Kaplan, and Debra Keates, 253–72. New York: Routledge.

Turner, Frederick Jackson. [1893] 1996. *The significance of the frontier in American history.* Madison: State Historical Society of Wisconsin.

UNIFEM. 2007. *A portal on women, peace and security.* http://www.womenwarpeace.org/info.htm.

Vecsey, Christopher, and Robert W. Venables, eds. 1980. *American Indian environments: Ecological issues in Native American history.* Syracuse, NY: Syracuse University Press.

Walker, Jeffrey. 1998. "Deconstructing an American myth: 'The Last of the Mohicans.'" In *Hollywood's Indian: The portrayal of the Native American in film*, ed. Peter C. Rollins and John E. O'Connor, 170–86. Lexington: University of Kentucky Press.

Wall, Derek. 2005. *Babylon and beyond: The economics of anti-capitalist, anti-globalist and radical green movements.* Ann Arbor, MI: Pluto Press.

Waring, Marilyn. 1999. *Counting for nothing: What men value and what women are worth.* Toronto: University of Toronto Press.

Warner, Melanie. 2006. "Wal-Mart eyes organic foods." *New York Times*, May 12. http://www.nytimes.com/2006/05/12/business/12organic.html?pagewanted=1&ei=5090&en=38ee8aa84d436d72&ex=1305086400&partner=rssuserland&emc=rss.

Warren, Karen J. 1987. "Feminism and ecology: Making connections." *Environmental Ethics* 9, no. 1: 3–20.

———. 1994. *Ecological feminism.* New Brunswick, NJ: Rutgers University Press.

———. 2000. *Ecofeminist philosophy.* Lanham, MD: Rowman and Littlefield.

Williams, Raymond. [1976] 1983. *Keywords.* New York: Oxford University Press.

Williams, Ted. 2000. "Classroom warfare." *Incite: Audubon Magazine.* http://audubonmagazine.org/incite/incite0009.html.

Wilson, Alexander. 1992. *The culture of nature: North American landscapes from Disney to the Exxon Valdez.* Cambridge, MA: Blackwell.

Zihlman, Adrienne. 1985. "Gathering stories for hunting human nature." *Feminist Studies* 11: 364–77.

Films, Television Shows, and Other Audio-Visual Materials

Alaska. 1996. Fraser Clarke Heston, dir. Castle Rock Entertainment.

America's Army: The Official Army Game. 2007. U.S. Army. http://www.americas army.com.

Babe. 1995. Chris Noonan, dir. Kennedy Miller Productions.

"Back by Popular Neglect." 1998. TV public service ad. Keep America Beautiful campaign. http://www.kab.org/uploadedFiles/KAB/popular-neglect-512k.wmv.

Balance: World Wall. 1990. Mural. Judith Baca.

Black Robe. 1991. Bruce Beresford, dir. Samuel Goldwyn Company.

Bowling for Columbine. 2002. Michael Moore, dir.

Brother Bear. 2003. Andre Blaise and Robert Walker, dirs. Walt Disney Productions.

Captain Planet and *The New Adventures of Captain Planet*. 1990–93. TV series. TBS Productions, DIC Productions, Hanna Barbera/Turner Enterprises.

Children of Men. 2006. Alfonso Cuarón, dir. Universal Pictures.

Core, The. 2003. Jon Amiel, dir. Paramount Pictures.

Courage under Fire. 1996. Edward Zwick, dir. Fox 2000 Pictures.

"Crying Indian." 1971. TV public service ad. Keep America Beautiful campaign. http://www.kab.org/uploadedFiles/KAB/crying-indian-512k.wmv.

"Crying Indian in Space." 2006. Plan4.blogspot.com. http://video.google .com/videoplay?docid=-22564191412515546955.

Dances with Wolves. 1990. Kevin Costner, dir. TIG Productions.

Day after Tomorrow. 2004. Roland Emmerich, dir. 20th Century Fox.

"Day the Violence Died." 1996. Episode of *The Simpsons* TV series. Matt Gruening, prod. Fox Network.

Democracy Now! 2006. Excerpt of debate on microcredit between Susan Davis and Vandana Shiva, aired Dec. 13. http://www.youtube.com/ watch?v=Vf9ioT4iKcM.

Dreamworlds II: Desire, Sex, Power in Music Video. 1997. Sut Jhally, dir. Media Education Foundation.

"Earthsong." 1995. Audio recording by Michael Jackson. On *HIStory—Past, Present and Future—Book 1*. Nicholas Brandt, prod. CD Epic Records.

Earth Song. 1995. Video by Nicolas Brandt, dir., with Michael Jackson. MJJ Productions.

"Elbow Room." 1976. Episode of *Schoolhouse Rock* TV series. Lynn Ahrens, Bob Dorough, David McCall, George Newall, Radford Stone, and Tom Yohe, prods. http://www.school-house-rock.com/history.html.

Emerald Forest, The. 1985. John Boorman, dir. Christel Films.

Ferngully: The Last Rainforest. 1992. Bill Kroyer, dir. Film/AS.

Fly Away Home. 1996. Caroll Ballard, dir. Columbia Pictures.

Franklin Templeton Is Making a Killing. 2008. Video by Save Darfur. http://www.youtube.com/watch?v=5jUxvk_Qu5E.

Free Willy. 1993. Simon Wincer, dir. Alcor Films.

Free Willy 2: The Adventure Home. 1995. Dwight H. Little, dir. Alcor Films.

Free Willy 3: The Rescue. 1997. Sam Pillsbury, dir. Donner-Shuler/Donner Productions.

Gattaca. 1997. Andrew Niccol, dir. Sony Pictures.

G.I. Jane. 1997. Ridley Scott, dir. Caravan Pictures.

Global Warming: What You Need to Know. 2006. Nicholas Brown, dir. Discovery Channel, BBC, and NBC.

Happy Feet. 2006. George Miller, dir. Kingdom Feature Productions.

Hidalgo. 2004. Joe Johnston, dir. Touchstone Pictures.

Incident at Oglala. 1992. Michael Apted, dir. Spanish Fork Motion Pictures.

Inconvenient Truth, An. 2006. Davis Guggenheim, dir. Paramount Vantage.

Independence Day. 1996. Roland Emmerich, dir. 20th Century Fox.

Jarhead. 2005. Sam Mendes, dir. Universal Pictures.

Jungle 2 Jungle. 1997. John Pasquin, dir. TF1 Film Productions.

Jurassic Park. 1993. Stephen Spielberg, dir. Universal Pictures.

Jurassic Park [II]: The Lost World. 1997. Stephen Spielberg, dir. Amblin Entertainment.

Jurassic Park III. 2001. Joe Johnston, dir. Amblin Entertainment.

Killing Fields, The. 1984. Roland Joffé, dir. Enigma Ltd.

King Kong. 1976. John Guillermin, dir. Dino de Laurentis Company.

KUMA/WAR. 2007. KUMA Reality Games. http://www.kumawar.com.

Last of the Mohicans, The. 1992. Michael Mann, dir. Morgan Creek Productions.

Last Samurai, The. 2003. Edward Zwick, dir. Warner Brothers.

Lion King, The. 1994. Roger Allers and Rob Minkoff, dirs. Walt Disney Feature Animation.

Little Big Man. 1970. Arthur Penn, dir. Cinema Center Films.

Mad Max. 1979. George Miller, dir. Kennedy Miller Productions.

Mad Max II: The Road Warrior. 1981. George Miller, dir. Kennedy Miller Productions.

Mad Max: Beyond Thunderdome. 1985. George Ogilvie and George Miller, dirs. Kennedy Miller Productions.

March of the Penguins. 2005. Luc Jacquet, dir. Bonne Pioche Productions.

Mighty Morphin Power Rangers. 1993–96. TV series. John Blizek and Vickie Bronaugh, prods. MMPR Productions.

Mission, The. 1986. Roland Joffé, dir. Enigma Productions.

Monoke-hime, or *Princess Monoke.* 1997. Hayao Miyazake, dir. Dentsu Music and Entertainment.

Once upon a Forest. 1993. Charles Grosvenor and David Michener, dirs. Hanna-Barbera.

Open Season. 2006. Roger Allers, Jill Culton, and Anthony Stacchi, dirs. Sony Pictures Animation.

Over the Hedge. 2006. Tim Johnson and Karey Kirkpatrick, dirs. Dreamworks Animation.

Pirates and Emperors (or Size Does Matter). 2004. Video. Eric Henry, dir. and prod. http://www.youtube.com/watch?v=_3zBV44vggM.

Planet of the Apes. 1968. Frank Schaffner, dir. 20th Century Fox.

Pocahontas. 1995. Mike Gabriel and Eric Goldberg, dirs. Walt Disney Feature Animation.

Pow-Wow Highway. 1989. Jonathan Wacks, dir. HandMade Films.

Reversal of Fortune. 1990. Barbet Schroeder, dir. Sovereign Pictures.

Rocky Horror Picture Show. 1975. Jim Sharman, dir. Twentieth Century Fox Film Corporation.

Silent Running. 1972. Douglas Trumbull, dir. Michael Gruskoff Productions.

Simpsons Movie, The. 2007. David Silverman, dir. Twentieth Century Fox.

Smoke Signals. 1998. Chris Eyre, dir. Shadowcatcher Entertainment.

SOCOMM: U.S. Navy SEALS. 2007. Sony Corporation. http://www.us.playstation.com/PS2/Games/SOCOM_II_U_S_Navy_SEALs.

Soylent Green. 1973. Richard Fleischer, dir. Metro-Goldwyn-Mayer.

Star Wars. 1977. George Lucas, dir. Lucasfilms.

Star Wars: The Empire Strikes Back. 1980. Irvin Kershner, dir. Lucasfilms.

Star Wars: Return of the Jedi. 1983. Richard Marquand, dir. Lucasfilms.

Teenage Mutant Ninja Turtles. 1987–93. TV series. Fred Wolf, prod.

300. 2007. Zack Synder, dir. Warner Brothers.

Through Arctic Eyes: Athabascan Observations on Climate Change. 2005. Tookie Mercredi, dir. Arctic Athabascan Council.

Thunderheart. 1992. Michael Apted, dir. Tribeca Productions.

Tough Guise: Violence, Media and the Crisis in Masculinity. 1999. Sut Jhally, dir. Media Education Foundation.

Triumph of the Will. 1935. Leni Riefenstahl, dir. Leni Riefenstahl-Produktion.

2001: A Space Odyssey. 1968. Stanley Kubrick, dir. MGM Studios.

Waterworld. 1995. Kevin Reynolds, dir. Davis Entertainment.

White Fang 2: The Myth of the White Wolf. 1994. Ken Olin, dir. Walt Disney Company.

Index

non-violent direct action movement, 163, 173
nuclear waste, 96

oil, 3, 5, 93, 161, 177
Once upon a Forest (film), 108, 110, 190n10
O'Neill, G. K., 81, 87
organic food, 3, 172, 175
organic labeling, 16, 41, 162, 179, 180
Outer Space Treaty, 97, 192n9
Over the Hedge (film), 107, 194n7

peace, 157–161, 169–170
penguins, 139–141, 144; environmentalism
    and, 132–136; *Happy Feet* and, 108, 113,
    134–136; heterosexism and, 135–136; *An
    Inconvenient Truth* and, 133–134; *March of the
    Penguins* and, 120, 126–128, 132–136, 145;
    Roy, Silo and Scrappy, 128–30; sexuality
    and, 126–136
people of color, 112, 150; division of labor
    and, 164–165; economic issues and,
    164–166; environmental justice and,
    9–10; female sexuality and, 37–38, 41;
    film industry and, 105, 111, 114–117;
    Gaiam and, 179–181; hippies and, 171;
    liberal multiculturalism and, 113–117;
    Michael Jackson and, 49; nature and,
    105; slavery and, 20; war and, 161
Perry, Ted, 65–66
PetroChina, 177
Pocahontas (film), 109, 190n10
policy: Anti-Ballistic Missile Treaty and, 87,
    97; Clean Air Act and, 162; exclusionary,
    21; extraterrestrialism and, 80–99; fair
    trade, 178–182; green initiatives and,
    173–185; immigration, 143; Manifest
    Destiny and, 55, 82, 89, 150; militarism
    in space and, 80–99; myth of the frontier
    and, 53–54; nature as tool of power and,
    19–23; Outer Space Treaty and, 97;
    population growth and, 141–144; U.S.
    expansionism and, 56
politics of the natural, 6; environmental
    reproductive justice and, 120–146; global
    feminist environmental justice analysis
    and, 3–16; liberal multiculturalism and,
    113–117; myth of the frontier and, 15;
    radical environmentalism and, 8–11;
    U.S. historical perspective on, 17–49
Pollan, Michael, 175–176
Pope, Carl, 93
popular culture: advertising and, 26–41;
    children's environmentalist, 103–119;
    dynamic nature of, 26; Earth as seen from
    space and, 42–43; Ecological Indian and,

53–79; environmentalist images of nature
    and, 41–49; extraterrestrialist global
    frontier myth and, 80–99; identity and,
    28–41; jeans and, 26–27; Manifest Des-
    tiny and, 55, 82, 89, 150; myth of frontier
    and, 39–40; post–cold war context and,
    103–104; U.S. influence on, 24–49
population growth, 141–144
poverty, 4, 14, 137, 167, 179
prostitution, 160

queer theorists, 125, 129–132, 195n1

race, 6, 15; advertising and, 29–39;
    children's popular culture and, 111–113;
    civil rights movement and, 184; environ-
    mental justice and, 9–10; ethnocide and,
    140; film industry and, 105, 114–117;
    inverted quarantine and, 178; liberal
    multiculturalism and, 113–117
rape, 159
Reagan, Ronald, 86, 95, 107, 166
recycling, 3, 42–44
Red Power, 62–63, 184
Reed, T. V., 188n3
refugees, 159–160
religion, 109; Catholics, 60; environmental
    reproductive justice and, 120, 124–136;
    hippies and, 172; Muslims, 28–29,
    168–169; right-wing fundamentalists
    and, 120, 126–128, 132–133, 135–136
reproductive rights, 121, 124
Riefenstahl, Leni, 111
Roche Pharmaceuticals, 136
Rocky Horror Picture Show, The (film), 111–112

Schoolhouse Rock (TV show), 88, 142,
    192nn7,8
Seager, Joni, 42, 161
Sea World/Busch Gardens Conservation
    Fund ad, 145
sexuality, 6–7, 155; advertising and, 29–41;
    critique of naturalizations and, 11–14;
    environmental reproductive justice and,
    120–146; female aggressiveness and,
    35–39; free love and, 172; gay/lesbian
    activists and, 21–22; heterosexism and,
    104–105, 123–126; militarism and, 80–99;
    myth of the frontier and, 55, 57; nature
    and, 103–104, 121–132; penguins and,
    126–136; prostitution and, 160; rape and,
    159; right-wing fundamentalists and, 120,
    122, 124–126; slavery and, 159–160, 168;
    violence and, 142–143, 155; virgin land
    and, 56

About the Author

Noël Sturgeon is a professor in the Department of Women's Studies and graduate faculty in the American Studies Program at Washington State University. She is the author of *Ecofeminist Natures: Race, Gender, Feminist Theory and Political Action* (Routledge 1997) and numerous articles on environmentalist, antimilitarist, and feminist movements and theories. She has been a Rockefeller Fellow at the Center for the Critical Analysis of Contemporary Cultures at Rutgers University and a visiting scholar at the Center for Cultural Studies, University of California, Santa Cruz; at the JFK Institute for North American Studies in Berlin; and at the Institute for Sustainability and Technology Policy at Murdoch University, Western Australia. At WSU, she has co-directed the Center for Social and Environmental Justice and the research group Gendering Research across the Campuses (GRACe). She lives in Pullman, Washington, with her partner, her son, and three companion species animals: Peanut Butter, Jelly, and Toast.

Library of Congress Cataloging-in-Publication Data

Sturgeon, Noël, 1956–
    Environmentalism in popular culture : gender, race,
sexuality, and the politics of the natural / Noël Sturgeon.
        p. cm.
    Includes bibliographical references and index.
    ISBN 978-0-8165-2581-2 (pbk. : acid-free paper)
    1. Environmentalism—Social aspects. 2. Ecofeminism.
I. Title.
GE195.S786   2009
304.2—dc22   2008036917